JUN 12 2013

ONONDAGA COUNTY PUBLIC LIBRARY
THE GALLERIES OF SYRACUSE
447 S. SALINA STREET
SYRACUSE, NY 13202-2494
WWW.ONLIB.ORG

CHOOSING A LASTING CAREER

The Job-by-Job Outlook for Work's New Age

CHOOSING A LASTING CAREER

The Job-by-Job Outlook for Work's New Age

James B. Huntington, Ph.D.

Royal Flush Press
Eldred, New York

Copyright © 2013 by James B. Huntington

All rights reserved. No part of this book may be reproduced or transmitted in any form or by any means, electronic or mechanical, including photocopying, recording, or by any information storage and retrieval system, without written permission from the author, except for the inclusion of brief quotations in a review.

Royal Flush Press
P.O. Box 190
Eldred, NY 12732

orders@royalflushpress.com
www.royalflushpress.com

Edition ISBNs:

Softcover	978-0-9835006-7-4
PDF	978-0-9835006-8-1

Printed in the United States of America

Publisher's Cataloging-in-Publication
(Provided by Quality Books, Inc.)

Huntington, James B.
Choosing a lasting career : the job-by-job outlook for work's new age / James B. Huntington.
p. cm.
Includes bibliographical references and index.
LCCN 2012922272
ISBN 978-0-9835006-7-4
ISBN 978-0-9835006-8-1
1. Vocational guidance. 2. Occupations.
I. Title.
HF5382.H86 2013
331.702
QBI12-600237

To Mary, as we approach our second anniversary of officially living and loving

Lasting Career Principles

1. Jobs that cannot reasonably be automated away are good.
2. Jobs dependent on obsolescent or endangered technology are bad.
3. Jobs that must be done locally are good.
4. Jobs that do not include health insurance are good.
5. Jobs producing less scalable goods and services MAY be good.
6. Jobs that seem to be maximized in efficiency already are good.
7. Jobs catering to the 1% are good.
8. Jobs that help people working very long hours are good.
9. Jobs related to personal, vacation, or recreational travel, especially custom-designed, exotic, or expensive, MAY be good.
10. Jobs that require highly unusual sets of aptitude MAY be good.
11. Jobs with artificially high or restrictive entry requirements MAY be good.
12. Jobs in skilled construction trades MAY be good.
13. Jobs connected with highway, road, bridge, or airport repair, design, or construction MAY be good.
14. Jobs with a high percentage of women working them, in perception or in reality, MAY be good.
15. Jobs in which Americans are particularly valued MAY be good.
16. Jobs doing extraction are bad.
17. Jobs doing manufacturing, except food products, are bad.
18. Jobs involving showing people how to do constructive unpaid activities are good.
19. Jobs connected with products disproportionately likely to be used by people over 65 MAY be good.
20. Jobs connected with health in any form MAY be good.

Table of Contents

Table of Figures

Acknowledgements

Chris DiNatale of DiNatale Design (http://www.dinataledesign.com/) shaped and put the book cover together. Editing and proofreading was by Mim Eisenberg of WordCraft (http://www.wordcraftservices.com/), Kendra Millis (khmillis@gmail.com) did the indexing, and Angela Werner (www.heyneon.com) the design and typesetting. Printing was done by Documation (http://www.documation.com/).

I thank my friends, relatives, and colleagues who served as an informal focus group on the book and provided other assistance: Sarah Chapin, Jim Diederich, Sam Huntington, Tony Kapsak, James Krot, Gloria Lang, Lance Marrou, Skip Nelson, Sallie Pine, Mark Raphaelson, John Reitz, Tim Ricke, Diane Rozek, Jane Ann Scott, Skip Yarian, and of course Mary.

Introduction: Which Careers Will Last?

There is a lot of people in the United States who say "isn't," and they ain't eating.
—Dizzy Dean, during the Great Depression[1]

Choosing a Lasting Career

We are now in a 250-year historical transition.

When the Industrial Revolution began, so did the idea that people would earn a living by formally working for others. One hundred and eighty-six years later, that notion began to lose steam. In 2012 I published *Work's New Age: The End of Full Employment and What It Means to You*, which documented that the jobs crisis was permanent and would not end with better economic times.

One thing I did to spread the word about Work's New Age, both the book and the idea, was to be interviewed on a large number of radio stations, in 42 states across the country. I talked about why the jobs would not come back, on the social effects the problem has had on Americans, on why both political parties misunderstood the crisis, and on which possible solutions were good, bad, and indifferent and why.

One type of question I was often asked was something I did not cover in *Work's New Age*. Many times the host or a caller would say something like, "My child is 16 years old. What career should he go into?" I answered based on the general causes of Work's New Age and on my business knowledge and intuition. By necessity, my recommendations were general and not to the standards I hold to my writing and research.

Choosing a Lasting Career: The Job-by-Job Outlook for Work's New Age was written to answer such queries definitively.

There is a lot of information available about the prospects for jobs and careers and on the college majors and other preparation they require. It will provide average salaries, number of positions expected, training involved, and so on. I cite some of that material here but have added three things about specific lines of work that make this book unique. First, using criteria more important than current earnings, I name the best careers for the next 20 years. Second, using combinations of those factors, I do the same for individual jobs. Third, I provide an alphabetical index of the 506 positions with statistics, specific ratings, and comments for each.

In the last chapter, I deal with probable or at least potential events which will not only affect career choices but may well obliterate them. What will happen to our livelihoods if we have the choice of being downloaded onto computers... if life expectancy skyrockets... if we can get "super powers" once only in the likes of Marvel and DC comic books... if none of these happen but technology continues on its accelerating pace? I will look at the main issues and brief you on things we will all need to think about.

Where This Book Fits In

On Amazon.com, on other sites, and at bookstores, you will see many different volumes on one topic and gigantic numbers on another. The first might be called personality career assessment; efforts in this area seek to connect the sort of person you are with a line of work. What are you good at? What do you like to do for fun? What tasks do you finish off without real difficulty, and which do you always avoid? The second subject is the detailed strategies of job-seeking: where you should look, how you should act, how you should care for and feed hiring managers, and of course a cacophony of opinions on interviews and résumés.

Choosing a Lasting Career is neither. Instead, it fits between these two categories.

Personality-to-career books are excellent at getting you to learn things about yourself. They offer thinking exercises, list-making projects, questionnaire after questionnaire, and much more, and they are usually quite informative. What they will not do, unfortunately, is say what lines of work are viable for you, personally or generally. Perhaps my aptitudes and disposition indicate that I should be a neurosurgeon, but at 56 with no medical training beyond Red Cross CPR, that simply isn't going to happen. Maybe I should become a computer operator, but those jobs, as we will see, are going away for almost all Americans. Some opportunities attract more people than others, but that will often change between a book's writing and publishing, let alone between writing, publishing, and going out of print. Such volumes are not intended to show what positions will and won't be in demand in a few years, not to mention the decade-plus most people have in mind for a career. You should not be spending time and money training for something humans soon won't need to provide, whether it's your dream job or not.

I may have seemed critical of tactical job-hunting books, and there are reasons for that. Interview stratagems are hardly set in stone, and will sometimes work and will sometimes not, depending on the interviewer. Although there are many good ways of writing résumés, the sources disagree, often strongly, on the right things to do, and always have. In the pre-email era, some experts thought résumés should be on plain white paper, while others said they should be almost any other color. More recently, there has been a controversy about sending thank-you letters or messages to interviewers, with one side saying they are courteous and allow reinforcement of points you made before, and the other maintaining they are blatantly self-serving nuisances. In the end, these sorts of things come down to the tastes of the people with whom you have interacted, and no fixed dogma will win every time. Some books, along with articles and viral emails, will give rather spectacular allegedly real-life examples of jobseeker gaffes: cover-letter statements about wanting to rule the world; applicants wearing X-rated T-shirts; people saying vile things about their former bosses; a man who openly and graphically lusted after a woman pictured on his interviewer's desk and had to be removed by security; and so on.

Beware! Before you put too much stock into any of this, understand four things:

1. What you need most to get hired are a) specific (not general) experience, and b) being personally liked by the interviewer.
2. Very few jobs are lost by choosing the wrong *reasonable* interview, résumé, or workplace behavior tactics.
3. Limiting your search to applying for widely advertised positions is unlikely to get you hired, even if your résumé looks like Mark Zuckerberg's and your interviewing skills resemble Oprah Winfrey's.
4. Avoiding massive blunders will only put you in a not-so-elite group of 99% of all jobseekers, most of whom are not finding work.

I do recommend books on both career assessment and job-hunting strategies.

For personality work, *The Pathfinder: How to Choose or Change Your Career for a Lifetime of Satisfaction and Success*, by Nicholas Lore (Touchstone Books). This multi-edition classic has the right idea on thinking about yourself and what would work for you.

Also for self-understanding, the often updated *What Color Is Your Parachute?: A Practical Manual for Job-Hunters and Career-Changers*, by Richard N. Bolles (Ten Speed Press)—but watch out! I recommend this standard for determining what careers would fit your disposition and interests and for insights on how employers actually fill jobs, but I warn against it for the tactical part. Much of its material on the latter has changed little since 1982, when applicants could actually sneak onto a payroll with "information interviews" (in which jobseekers purport to be interested only in the nature of a position or company) and could impress hiring managers by doing no more than dressing well, acting intelligently, and seeming to have aptitudes transferrable to higher-level jobs. It's been many decades since those looking for work had the best of the overall market, and employers are tougher these days—they've seen it all before. Without experience pertaining to the exact position—for example, if a bill-paying company wants a project manager who uses Primavera and has worked in that industry, a telecommunications PM expert at Microsoft Project won't be chosen—you'll need a lot of luck, no matter how smart or skilled you are.

A third good volume on self-examination for work is *I Could Do Anything If I Only Knew What It Was: How to Discover What You Really Want and How to Get It*, by Barbara Sher (Delacorte Press). It is from 1994, ancient by the standards of career books, but most of its material is timeless, and you can get a used copy for almost nothing (plus shipping) on the likes of Amazon.com.

For interviews, *Sweaty Palms: The Neglected Art of Being Interviewed*, by H. Anthony Medley (Warner Business Books) is thorough and well reasoned. It has a large number of sections on interview stratagems, with controversial but good advice.

On tactics in general, the finest I've ever seen, and my candidate for the best book overall on seeking employment, is *What Does Somebody Have to Do to Get a Job Around Here?: 44 Insider Secrets That Will Get You Hired*, written by Cynthia Shapiro and published by St. Martin's Griffin. I bought it in 2010 when I wasn't even looking for work, after paging through it at a bookstore (in Korea of all places), and I was stunned. Here is what I wrote about it on Amazon, which should give you an idea about my views on the field in general:

> This book is a fifth-level response to a) employers having certain standards and many biases, b) applicants finding out how to overcome them and display their best picture, followed by c) employers seeking to overcome said overcoming themselves, and topped off by d) strict laws forbidding discrimination of various kinds, which employers, out of nothing more than perceived self-interest, see it in their interest to do.
>
> The work is made up of many, many outstanding insights that ring true about how getting hired ACTUALLY works. Maybe 2/3 of the book I knew already (I'm a bit of an old graybeard at this stuff), but, even (especially) for me, the remaining 1/3 is worth many times the purchase price. Some tips were hard to swallow, but of course that is to be expected with this super-stressful non-merit-based endeavor, in which the other side has almost all the cards and knows it.

> Two minor quarrels. First, people would not try stunts such as wearing gorilla suits, wrapping resumes in champagne, and so on if they didn't sometimes work. While someone as experienced and sophisticated as the author would refuse to pay off to them, maybe if it's a job you badly want AND there are vast numbers of applicants AND you don't think your qualifications put you in the top category AND the gatekeeper is a woman in her 20s (sorry, but such ploys are similar to those corny bar pickup lines which all women blast but so often work), you might still go for one of those. Second, in one section she gave a recipe for success for something using four concepts that began with the letter C – as the rest of the book was so far above that level, that part seemed to me incongruous and even destructive. So knock it down from 5+ stars to just 5.
>
> All in all, the perfect job-seeking book for the Great Recession. It absolutely buries the likes of *What Color Is Your Parachute*, with its long-obsolete ideas that you can impress employers so much as a general resource they will do anything to get you, even create a position for you. The author shows she knows, as do many of the rest of us, that human resources departments should go back to calling themselves 'personnel,' as what they want are cogs. And no other writer, in any of the 50+ pertinent books I've read or read about, does as well at showing how to get there. This book is not only an unqualified tour de force, but a major milestone in the field.

So that's what we're facing. These volumes, possibly augmented by newer ones, will get you personally grounded and ready to implement, and the book you're reading now will help you make the strongest real-life choice.

Now, let's look at where we are, how we got there, and where we are going with work, jobs, and careers in the United States.

Part I: Our Situation

Chapter 1:
Work's New Age

Can either Move-On.org or the Tea Party get us back to 1957? In my view, no. A tipping point has been reached, a line crossed. To stay with the car analogy, the job system has already replaced the engine, the transmission, the windshield wipers, and just about every other part — and it still isn't running well. —Frank Joyce[2]

What is happening with jobs, and why is the lack of them going to continue?

Full Employment's End: How the Change Occurred

Before the Industrial Revolution started in America in 1787,[3] people seldom worked for a living in the same sense we do now. They joined the military, entered the priesthood, owned farms or other small businesses, or cadged and foraged around or beyond the edges of the law.[4] With the rise of industry, most people exchanged their labor for money, on which they lived.[5] As late as the 1910s, people without jobs were usually called "idlers" or "loafers," as the term "unemployed" implied they were not responsible for that.[6]

The problems with work in general and industrial positions in particular started in 1929 with the Great Depression, when personal monetary failures, with investments on margin being completely lost, were much more common than in any recessions since. In 1944, the G.I. Bill became law, and millions then in the service would use it to get the college educations they had never expected. In 1946, the first modern computer, ENIAC, was produced,[7] which had little immediate effect but started a series of events leading to widespread automation. As university enrollment became more and more common, graduates got a variety of good jobs, but within a couple of decades their schooling began to surpass the needs of the marketplace. During the 1960s, only 10% of those just finishing college took positions requiring less education,[8] but that soared quickly to 33% in 1970 and 1971,[9] due at least in part to an increase in enrollment driven by the Vietnam-era draft.

Economies in Europe and elsewhere had been getting more competitive with America's, when events in the Middle East ushered America into Work's New Age. In 1973 the leaders of Saudi Arabia and Egypt manipulated the price and supply of oil as a war weapon, after which other Arab countries embargoed it and boosted rates, leading to a per-barrel price quadrupling the next year.[10] The effects on Americans included manufacturing slowdowns, occasional gasoline outages along with the start of its rationing, and a recession. Those things did not last long, but no longer would unemployment stay at the levels of the 1960s.

Over the next decades, job growth in non-recession years progressively lessened. While during economic expansion times from 1950 through 1979 the number of non-government positions increased an average of 3.5% per year, that dropped to 2.4% during similarly prosperous times from 1980 to 1999 and to 0.9% for the years of greatest progress in the next decade.[11] Job losses in recessions exceeded the gains at other times, and, from December 1999 to December 2009, 944,000 net positions disappeared.[12] More women went to work, causing the labor force, as shown in Figure 1, to grow in both number and percentage almost every year from 1973 to 1999.[13]

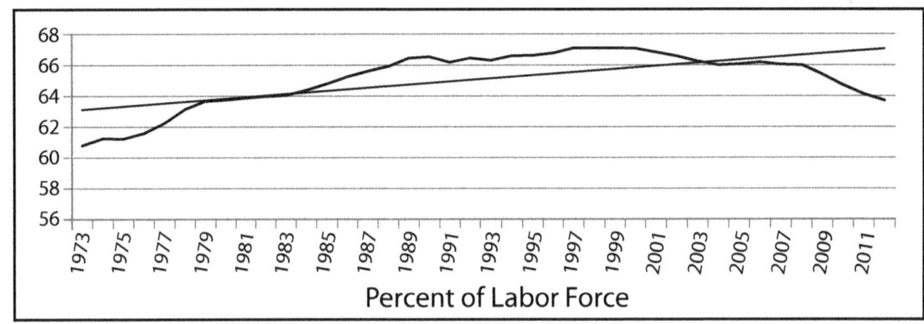

Figure 1: Overall Labor Force Participation Rate, 1973–2012—1947–1972 average: 59.3%

With Mao Zedong's death, China began exporting massively more, and with the invention of the World Wide Web, computers became more connected and globalization as we know it today began. The prosperity of the 1990s, the dot-com securities boom around 2000, and the real-estate-led consumer spending spree around 2005 concealed these job-reducing factors, but when housing prices dropped to those of years before, the reality became clear.[14]

Since 1980, post-recession recoveries have taken longer each time. In 2009, 44% of American families had at least one person whose pay was reduced, had their hours cut, or lost their job.[15] The 2000s were the first decade for median United States household income to drop.[16] The portion of adult Americans working shrank from 63.3% in March 2007 to 58.7% in September 2009, and has been between 58% and 59% ever since.[17] The number of net new positions needed per month just to cover labor force entrants has been estimated since 2010, by eight different sources, as between 90,000 and 150,000.[18]

Figure 2 gives overall unemployment rates since 1973.[19] Figure 3 shows the average number of weeks for those officially jobless and the share of them looking for 27 or more.[20]

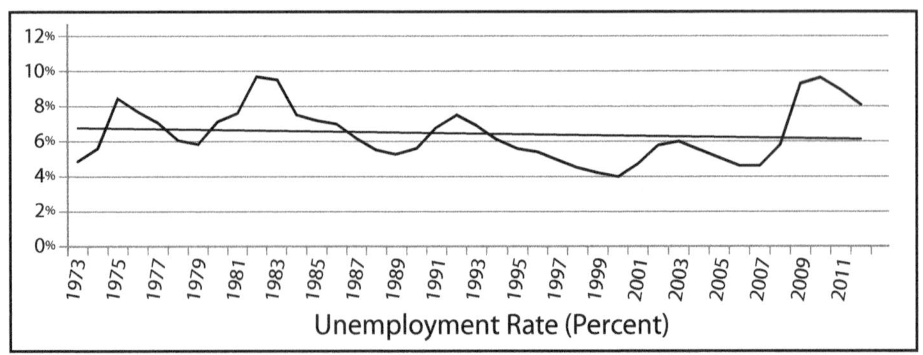

Figure 2: Unemployment Rate, Percent, 1973–2012—1947–1972 average: 4.74%

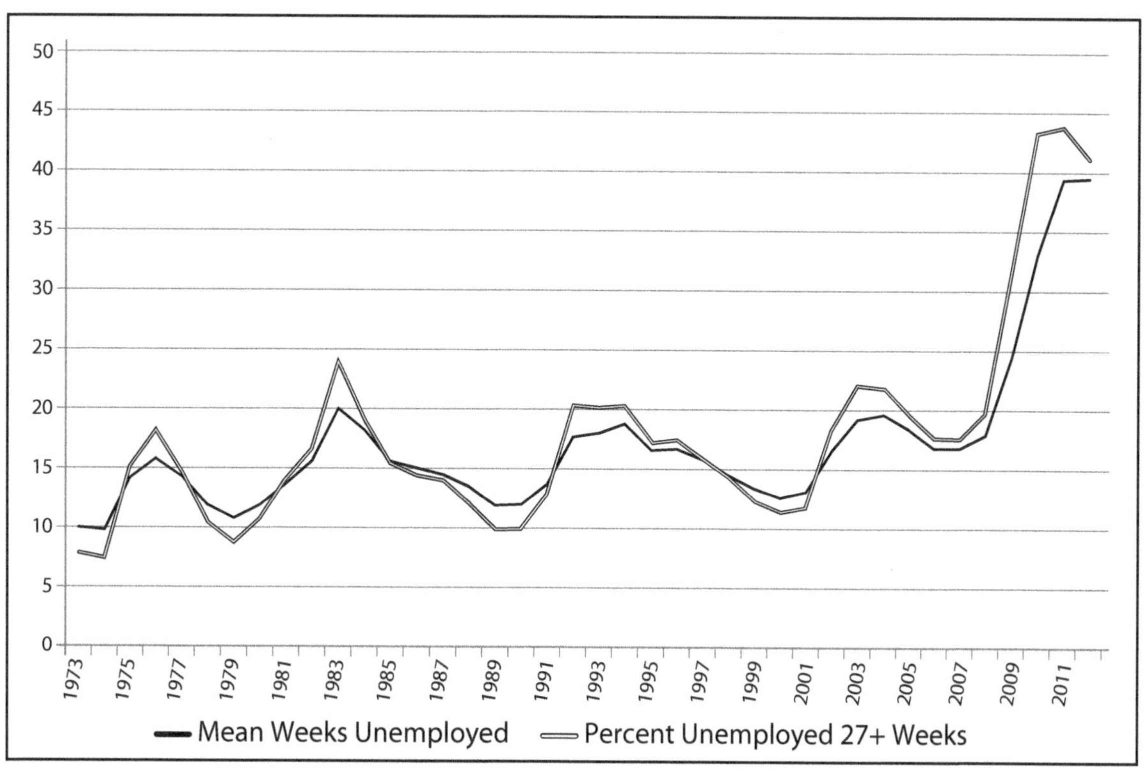

Figure 3: Mean Weeks Unemployed, and Percent of Jobless People Unemployed for 27 Weeks or More, 1973–2012—1948–1972 averages: 11.2 weeks and 9.5%

In Figure 2, we see a slightly descending trend line over the 40 years, which is likely to flatten or increase soon. Figure 3 indicates that the proportion of long-term unemployed is more extreme than the mean jobless lengths, lower at good points and higher at bad ones.

How has working, or looking for work, differed by age since 1973? Figure 4 gives labor force participation rates among age groups.[21]

As the chart shows, for more than 20 years labor involvement for those 16 to 19 has plummeted through good economic times and bad, and it has also fallen for those 20 to 24, both declines happening at times when overall participation increased. The rates for people 16 to 19 and 55 to 64, within 1% throughout the 1980s, have since diverged, as have those for 20 to 24 and 25 to 54. If these trends continue, the shares for those 20 to 24 and 55 to 64 will converge, as will those for ages 16 to 19 and 65-plus, which have not been at all close.

Another trend worthy of attention is the education level of the American workforce. The portion with a college degree, only 11% in 1969,[22] has risen steadily since 1990, as shown in Figure 5.[23]

Will United States workers, as a group, continue to get more and more educated? What does that mean for careers? We will discuss these issues in Chapters 2 and 3.

The Job Situation Now, and the American Job Shortage Number (AJSN)

As of December 2012, official American unemployment stood at 7.8%, with 3,290,000 fewer jobs than at the November 2007 peak. The median December 2012 jobless time was 18 weeks, well below the maximum of 22.4 reached in May 2010, but still more than any from 1948 to 2008; the mean was far worse at 38.1 weeks, compared with the November and December 2011 all-time extreme of 40.7. The civilian labor force in July 2012 numbered 155,511,000 with 143,305,000 working, of

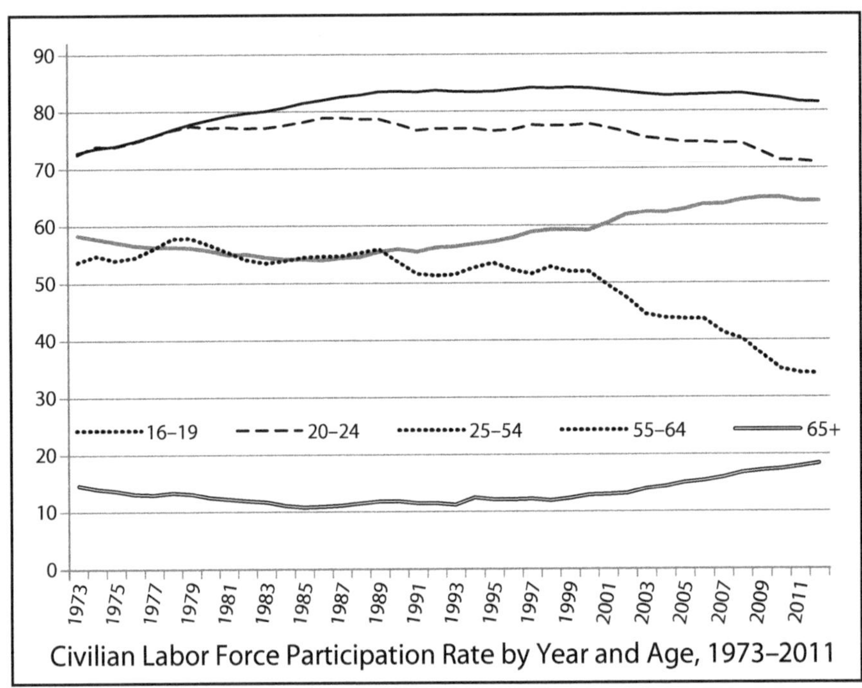

Figure 4: Labor Force Participation Rate by Age, 1973–2012—1948-72 averages: 48.9% for 16-19, 65.5% for 20-24, 68.8% for 25-54, 60.2% for 55-64, and 21.0% for 65+

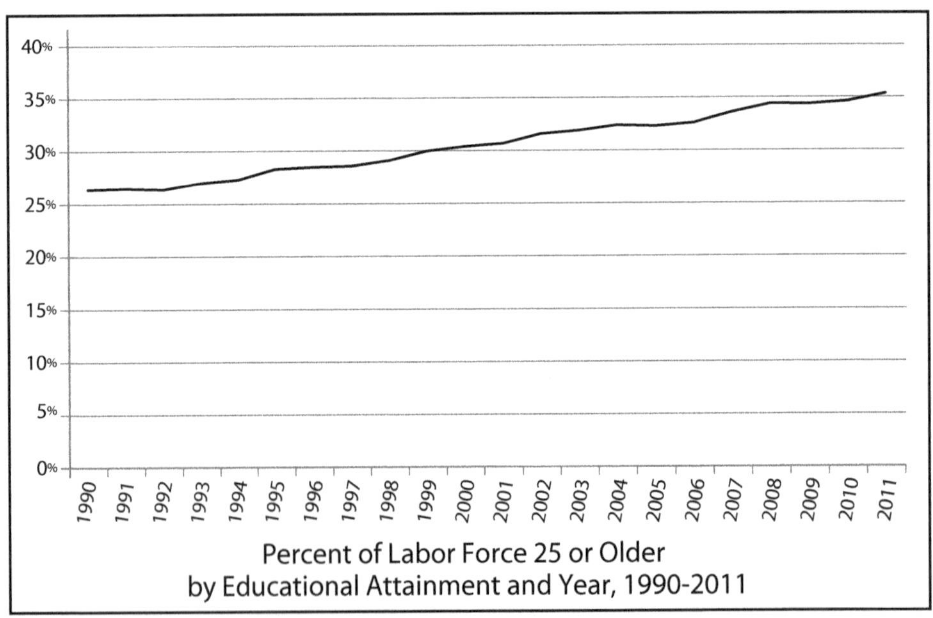

Figure 5: Percentage of Labor Force with at Least a Four-Year College Degree, 1990–2011

whom 7,918,000 were employed part-time but wanted to work full-time.[24] High school and college graduates from 2011 had a 17% unemployment rate that year, and that for those age 23 or less had increased each of the previous four.[25] The drop in the labor force has been so large, and affects official unemployment so much, that the April 2012 figure of 8.1% would have been 11.1% or 13.1% if the participation rate were the same as in January 2009 or January 2001, respectively.[26]

In *Work's New Age*, I identified 15 different employment statuses: unemployed; working part time for economic reasons; underemployed due to money, skill, or values; solidly employed; discouraged; family responsibilities; in school or training; ill health or disability; other; did not search for work in previous year; not available to work now; do not want a job; under age 15; non-civilian and institutionalized, 15+; and American expatriates.[27] Most are directly from the Bureau of Labor Statistics (BLS); the others are underemployed due to money, skill or values (working full time, but at jobs that fall below the worker's qualification level in terms of pay, use of abilities, or productive values gained);[28] solidly employed (those working and neither underemployed in any of these ways nor working part time while wanting to work full time); under age 15 (from Census Bureau statistics); non-civilian and institutionalized (subtracted from all other groupings); and American expatriates (United States citizens living in other countries, their number estimated from various sources).[29] Each of these categories has its own posture toward work. I assigned each a percentage of those who would take employment if jobs were readily available,[30] which, when added together, became the American Job Shortage Number (AJSN), the definitive measure of latent demand for jobs in the United States.[31]

Employment Status	Number	Percent of Total	Number Working in USA	Latent Demand Percent (Est.)	Latent Demand Number (Est.)
Unemployed	11,844,000	3.69%	0	90%	10,659,600
Working Part Time for Economic Reasons	7,918,000	2.47%	7,918,000	0%	0
Underemployed Due to Money, Skills, or Values	57,189,600	17.84%	57,189,600	0%	0
Solidly Employed	77,866,400	24.29%	77,866,400	0%	0
Discouraged	1,068,000	0.33%	0	90%	961,200
Family Responsibilities	222,000	0.07%	0	30%	66,600
In School or Training	346,000	0.11%	0	50%	173,000
Ill Health or Disability	181,000	0.06%	0	10%	18,100
Other	797,000	0.25%	0	30%	239,100
Did Not Search for Work In Previous Year	3,252,000	1.01%	0	80%	2,601,600
Not Available to Work Now	667,000	0.21%	0	30%	200,100
Do Not Want a Job	82,914,000	25.86%	0	5%	4,145,700
Under Age 15	63,085,752	19.68%	0	0%	0
Non-Civilian and Institutionalized, 15+	6,940,248	2.16%	0	10%	694,025
American Expatriates	6,320,000	1.97%	0	20%	1,264,000
Total	320,611,000	100.00%	142,558,000		
AJSN					21,023,025

Figure 6: The 15 Employment Categories, with Total Numbers, Percentages, and Latent Demand for Jobs, and the AJSN, December 2012

Figure 6 shows the number of people in each grouping as of December 2012, the percent of the combined population of American residents and expatriates, and the number currently working in the United States,[32] along with the estimated portion of who would accept positions, and total, or AJSN, of just over 21 million.

Hidden desire for jobs is hardly exclusive to America. Worldwide, Gallup polls have shown that of the 5 billion people 15 or older, 3 billion want to work full time, but there are now only 1.2 billion regular jobs.[33] Clearly, the rest of the world, taken as one unit, is even worse off.

Why It's Permanent This Time

So how do we know that we won't be back to 5% unemployment before we know it? Federal Reserve Chairman Ben Bernanke's January 2011 prediction that the jobless rate would likely be about 8% two years later[34] has proven quite accurate. *U.S. News & World Report* editor Mortimer P. Zuckerman, who noted in late 2010 that that the country's nongovernmental employment "machine is clanging to a halt,"[35] and also wrote in early 2011, actually after a drop in the unemployment rate, that there was "no life in our jobs market," stated that "millions of men and women are willing and eager to work, but their skills, brainpower, and energies are wasted," and maintained that though the Great Recession had ended, "the Great Job Recession continues apace."[36] Since 1980, large, profitable companies have become less and less likely to hire;[37] according to economist Robert J. Samuelson, they "are doing much better than workers; that's a defining characteristic of today's economy."[38] A cartoon by Tom Toles in *The Washington Post* depicted a magician labeled "The Amazing Corporate America," after sawing a person portrayed as "workforce," saying, "There is no 'rest of the trick.' I cut you in half and I got record profits!"[39] Another presented a sealed-off factory marked "The Economy" telling a large group of unemployed people outside, "Don't take this the wrong way, but we discovered it works better without you."[40]

So why are all recoveries now jobless,[41] and why won't the work come all the way back?

Automation—Technical Progress in One Direction

Automation, the ability of technology to take over functions once performed by people, has been progressing since the beginning of the Industrial Revolution and before.[42] Ever more sophisticated machinery and software, especially in this century, has thinned out and replaced people in many fields, from doctors swapped for diagnostic packages[43] to property assessors giving way to programs using data such as neighborhood statistics and square feet.[44] Accountants,[45] business analysts, physicians,[46] commercial artists and advertising designers,[47] and many of America's once 3.5 million cashiers[48] are now endangered. Through document analyzing software, as many as 500 lawyers can be replaced by one.[49] From 2000 to 2010, mechanization was partially or completely responsible for the loss of 5.6 million jobs in manufacturing alone,[50] and in 2004 economist and writer Jeremy Rifkin assessed that more than 70% of the workforce had positions at risk of being automated away.[51] In 2011 Mortimer P. Zuckerman wrote that automation had such great perils that it could subvert the country.[52] Yet, per software company founder Martin Ford, author of *The Lights in the Tunnel*, many economists in 2009 still judged technology-driven high unemployment to be "unthinkable."[53]

There will be even more job losses from mechanization in the future. Work now ready for automation includes financial auditing, more teaching, and more health care providing,[54] including highly-trained professional specialties such as radiology, which consists mostly of pattern recognition in an abstract environment.[55] Most at risk to be mechanized are higher-paid jobs where accumulated knowledge can be defined algorithmically.[56] More complex technical positions will be needed and filled, but their numbers will be tiny compared with those they and their machines displaced.[57] Any products as popular as cars or computers would create opportunities but would be produced in ways too automated to provide huge amounts of work.[58] As of 2010, the companies of eBay, Facebook, and Twitter, all among the most popular innovations of recent decades, employed 17,000, 2,000, and 300 people, respectively.[59] As Martin Ford, who called such positions "software jobs," wrote, "At some point in the future—it might be many years or decades from now—machines will be able to do the jobs of a large percentage of the 'average' people in our population, and these people will *not* be able to find new jobs."[60] We can see that coming now, and it will have gigantic implications for which careers will last and which will not.

A few positions will remain untouched by automation, but they will be a tiny minority. Even taxi drivers, whose working tactics are manual and nonalgorithmic, benefit from GPS devices. The future of mechanization could approach that described by Kurt Vonnegut Jr. in his 1952 future-set novel *Player Piano,* in which manicures and haircuts were performed by machines programmed by recording the precise movements of human experts.[61] Automation, without a doubt, is the greatest single cause of Work's New Age.[62]

Globalization—More Progress All the Time

Globalization, or freer cross-border trade along with development of related economic systems,[63] has progressed steadily since 1973. In 2007, the International Monetary Fund determined that the number of worldwide workers suitable for tasks performed in American jobs had increased fourfold since 1980.[64] A 2009 study found that 71% of United States employees were threatened by dwindling demand for their services, a growing supply of those able to provide them, or both.[65] Around that time, Princeton professor Alan Blinder predicted a reduction of 40 million more American white-collar jobs over the subsequent few decades from globalization.[66] Foreign workers are becoming increasingly capable; as *Time* assistant managing editor Rana Foroohar wrote about the company that prepared a related study, "Even million-dollar-a-year McKinsey consultants should be worried; how much longer will it be before $200,000-a-year partners at India's Infosys eat their lunch?"[67]

Another set of positions that will continue to be sent overseas in large number are those manual and non-repetitive.[68] With a video screen and controls, lower-paid workers elsewhere could operate devices in American workplaces. This technology, which has actually been used for "teaching robots" in some Korean public schools,[69] is already employed in America, both in the armed services and in law enforcement.[70]

Globalization has been tremendously beneficial in many ways, but as it has been similarly effective in providing cheaper alternatives to American labor, it is second only to mechanization in making jobs disappear. From the perspective of American workers, globalization and automation seem the same—opportunities go away, and the goods and services continue.[71]

Other Shifts: Scalability, Health Insurance Costs, and Efficiency

Before the Industrial Revolution, almost no production was scalable, meaning that every horseshoe, bowl, or drinking glass was made individually.[72] The arrival and spread of machines changed that. More things could be made more quickly, but it took time and labor to set up a factory and to start and stop a production run. With the post-industrial age came products with even longer startup periods and much lower marginal labor needs, such as software, which can take thousands upon thousands of hours to develop, but with each copy sold necessitating at most a CD, paper, case, and packing, all mass-produced and barely related to the real product cost. Pre-industrial, industrial, and post-industrial production have relationships between work and value created of, roughly, straight-line, exponential, and logarithmic, respectively.[73] If Microsoft uses 40,000 hours of labor to produce 10,000 copies of Excel, it may well need only 60,000 for one million, or 90,000 for one billion. This is scalability, which, when combined with automation, breaks the link between work needed and the amount of a product consumed. When another million people buy the latest TurboTax program, the additional number of employees needed to deal with this extra business, when compared with Intuit's revenues, is minuscule. Therefore, as the labor portion of a product's price declines, greater sales of it cause fewer additional people to be hired.[74]

Another driver toward the reduction in jobs is rising health insurance rates. For 40 years, the escalating cost of health care has pushed up the cost of employment and stopped unknown numbers of positions from being offered and filled.[75] There will not be much relief from the Affordable Care Act of 2010 (commonly known as Obamacare), which addresses neither problem prevention nor runaway costs.[76] These expenses are often a result of another issue: per Gallup chairman Jim Clifton, although Americans end up with lower life expectancies than those in Great Britain, France, Canada, or Germany, they "grossly overuse" medical resources.[77] Employer-based health insurance is burdensome on both employees and companies, in pricing as well as in cost structures.[78] Such obligations also encourage United States companies, which pay per worker, to remove jobs instead of reducing hours.[79]

One more work-decreasing element is greater and greater efficiency. Organizations often find, when they cut staff, that their tasks require fewer employees. As business improves, the jobs lost may not return. In fact, corporate sales at the end of 2010 were similar to those in mid-2009, but 5% of company positions had vanished.[80] Efficiency, and its one-way progress, is easy to understand; if you consider your experiences of being short on time, money, or other resources and changing what you

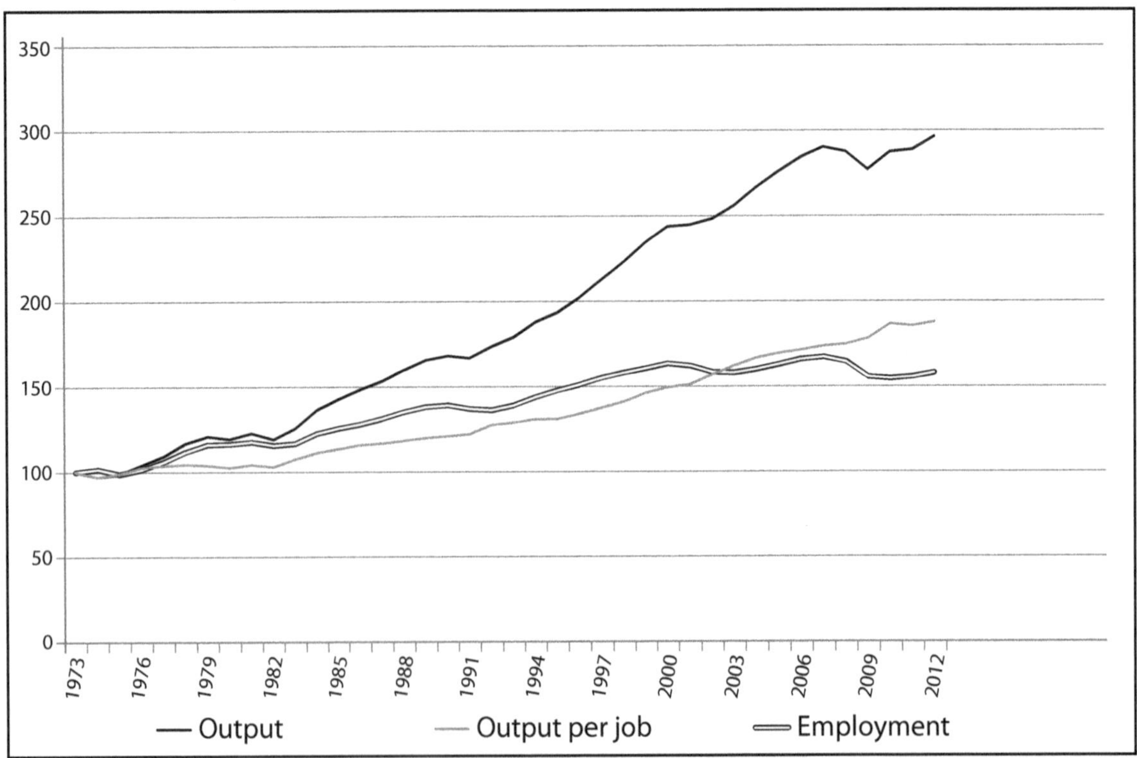

Figure 7: Productivity Indexes—Output, Output per Job, and Employment (1973=100). 1947–1972 averages: Output 59.6, Output per Person 71.3, Employment 82.4

did or how you did it, you probably remember things you discovered that were so good that you continued doing them even when the time or money returned. Businesses do that as well.

Efficiency can be quantified, economically, as productivity. So how much more productive has American business become, and how much has that helped its workers? From 1980 to 2000, workplace productivity consistently increased, while inflation-adjusted earnings for 80% of employees declined.[81] From September 1999 to May 2010, the economy grew by 20%, while the number of jobs ended up the same.[82]

Figure 7 shows the 39 years ending in 2011 in output, output per person, and employment, adjusted to 1973 values of 100.[83] Output, measured from weighted indexes provided by various industries and usually including inflation-adjusted sales statistics,[84] has moved far above the other two variables, indicating that providing goods and services usually involves fewer and fewer workers; although employment in 2012 was about the same as in 1998, output has surged since. At the same time, average inflation-corrected hourly wages, which increased 72% between 1947 and 1979, were up only 8% from 1979 to 2009, and total compensation rose 100% for the first period but only 7% in the second.[85]

No Relief from Retiring Baby Boomers, Unfilled Jobs, or Any Skills Gap

Observers have named three things that could make jobs more available in the future, specifically the baby boom generation retiring in massive numbers, more advertised positions, and an end to what some have called either "structural unemployment" or a "skills gap," in which employers cannot find able people to fill open jobs. Unfortunately, none of those offer much help.

Baby boomers have long held different opinions on aging from those in previous generations, views which have recently become more justified. In a 2002 survey, three-fifths of baby boomers aged 48 and older and 65% of those younger reported that they expected to work part time after retirement.[86] A 2003 AARP study, long before the 2008–2009 Great Recession housing and stock market price decreases, revealed that only one-fifth considered retirement time to be unproductive.[87] Other research has shown that baby boomers perceive themselves to have been more financially hurt by the Great Recession than any other age group, with many having relied on home equity in particular to facilitate their retirements.[88] Older employees' unemployment and workforce participation both reached all-time peaks in 2010,[89] and mean 2011 jobless time for those 55 and older was more than one year, roughly three months longer than the average for all ages.[90] In late 2010, about 60% of 50- to 61-year-old survey respondents claimed they had decided to retire later than they had expected, while 35% of those older had already postponed it.[91] In all, *U.S. News & World Report* chief business correspondent Rick Newman's early 2010 assessment that most Americans might want to work 10 to 15 years later than previous generations[92] seems spot-on.

The simple number of baby boomers alone means that there will be far more older people working. Figure 8 shows how many aged 55 and beyond, in three groups, have been in the labor force, extended with BLS predictions made in 2012 for the year 2020.[93]

The second often discussed relief factor is the number of publicized work opportunities. However, in the year from middle 2009 to middle 2010, though job postings increased 26%, there was no growth in actual hiring.[94] It is well known to people looking for work at different times in the past decade that ability and experience requirements have become more stringent.[95] Robert J. Samuelson held that as the economy weakens, employers "become more picky and cautious" and will often not add workers even after advertising positions if their sales are much the same, or they will hire only particularly outstanding candidates.[96] Likewise, specific knowledge or skills for which companies once

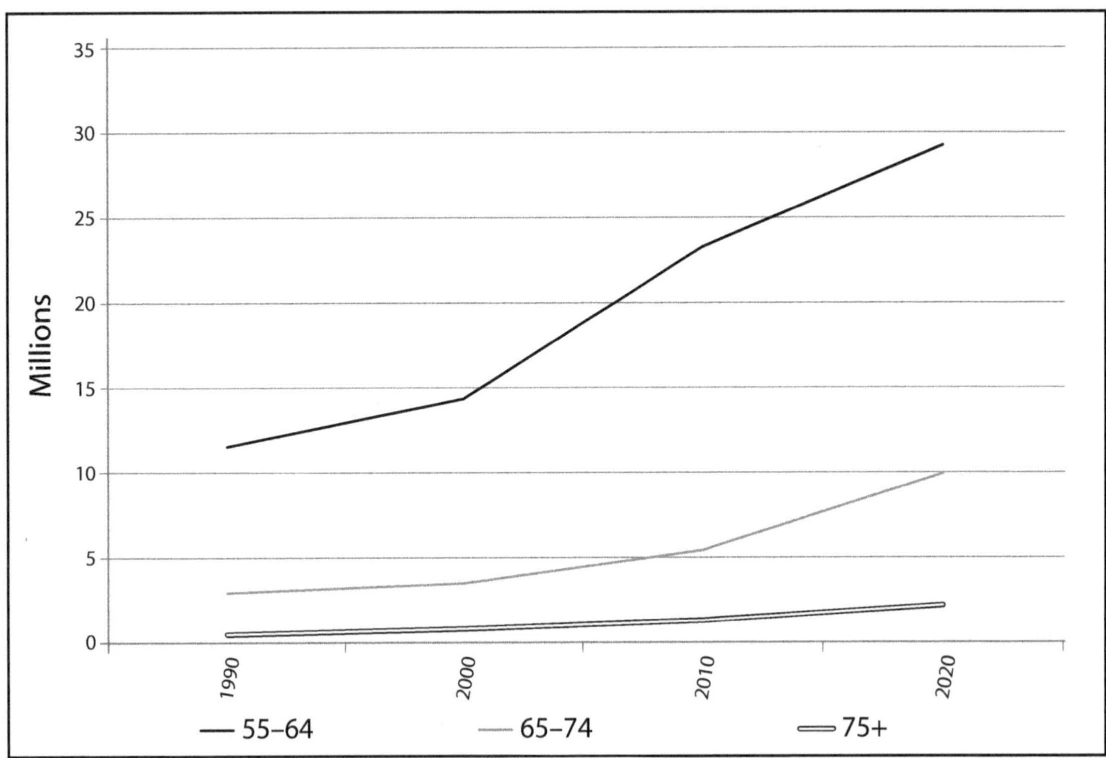

Figure 8: Number Aged 55+ Participating in the Labor Force by Age Group for 1990, 2000, and 2010, and Projected for 2020

only hoped are often now rigid requirements. Organizations' inclination to train incoming employees has also fallen drastically,[97] and specific capabilities, even if easily gained on the job, are increasingly needed in advance.[98] For these reasons, along with a rising tendency for businesses to use multiple methods to identify potential workers with possibly expensive health concerns,[99] more and more open positions are not filled.

Third, various articles since 2010 have claimed that much unemployment has been due to a mismatch between employees and employers. Many jobs, writers have contended, go unfilled, as they are needed in places with too few seekers or not enough with the aptitudes and experience required.[100] Although there is always some of this geographical structural unemployment, and real estate price decreases have cut mobility by making it harder to sell houses and move,[101] there is no skills gap now critical.[102] Wharton management professor Peter Cappelli pointed out that these so-called shortages were the same to businesses as not being able to get other resources at the price they wanted to pay, so often they simply needed to offer more money.[103] Cappelli also determined that employees were not missing basic educational skills as some companies claimed, but abilities related to workplace time.[104] Nobel Prize-winning economist Paul Krugman wrote that structural unemployment was also blamed during the Great Depression, but when demand came forward with World War II, it vanished as a problem.[105] To see that this problem is small, we need only view the numbers of jobs and job seekers; even if every one of September 2012's 3,547,000 advertised nonfarm positions were filled by one of that month's 12,082,000 officially jobless, the unemployment rate would still be over 5.5%[106]—and that with no advertised opportunities at all.

Upshot: What We Have Now Is What We're Going to Face

Philosophers and others have long debated the proper role of labor. Aristotle said the purpose of work was to gain leisure, the stuff of happiness, but time off, our main objective, should be productive, though for its own sake,[107] much as futurist Herman Kahn wrote about quaternary or unpaid activity.[108] Bertrand Russell even saw its virtuous reputation as damaging, equated professional labor to slavery, and said that "the road to happiness and prosperity lies in an organized diminution of work."[109] Long-time author Frank Joyce wrote in 2012 that the job system was not sustainable and not "the best we can do."[110]

Now, many more Americans want work than can get it, and the disparity will only grow, continuing a vicious circle in which lower demand for workers means less job income so sales are lower and even fewer employees are needed. As Martin Ford put it, "The skills and capabilities of many experienced workers are simply no longer demanded by the future."[111] It has also been a generation or more since people could easily get low-end "survival jobs." Overall, economically speaking, the United States now has excess capacity—in its workforce.[112]

So what can people do? Fortunately, not every viable lifestyle requires a full-time job. In *Work's New Age*, I wrote that millions of Americans had been independently surviving without one for a long time. Generally, their lives fit into two general schemes:

1. What could be called "living off the land," often without government-provided utilities,[113] by growing food, making things or obtaining them used whenever possible, living in non-standard houses, and generally minimizing both production and consumption.[114]
2. Living in a town or city, usually cooking from fresh ingredients, buying used in general, sharing living quarters, and getting around by walking, riding bicycles, or using public transportation,[115] reminiscent of how many lived during the Great Depression.[116]

Under these lifestyles, work, when available or chosen, can be steady but low-paying, part-time and occasional, or sporadic, but in any case is more peripheral to those involved.[117] Leisure time is more plentiful, but its activities need to be much less expensive than those practiced by most well-employed Americans.[118] More people have long been bending in this direction, even through good times; the share of those in the United States considering their paid labor the most important thing for them dropped from 38% in 1955 to 18% in 1991.[119]

The crux of the matter is for people to be aware of the transition we are now in. As before, prior to the Industrial Revolution, work was not the same, and it will not be again. Many studies have shown that relationships are more emotionally important to people than their jobs.[120] Involvement in communities will become more important to many, as the closeness more characteristic of small towns, valuable from many physical and mental health standpoints, figures to spread to cities as well.[121] In a backhanded way, jobs will return to the lack of significance they had before 1800—less common, less important, and much less obtainable, and we will learn to survive and even prosper without them.

So what can we expect for the next decade and beyond, in and around the world of work? That is the subject of Chapter 2.

Chapter 2:

What's Ahead for Workers and the Rest of Us

America is divided on many economic issues in name only. —Adam Davidson[122]

Events in the years to come are both predictable and unpredictable. The official unemployment rate and the AJSN will fluctuate, the latter moving more up than down. Automation, globalization, scalability, and efficiency will march on, absent huge and catastrophic world events. The rising cost of health care, and its continuing provision by employers, may or may not change legislatively.

The Next Four Years

Now that President Barack Obama has been re-elected and Republicans maintain a majority in the House of Representatives but not in the Senate, what will happen with American jobs?

During the 2012 campaign, neither candidate voiced much of substance about how to create more positions, which were then logging monthly gains but not enough to cover population increases. Barack Obama's acceptance speech at the 2012 Democratic National Convention proposed no significant action on employment.[123]

What difference was there between Obama and Republican candidate Mitt Romney on jobs and related issues? On tax rates, their most significant disagreements were on people with the highest incomes; on corporate tax levels, in 2009 we inaugurated a president who supported a 28% top rate, instead of a 2012 challenger who wanted 25%. We failed to vote in someone who thought the highest capital-gains tax should be 15%, and we chose one who said it should be 20%. We passed up a possible president who advocated little change in welfare and Social Security payments along with more free trade, and we got one who, during the campaign, supported the same.[124] We chose a candidate who said he wanted to "create opportunities for hard-working Americans to start making stuff again," and we rejected one who said he would "work to bring manufacturing back."[125] We did not elect Romney, who had "energy independence" listed first among his five-point plan for American jobs,[126] and we got Obama, who publicly wished, early in his 2012 State of the Union Address, for "a future where we're in control of our own energy" and later said he was ordering his "administration to open more than 75 percent of our potential offshore oil and gas resources." We declined a politician with conservative views and re-elected one who had said earlier in the year that he believed, as had Republican Abraham Lincoln, that "government should do for people only what they cannot do better by themselves, and no more."[127]

How liberal is our president, actually, on employment? Consider the following statements he made during 2012:

- "We should start with our tax code. Right now, companies get tax breaks for moving jobs and profits overseas. Meanwhile, companies that choose to stay in America get hit with one of the highest tax rates in the world. It makes no sense, and everyone knows it."[128]
- "We can give more tax breaks to corporations that ship jobs overseas, or we can start rewarding companies that open new plants and train new workers and create new jobs here, in the United States of America."[129]
- "I will go anywhere in the world to open new markets for American products."[130]
- "Michelle [Obama] and Jill Biden have worked with American businesses to secure a pledge of 135,000 jobs for veterans and their families."[131]
- "I've approved fewer regulations in the first three years of my presidency than my Republican predecessor did in his. I've ordered every federal agency to eliminate rules that don't make sense. We've already announced over 500 reforms, and just a fraction of them will save business and citizens more than $10 billion over the next five years."[132]
- "Right now, our immediate priority is stopping a tax hike on 160 million working Americans while the recovery is still fragile. People cannot afford losing $40 out of each paycheck this year."[133]

It is true that, though both Barack Obama and Mitt Romney asked for tax cuts on companies creating jobs, it was Obama who emphasized that they should be "good" positions.[134] A larger difference we should be aware of is on environmental issues, on which a 2012 Pew survey showed that 93% of Democrats wanted stricter laws, compared with a perhaps surprising but much lower 47% of Republicans,[135] boding well for jobs related to environmental controls.

Given that Barack Obama's labor philosophy is actually moderate, will the lack of cooperation between Democrats and Republicans in Congress still continue? The "fiscal cliff" negotiations called for both tax increases and spending cuts, effective in January 2013, if the two sides could not negotiate a solution,[136] which they achieved, with unemployment benefit extensions continued but a payroll tax reduction ended.[137] Political blogger and columnist Matthew Yglesias expected little teamwork, though Obama would get "concrete leverage" from what without negotiation, would be the end of various corporate tax reductions.[138] Yglesias noted that "expecting Republicans to surrender when Obama is returned with a weaker mandate and minorities in Congress is naïve,"[139] a sentiment echoed by *New York Times* columnist Ross Douthat, who wrote in September 2012 that "a re-elected Obama will be a permanently diminished Obama, with no magic left in his public persona and no mandate save to stay the current economic course."[140] Yglesias suggested that the president use his tax-cut leverage to get assistance on other issues,[141] which could materialize, but may not; if, as many charged, Republican federal lawmakers wanted to stop anything from passing in order to improve the perceived chance of Mitt Romney winning,[142] they may do the same thing with the 2016 election in mind.

So overall, what can we expect on the jobs front during Barack Obama's second term? Ross Douthat said he would be "already essentially a lame duck" by February 2013.[143] Author and columnist David Brooks asked if there was anything in Obama's nomination acceptance speech to convince us that the next four years would be different and wrote that at the 2012 Democratic National Convention he had asked "governors, mayors, and legislators" to state any important law they wanted passed in a second Obama term, and none could name any.[144] During the campaign, *Washington Post* blogger and columnist Ezra Klein said that voting for the president's agenda would constitute a vote for an attempt to return to pre-2008 normalcy,[145] something without a real chance, especially in the area of manufacturing, for which Obama has expressed expectations to provide 20th-century levels of jobs.[146] *Los Angeles Times* columnist Doyle McManus concurred in August 2012, citing the then-expected indecisive election outcome as incompatible with any perception of a mandate for action.[147] Ben Bernanke's December 2012 decision to maintain low interest rates until inflation reaches 2.5% or the unemployment rate drops below 6.5%[148] has been deemed by economists on both sides unlikely to significantly help the jobs situation.[149] In all, though we may get, as Brooks put it, "incremental improvement,"[150] we have every reason to expect the years 2013 through 2016, on jobs-related legislation, to be much the same as the previous four.

College Debt: The Next Bubble to Burst?

In June of 2012, President Obama told a university group that "making college affordable" was "one of the best things we can do for the economy."[151] So what has been happening financially with higher education?

Student borrowing started to rise along with large tuition increases in the 1980s.[152] By 2008, the mean educational loan debt among college seniors was more than $23,000, along with an average of $4,138 owed on credit cards.[153] The share of students with loans increased from 47% of those starting college in 1995 to 53% in 2003,[154] with the portion of bachelor's degree recipients owing money on them up from 45% in 1992 and 1993[155] to 66% in 2008 and 2010.[156] The average amounts they had to pay increased from $24,000 in 2009[157] to $25,250 the next year[158] and $26,600 in 2011,[159] the latter representing an 83% inflation-adjusted jump since 1993.[160] For-profit universities have much higher rates.[161] Funding from private sources has also become more common since 2002, as borrowers have responded more to direct marketing efforts.[162] Additionally, many have debt they will pay back to parents, which according to one estimate averaged $6,800 per graduate.[163]

Defaults on student loans, though still far behind the 1990 historical high of over 20%,[164] have become more common since the Great Recession,[165] increasing from 7% in the 2009 fiscal year to 8.8% the next,[166] and were close to 10% for those starting payments in 2009.[167] Those who fail to complete college were, as of 2012, over four times as statistically likely to default as those who obtained their degrees, with a rate of 16.8% compared with 3.7% of graduates. More borrowers have been dropping out as well, from 23% of those starting their studies in 1995 to almost 30% eight years later.[168] Approximately twice as many who have defaulted outright are in arrears, and only 37% of those who started repayment in 2005 have done so in full and on time.[169]

Recently, total national student loan debt overtook the amount owed on credit cards.[170] As of the middle of 2012, Americans had a total of more than $1 trillion, of which more than $850 billion was extended by the federal government. More loans have been cosigned, the share increasing from 67% in 2008 to more than 90% just three years later.[171] Federal student liabilities cannot easily be erased in bankruptcy and are cause for garnishment of Social Security checks and tax refunds.[172] As Mark Kantrowitz, proprietor of two college-payment websites put it, "student debt goes up and it doesn't ever go down."[173] However, those borrowing often see it as positive, with one study showing the self-esteem of those aged 18 to 27 correlating positively with the amount they owed on student loans and credit cards. Many just older, though, were less optimistic about it.[174]

In response to the state of the economy, the Obama administration reduced the requirement for minimum federal Stafford student loan payments to 10% of a borrower's disposable income, down from 15%, along with forgiving all balances owed, if sufficient payments have been made, after 20 years instead of the previous 25,[175] effective December 21, 2012.[176] The interest rate on current loans, though, increased from a temporary 3.4% to the former 6.8% on July 1 of that year,[177] a rise not as significant as it may seem, as it only affected money borrowed for school years starting in 2012 and will amount to an average of only $6 per month per loan year.[178]

What does the growth of student debt, often unpayable, mean for the choice to go to college? While higher education still correlates with higher income, covering its cost can cause severe problems. Non-federal governmental financing for college dropped 24% from 2001 to 2011, while tuition at state schools rose an average of 72%.[179] Average annual inflation-adjusted tuition and nonresidential fees increased, from about $1,000, $2,500, and $10,500 for public two-year, public four-year, and private four-year colleges in the 1980 to 1981 school year to $2,963, $8,244, and $28,500, respectively, in 2011-2012.[180] Typical annual costs for tuition, other fees, room, board, and other living expenses at Ohio State University are now about $25,000, with the University of Dayton, which advertised itself as affordable, costing about $48,000 and Oberlin, $60,000.[181] According to Mark Kantrowitz, lower-income students already are more often choosing community colleges over more expensive four-year schools.[182] Despite the perception of increased future income, in a 2012 *Time*/Carnegie Corporation survey, 80% of respondents agreed somewhat or slightly that "at many colleges, the education students receive is not worth what they pay for it."[183]

What will happen with all of this money owed? Without a large increase in the number of jobs, it seems clear that a lot of it will not be paid off. The chances are good that the Obama administration, or one later, will forgive even more of it. That will mean more losses to be absorbed, and, as has happened with mortgages and housing loans, it will then become more difficult to get money for college. Nongovernmental lenders will drop out. The number attending four-year schools will do what it has not done since before World War II: It will fall, maybe substantially. Private, four-year schools will face the issue of how much of their often ample endowments to spend supporting students who would otherwise not have a chance of attending. That will put the problem where it truly belongs, in the hands of organizations with more disposable income, in effect, than government agencies. Yet the result will be lower education levels, in general, for Americans.

2016, 2020, and Beyond

By 2016, most observers will at least wonder if the jobs crisis is permanent. Many Republicans will think that the measures advocated by Mitt Romney in 2012 and not implemented since, such as lower tax rates for those in the highest brackets, might help the crisis, but fewer will honestly expect any small or moderate change to solve the problem. One issue becoming plain, if hard to accept, is that America is not unique for either business climate or standard of living. It was before the "Winning by Default Years" ended in 1973,[184] but since then, though the strongest militarily and still the most influential, the United States has become only one of a growing set of 30, 40, or more free, prosperous, generally Western countries. Many Americans will still consider theirs the best, but ever fewer with overseas experience will consider it superior by a wide margin. The economy, meanwhile, will continue on the same pace, not in recession but, due to the realities of Work's New Age, seeming that way. The competitive sector, called "Economy I" by David Brooks, will continue improving productivity while cutting more jobs, while noncompetitive fields such as health care and government functions, Brooks's "Economy II,"[185] will provide a growing share of work.

Politically, the United States will be ready for a change. A charismatic Republican, possibly Marco Rubio or Bobby Jindal, will probably be elected in 2016 and will be more able than Barack Obama had been to push through legislation to alleviate the nation's largest problems, namely still-rising health care costs, a national debt well over $20 trillion, and, whatever the official employment rate, enormous numbers of Americans without work who would take it if readily available, as measured by an AJSN of 23 to 25 million.[186] The new laws and policies will help, but not enough to solve the jobs crisis, which even more commentators will realize is stable. A national discussion will pick up speed and get serious in the late 2010s, with debate on options such as guaranteed income and officially reduced work hours. With costs continuing to rise, compounded by the massive increase of enrollees from Obamacare, there may be serious calls for increased personal responsibility, a factor in, according to a Centers for Disease Control and Prevention 2011 study, as much as 75% of health care expenditures.[187]

One set of issues that may see some resolution in the late 2010s and early 2020s is the status of women in the workplace. Despite laws guaranteeing equal rights for both sexes, results have not been equal, especially in average pay. Though authors such as Warren Farrell[188] have documented that occupational choices explain most of the disparity and others have noted that it disappears or is even reversed when factors such as education and presence or absence of small children are controlled for, it remains a political issue, and one where almost all widely publicized observations have been in the direction of alleged anti-female discrimination. That may change. A landmark 2012 article by professor and public commentator Anne-Marie Slaughter in *The Atlantic*, "Why Women Still Can't Have It All," put forth the idea that women are inherently more involved in child-raising, and therefore, as long as high-level jobs have family-unfriendly requirements such as extensive travel and very long hours, they will not reach the same average workplace success as men. Slaughter called for industry-wide changes in these obligations,[189] which may at least partially materialize. There could also be appeals for affirmative action of sorts, mandating higher pay for women until their average income is the same; that is not likely to be passed into law, but it will influence public policy to the point where related things may occur.

Also more discussed will be the status of the Singularity, a possible event which author, inventor, and futurist Ray Kurzweil summarized as "extending our intelligence by reverse engineering it, modeling it, simulating it, reinstantiating it on more capable substrates, and modifying and extending it,"[190] and in which we may "transcend all of the limitations of our biology"[191] by merging our minds and bodies with computers. Kurzweil projected that by the late 2020s, products would be so cheap to produce that their value would be contained almost exclusively in their information, and with the economic power of genetics, nanotechnology, and robotics, the American underclasses would "largely disappear" between 2024 and 2034.[192] By the early 2030s, Kurzweil contended, there will be little difference between "human and machines, between real and virtual reality, or between work and play."[193] By the late 2010s, this possibility and the status of its progress will be better understood, and the richness of its philosophical issues will provide an immense area for national discourse.

How can we assess whether the Singularity as Ray Kurzweil saw it is taking hold? Author and reporter Joel Garreau outlined three general courses technology, people, and their interaction could follow, which he called the Heaven, Hell, and Prevail scenarios.[194] The Heaven scenario is continued exponential improvement in computer capacity and speed with almost exclusively good results, as Kurzweil predicted. Garreau wrote that if "almost unimaginably good things are happening," and if "predictions that recently seemed like science fiction are routinely exceeded," with technology taking the lead role, we would be seeing early indications of the Heaven development coming true.[195] The Hell possibility has the same acceleration in computing but with unstoppable "unspeakable evil," which would seem to be happening if the nearly unbelievable occurrences were bad instead of good, and the science-fiction-seeming results were disasters, out of control of humans.[196] In the Prevail scenario, which Garreau attributes to the work of philosopher and computer scientist Jaron Lanier, people will successfully regulate the rate of technological change and will agree to slow down or halt progress in dangerous areas, as happened with nuclear weapons technology in the mid-20th century. A slowing of the curve of computer-related advancement or software failing to keep pace, along with "little correlation between any exponential change in technology and the development of human society," would also mean that the Prevail situation is unfolding.[197]

When could possible inventions be in use? A *New York Times* 2011 reader survey started with predictions from a team of futurists and asked readers to move their expected implementation times forward or backward. Events and dates projected included a universal medical database by 2019, personalized genetic-based cures for cancer by 2023, practical driverless cars by 2024, designed and manufactured life-forms by 2026,[198] and recording devices to routinely capture both audio and video of entire lives by 2031.[199]

A more down-to-earth trend almost certain to continue is aging. By 2030, the United States average is projected to be as high as Florida's was in 2004, with 35.5 Americans aged 65 or older for each 100 who are 20 to 64, an increase of 67% from 2010.[200] The older population, from people living ever longer and birth rates not rising, will profoundly affect jobs, on both the supply and demand sides.

In all, there will be many differences between 2013 and 2033, the date I am using to predict the viability of careers. How can we fashion knowledge about the trends we have now and may see soon into influences on jobs? We will do that in Chapter 3.

Chapter 3:

What All This Means for Our Career Choices

I skate to where the puck is going to be, not where it has been. —Wayne Gretzky[201]

Careers, careers, careers. There are hundreds of them in the United States. They pay different amounts. They have widely varying working conditions. Their job security is not the same. Their benefits are unlike, along with their effects on lifestyles. A lot has been written about them. So what is original here?

We are in Work's New Age. Overall, fewer and fewer people are needed for jobs, and that won't change. Yet the effect of today's and tomorrow's economic realities will hardly be the same on each. We can summarize the trends into five main areas, in order of importance, as such:

- Automation—the ability of machines, software, and other technological tools to replace workers
- Globalization—the presence and availability of foreign employees more cost-effective than Americans
- Health Insurance—the burden on employers to cover their workers' medical expenses
- Scalability—the capability of a product to be produced in exponentially or logarithmically larger quantities with only linear increases in labor
- Efficiency—the one-way process of discovering methods to complete tasks with less work.

From these, we can start with six career principles:

1. Jobs that cannot reasonably be automated away are good.
2. Jobs dependent on obsolescent or endangered technology are bad.
3. Jobs that must be done locally are good.
4. Jobs that do not include health insurance are good.
5. Jobs producing less scalable goods and services MAY be good.
6. Jobs that seem to be maximized in efficiency already are good.

Other patterns which will affect the value and life remaining in careers are as follows:

A. Income inequality, often described as dividing people into "the 1%" and "the 99%," will continue and even increase. While it is not a problem in itself (Americans able to sell their labor for a good living have historically neither worried about nor been damaged by others earning much more), it is a natural consequence of work being done by a declining number of people, who will have dramatically more money and less time than most of their countrymen. As a luxury with ever-increasing possibilities, travel will be even more popular among the 1% and many others.

B. As described in Chapters 1 and 2, education levels have continued to rise but will soon level off or even decline. Community colleges, massive open online courses or MOOCs,[202] and other lower-priced alternatives to four-year universities will fill some of the gap, yet with many graduates unemployed and the pool of good entry-level jobs continuing to shrink, bachelor's degrees by themselves will increasingly be insufficient, as more jobs will require master's degrees[203] or even doctorates. To a great and growing extent, the more common the skills required for a position, the less it will pay.[204] Few artificially high hiring standards will actually be removed, for fear of making the set of applicants unworkably large.[205]

C. The problem of deteriorating American infrastructure, for which the American Society of Civil Engineers in 2009 gave the United States a summary grade of D[206] and per the World Economic Forum has dropped world wide from a rank of first to 14th from 2005 to 2012,[207] must be solved, and neither conservatives, who don't want America to fall further by world standards, nor liberals, who are most willing to spend the money, will let it get much worse. Whatever the source of funding, there will be extensive work on American highways, bridges, roads, and airports in the late 2010s and 2020s.

D. Although women are passing men in many career-related areas, such as graduation rates and income in their 20s,[208] they, per Chapter 2, will still be perceived as a group needing protection, so, to some extent in defiance of market forces, pay for and number of opportunities in jobs regarded as "women's work" will often do better than other events would indicate.

E. There will be a rising ability of companies to charge more or to otherwise gain an advantage with customers, if they can certify their goods and services were made in America or provided by Americans. (In late 2012, after first writing this sentence, the author heard help-desk workers at three different companies announce their cities and states on each call.[209] We can expect that sort of thing to become even more commonplace.)

F. The primary (extracting raw resources through such means as farming or mining) and secondary (manufacturing) sectors, except for food production, which must often take place locally and nationally, will continue to shed jobs faster than the national average. The number of positions in the tertiary (service) sector, which provided 80% of jobs as of 2008,[210] will generally drop as well, but at different rates and slower overall. More and more people will be productive in the quaternary sector—constructive activities for their own sake, such as religious practices, reading, playing games, tourism, outdoor recreation, nonvocational skill acquisition and use, and political discussions,[211] as well as community tasks[212]—but these undertakings will still be unpaid.

G. As described in Chapter 2, the American population, as a unit, will continue to age. Older people will have younger characteristics than before, but there will be far more of them, and they will still consume a disproportionate amount of health care resources. Between that and Obamacare, which will allow an increasing number of people to get insurance coverage, jobs in the health care field, which as a relatively inelastic area of spending was affected remarkably little by the Great Recession,[213] should generally grow greatly.

From these, we can derive a variety of principles. From the first pattern above:

7. Jobs catering to the 1% are good.
8. Jobs that help people working very long hours are good.
9. Jobs related to personal, vacation, or recreational travel, especially custom-designed, exotic, or expensive, MAY be good.

From the second:

10. Jobs that require highly unusual sets of aptitude MAY be good.
11. Jobs with artificially high or restrictive entry requirements MAY be good.

From the third:

12. Jobs in skilled construction trades MAY be good.
13. Jobs connected with highway, road, bridge, or airport repair, design, or construction MAY be good.

From the fourth:

14. Jobs with a high percentage of women working them, in perception or in reality, MAY be good.

From the fifth:

15. Jobs in which Americans are particularly valued MAY be good.

From the sixth:

16. Jobs doing extraction are bad.
17. Jobs doing manufacturing, except food products, are bad.
18. Jobs involving showing people how to do constructive unpaid activities are good.

From the seventh:

19. Jobs connected with products disproportionately likely to be used by people over 65 MAY be good.
20. Jobs connected with health in any form MAY be good.

All seven of these patterns, or trends, will bring in business opportunities, some for goods and services rare or nonexistent today. Yet, although some jobs over the next 20 years will be new or almost new, it is stunning to see how many are not. Of the 26 Bureau of Labor Statistics categories in which at least a million people were working in 2006, only part of one—the last three words of "combined food preparation and serving workers, including fast food"—was new since 1930.[214] It is also noteworthy that none of the 26 centers on computers.[215]

More than any other consideration, it is essential that people deciding among careers be aware of the *future* situation, not the nature of the past or even the present. Therefore, we should not overemphasize possibly temporary advantages, or look at an insufficient upcoming timespan. One large 2012-copyrighted book on the "best jobs" names as its first- and third-highest-ranking ones developers of applications and systems software, citing their average annual earnings of more than $80,000, high expected growth percentages through 2018, and 15,000 openings apiece each year.[216] Developers of uncategorized software ranked first on the CareerCast website in its piece on the 200 best jobs of 2012, and second in a like *U.S. News & World Report* article.[217] These sources do not incorporate any outlook later on and fail to consider that software development can be done from anywhere in the world, by people willing to be paid a lot less. The Forecast for 2033 ratings in Part II reflect projected changes in the number of American jobs over the next 20 years, so to the corresponding BLS occupation, named Software Developers, I give a rating of Poor.

Similarly, other positions look different from this longer future perspective. This same career volume rates pharmacists, with annual earnings more than $100,000, 17% growth projected through 2018, and more than 10,000 annual openings, at 13th overall. I also rate this job as Poor, since pharmacy as a profession is currently buoyed by outdated prescription-filling requirements and the lack of comprehensive electronic-based medical records, and when these situations end a long time before 2033, far fewer will be needed. Another is accountants and auditors, 11th out of 400 "best jobs overall" with growth more than 20% and almost 50,000 annual openings,[218] and mentioned first in another *U.S. News & World Report* piece, about six "hot jobs"[219]—I again say Poor, since auditing and accounting, even if demand is currently strong, are very susceptible to both automation and globalization. People may do well with these positions for the next five years, and that's all there are until 2018, but spending much time and money for, say, pharmacy education, in expectation of a solid career for life, would now be a serious mistake. Many people graduating college this year will be 27 in 2018, and numerous new high school graduates will be 23, hardly optimal horizons for their career planning. Much other writing takes the same positions, considering the best jobs as those with good working environments, relatively high pay, and exceptional short-term hiring expectations,[220] any or all of which will probably change long before today's younger applicants even approach midlife.

The opposite can also be true, as positions considered poor in most sources can look much better for 2033. In the CareerCast listing of "the 10 worst jobs of 2011," the fifth and sixth ones named, taxi driver and emergency medical technician, received rankings here of Very Good and Excellent. The CareerCast article acknowledges that hiring prospects for some positions listed are good[221] but is more concerned with work conditions, which are not connected with job longevity and are judged by individual preference anyway.

Another disagreement I have with other things you may read is on science-related opportunities. Some score high in the chapters to come, but the field is hardly the wide-open hiring area implied by those who say American universities do not produce enough science graduates.[222] Many want to work in academia, but as of 2009, only 14% of new degree holders in the life sciences were able to get university positions teaching or researching within five years, a share shrinking steadily since 1979,[223] and reports published in 2010 and 2011 show that private industry has not hired enough science doctorates to make the degrees financially worthwhile.[224] For one example, between 2000 and 2012, American drug companies cut 300,000 jobs, many formerly providing work for Ph.D.s in chemistry.[225] As a result of poor opportunities, many scientists with doctoral degrees in various disciplines have now been working as low-paid postdoctoral fellows, customarily one- to two-year apprenticeships of sorts, for as long as ten.[226]

One factor maybe surprising by its nonincorporation in this book's 2033 forecasts is level of pay. I list it in a general range and have some comments about where I expect compensation for a position to go, but it is not included in the overall predictions. There are four reasons for this. First, amount of income will increasingly become an individual issue, as all jobs will allow survival. Second, more money means more competition, which means positions that pay more will be harder to get for that reason alone. Third, high-income jobs have the disadvantage of attracting replacement by robots, computer systems, and lower-compensated foreign workers. Fourth, in order to get the money involved, you must be *employed* in the field—a jobless nurse's aide has the same work income as an unemployed computer systems manager—so the chances of actually working at a given position can be as important, if not more so, as how much it pays. I document the overall chance for earning enough for what most people would consider a reasonable living, for quality of work conditions, and for compatibility with other involvements, but none are incorporated into the 2033 prospect ratings. It is up to you to decide how important they are.

Now that we know how to judge the compatibility of careers and jobs with the future, which ones are good, bad, and indifferent? We will explore that in Part II.

Part II: Careers and Jobs that Will and Won't Last

Chapter 4:
The Careers: How They Compare

Don't confuse having a career with having a life. —Hillary Clinton[227]

The BLS, within the U.S. Department of Labor, recognizes 25 "occupation groups"[228] or career fields. Within them there are 502 jobs, or "detailed occupations,"[229] for which the BLS maintains statistics, including the number of people employed and a projected ten-year increase or decrease.[230] I have added four more, which are currently nearly nonexistent or generally illegal but which will be more prominent by 2033.

Figure 9 shows the occupation groups, along with the number of jobs they include in this book.

Occupation Group	#	Occupation Group	#
Architecture and Engineering	30	Legal	6
Arts and Design	10	Life, Physical, and Social Science	31
Building and Grounds Cleaning	6	Management	28
Business and Financial	25	Math	5
Community and Social Service	10	Media and Communications	10
Computer and Information Technology	8	Military	1
Construction and Extraction	40	Office and Administrative Support	27
Education, Training, and Library	17	Personal Care and Service	25
Entertainment and Sports	8	Production	59
Farming, Fishing, and Forestry	7	Protective Service	14
Food Preparation and Serving	8	Sales	17
Healthcare	48	Transportation and Material Moving	29
Installation, Maintenance, and Repair	37	Totals	506

Figure 9: Number of Jobs Included in Choosing a Lasting Career, *by Bureau of Labor Statistics Occupation Group*

There are many different ways of comparing occupations. I name 15 for each:

1. Job Name, the same as the BLS's Detailed Occupation when available[231]
2. Occupation Group, also matching BLS wording[232]

3. Local-Boundness, expressed as Low, Medium, or High
4. Resistance to Robotics, expressed as Low, Medium, or High
5. Resistance to Computing and Connectivity, expressed as Low, Medium, or High
6. Pertinent Principles (Good), naming each of the applicable Lasting Career Principles that are consistently positive
7. Pertinent Principles (Maybe Good), naming each of the applicable Lasting Career Principles that are usually positive
8. Pertinent Principles (Bad), naming each of the applicable principles that are consistently negative
9. 2010 Number of Workers, as reported by the BLS[233]
10. Chance for Good Living Wage, expressed as Low, Medium, or High
11. 2010 Median Pay, as reported by the BLS: Low for below $40,000 annually, Medium for $40,000 to $80,000, and High for over $80,000[234]
12. Median Quality of Work Conditions, expressed as Low, Medium, or High
13. Family and Outside Activities Compatibility, expressed as Low, Medium, or High
14. Forecast for 2010–2020 Change, in percentage, as reported by the BLS[235]
15. Forecast for 2033, expressed as Poor, Fair, Good, Very Good, and Excellent.

All of these are listed for each of the 506 jobs, along with comments, in Chapter 7. The Appendix contains definitions of the meaning of everything in these 15 fields.

Which careers have jobs most likely to require local work? Figure 10 presents the average ratings within each of the occupation groups, weighting each position within each group equally, using ratings of 1 for low local boundness, 2 for medium, and 3 for high, in order from most to least locally bound.

Occupation Group	1 to 3 Scale	Average Result
Building and Grounds Cleaning	3.00	Very Locally Bound
Construction and Extraction	3.00	Very Locally Bound
Food Preparation and Serving	3.00	Very Locally Bound
Personal Care and Service	2.88	Very Locally Bound
Farming, Fishing, and Forestry	2.86	Very Locally Bound
Installation, Maintenance, and Repair	2.78	Very Locally Bound
Community and Social Service	2.70	Very Locally Bound
Healthcare	2.69	Very Locally Bound
Protective Service	2.57	Very Locally Bound
Transportation and Material Moving	2.31	Somewhat Locally Bound
Education, Training, and Library	2.29	Somewhat Locally Bound
Entertainment and Sports	2.25	Somewhat Locally Bound
Management	2.07	Somewhat Locally Bound
Sales	2.06	Somewhat Locally Bound
Production	1.90	Somewhat Locally Bound
Office and Administrative Support	1.89	Somewhat Locally Bound
Legal	1.67	Somewhat Locally Bound

Life, Physical, and Social Science	1.65	Somewhat Locally Bound
Media and Communications	1.60	Somewhat Locally Bound
Architecture and Engineering	1.30	Not Locally Bound
Arts and Design	1.30	Not Locally Bound
Business and Financial	1.28	Not Locally Bound
Computer and Information Technology	1.00	Not Locally Bound
Math	1.00	Not Locally Bound
Military	1.00	Not Locally Bound
Overall Average	2.18	Somewhat Locally Bound

Figure 10: Average Local-Boundness by Career, Measured by Average of Included Jobs

As well, the occupation groups have different chances of being hurt by probable robotics developments. How do they compare? Using the same 1-2-3 system, and also averaged among jobs within each career, Figure 11 gives the results.

Occupation Group	1 to 3 Scale	Average Result
Business and Financial	3.00	Very Resistant to Robotics
Community and Social Service	3.00	Very Resistant to Robotics
Computer and Information Technology	3.00	Very Resistant to Robotics
Education, Training, and Library	3.00	Very Resistant to Robotics
Entertainment and Sports	3.00	Very Resistant to Robotics
Legal	3.00	Very Resistant to Robotics
Life, Physical, and Social Science	3.00	Very Resistant to Robotics
Management	3.00	Very Resistant to Robotics
Math	3.00	Very Resistant to Robotics
Architecture and Engineering	2.93	Very Resistant to Robotics
Healthcare	2.81	Generally Resistant to Robotics
Arts and Design	2.80	Generally Resistant to Robotics
Farming, Fishing, and Forestry	2.71	Generally Resistant to Robotics
Personal Care and Service	2.68	Generally Resistant to Robotics
Media and Communications	2.60	Generally Resistant to Robotics
Sales	2.59	Generally Resistant to Robotics
Food Preparation and Serving	2.50	Generally Resistant to Robotics
Protective Service	2.50	Generally Resistant to Robotics
Installation, Maintenance, and Repair	2.49	Generally Resistant to Robotics
Building and Grounds Cleaning	2.17	Somewhat Resistant to Robotics
Office and Administrative Support	2.11	Somewhat Resistant to Robotics
Transportation and Material Moving	2.03	Somewhat Resistant to Robotics
Military	2.00	Somewhat Resistant to Robotics
Construction and Extraction	1.80	Somewhat Resistant to Robotics
Production	1.19	Not Resistant to Robotics
Overall Average	2.45	Generally Resistant to Robotics

Figure 11: Average Resistance to Robotics by Career, Measured by Average of Included Jobs

The next assessment shows vulnerability to being automated through computing systems and connectivity, or through the ability of computers to communicate with minimal human involvement. Applying the same 1-2-3 scale job by job produces Figure 12.

Occupation Group	1 to 3 Scale	Average Result
Building and Grounds Cleaning	3.00	Very Resistant to Computing and Connectivity
Farming, Fishing, and Forestry	3.00	Very Resistant to Computing and Connectivity
Food Preparation and Serving	3.00	Very Resistant to Computing and Connectivity
Installation, Maintenance, and Repair	3.00	Very Resistant to Computing and Connectivity
Military	3.00	Very Resistant to Computing and Connectivity
Personal Care and Service	3.00	Very Resistant to Computing and Connectivity
Protective Service	3.00	Very Resistant to Computing and Connectivity
Construction and Extraction	2.98	Very Resistant to Computing and Connectivity
Management	2.93	Very Resistant to Computing and Connectivity
Life, Physical, and Social Science	2.74	Generally Resistant to Computing and Connectivity
Community and Social Service	2.70	Generally Resistant to Computing and Connectivity
Transportation and Material Moving	2.69	Generally Resistant to Computing and Connectivity
Healthcare	2.69	Generally Resistant to Computing and Connectivity
Production	2.68	Generally Resistant to Computing and Connectivity
Math	2.60	Generally Resistant to Computing and Connectivity
Entertainment and Sports	2.50	Generally Resistant to Computing and Connectivity
Education, Training, and Library	2.35	Somewhat Resistant to Computing and Connectivity
Sales	2.35	Somewhat Resistant to Computing and Connectivity
Media and Communications	2.30	Somewhat Resistant to Computing and Connectivity
Arts and Design	2.20	Somewhat Resistant to Computing and Connectivity
Architecture and Engineering	2.07	Somewhat Resistant to Computing and Connectivity
Legal	1.83	Somewhat Resistant to Computing and Connectivity
Business and Financial	1.80	Somewhat Resistant to Computing and Connectivity
Office and Administrative Support	1.74	Somewhat Resistant to Computing and Connectivity
Computer and Information Technology	1.38	Not Resistant to Computing and Connectivity
Overall Average	2.58	Generally Resistant to Computing and Connectivity

Figure 12: Average Resistance to Computing and Connectivity by Career, Measured by Average of Included Jobs

How about prospects for a reasonably comfortable living wage? Figure 13 shows that, using the same method.

Occupation Group	1 to 3 Scale	Average Result
Management	2.89	Very High Chance of Good Living Wage
Architecture and Engineering	2.87	Very High Chance of Good Living Wage
Computer and Information Technology	2.75	High Chance of Good Living Wage
Life, Physical, and Social Science	2.68	High Chance of Good Living Wage
Math	2.60	High Chance of Good Living Wage
Business and Financial	2.56	High Chance of Good Living Wage

Legal	2.50	High Chance of Good Living Wage
Education, Training, and Library	2.35	Medium Chance of Good Living Wage
Healthcare	2.29	Medium Chance of Good Living Wage
Community and Social Service	2.20	Medium Chance of Good Living Wage
Transportation and Material Moving	2.14	Medium Chance of Good Living Wage
Installation, Maintenance, and Repair	2.03	Medium Chance of Good Living Wage
Construction and Extraction	2.03	Medium Chance of Good Living Wage
Military	2.00	Medium Chance of Good Living Wage
Protective Service	2.00	Medium Chance of Good Living Wage
Arts and Design	1.90	Medium Chance of Good Living Wage
Media and Communications	1.90	Medium Chance of Good Living Wage
Sales	1.76	Medium Chance of Good Living Wage
Entertainment and Sports	1.38	Low Chance of Good Living Wage
Building and Grounds Cleaning	1.33	Low Chance of Good Living Wage
Production	1.32	Low Chance of Good Living Wage
Personal Care and Service	1.32	Low Chance of Good Living Wage
Farming, Fishing, and Forestry	1.29	Low Chance of Good Living Wage
Office and Administrative Support	1.22	Low Chance of Good Living Wage
Food Preparation and Serving	1.13	Low Chance of Good Living Wage
Overall Average	2.04	Medium Chance of Good Living Wage

Figure 13: Average Chance of Good Living Wage by Career, Measured by Average of Included Jobs

Next, we have working environments, determined similarly in Figure 14.

Occupation Group	1 to 3 Scale	Average Result
Architecture and Engineering	3.00	Excellent Median Quality of Work Conditions
Computer and Information Technology	3.00	Excellent Median Quality of Work Conditions
Education, Training, and Library	3.00	Excellent Median Quality of Work Conditions
Legal	3.00	Excellent Median Quality of Work Conditions
Math	3.00	Excellent Median Quality of Work Conditions
Media and Communications	3.00	Excellent Median Quality of Work Conditions
Business and Financial	2.96	Excellent Median Quality of Work Conditions
Life, Physical, and Social Science	2.94	Excellent Median Quality of Work Conditions
Arts and Design	2.90	Excellent Median Quality of Work Conditions
Community and Social Service	2.90	Excellent Median Quality of Work Conditions
Management	2.89	Excellent Median Quality of Work Conditions
Healthcare	2.85	Excellent Median Quality of Work Conditions
Office and Administrative Support	2.78	Very Good Median Quality of Work Conditions
Entertainment and Sports	2.75	Very Good Median Quality of Work Conditions
Personal Care and Service	2.72	Very Good Median Quality of Work Conditions
Transportation and Material Moving	2.41	Good Median Quality of Work Conditions
Sales	2.41	Good Median Quality of Work Conditions
Installation, Maintenance, and Repair	2.35	Good Median Quality of Work Conditions
Protective Service	2.14	Fair Median Quality of Work Conditions

Production	2.05	Fair Median Quality of Work Conditions
Food Preparation and Serving	2.00	Fair Median Quality of Work Conditions
Building and Grounds Cleaning	1.83	Fair Median Quality of Work Conditions
Construction and Extraction	1.75	Fair Median Quality of Work Conditions
Farming, Fishing, and Forestry	1.71	Fair Median Quality of Work Conditions
Military	1.00	Poor Median Quality of Work Conditions
Overall Average	2.56	Good Median Quality of Work Conditions

Figure 14: Average Quality of Work Conditions by Career, Measured by Average of Included Jobs

The final detailed measure we will look at by occupation group is suitability with families and other efforts, shown in Figure 15.

Occupation Group	1 to 3 Scale	Average Result
Building and Grounds Cleaning	3.00	Excellent Compatibility with Family Life and Outside Activities
Community and Social Service	3.00	Excellent Compatibility with Family Life and Outside Activities
Computer and Information Technology	3.00	Excellent Compatibility with Family Life and Outside Activities
Education, Training, and Library	3.00	Excellent Compatibility with Family Life and Outside Activities
Food Preparation and Serving	3.00	Excellent Compatibility with Family Life and Outside Activities
Math	3.00	Excellent Compatibility with Family Life and Outside Activities
Office and Administrative Support	3.00	Excellent Compatibility with Family Life and Outside Activities
Production	2.98	Excellent Compatibility with Family Life and Outside Activities
Healthcare	2.98	Excellent Compatibility with Family Life and Outside Activities
Construction and Extraction	2.95	Excellent Compatibility with Family Life and Outside Activities
Arts and Design	2.90	Excellent Compatibility with Family Life and Outside Activities
Life, Physical, and Social Science	2.84	Very Good Compatibility with Family Life and Outside Activities
Media and Communications	2.80	Very Good Compatibility with Family Life and Outside Activities
Management	2.79	Very Good Compatibility with Family Life and Outside Activities
Protective Service	2.79	Very Good Compatibility with Family Life and Outside Activities
Personal Care and Service	2.76	Very Good Compatibility with Family Life and Outside Activities
Installation, Maintenance, and Repair	2.70	Very Good Compatibility with Family Life and Outside Activities
Sales	2.65	Very Good Compatibility with Family Life and Outside Activities
Business and Financial	2.64	Very Good Compatibility with Family Life and Outside Activities
Farming, Fishing, and Forestry	2.57	Good Compatibility with Family Life and Outside Activities
Architecture and Engineering	2.53	Good Compatibility with Family Life and Outside Activities
Legal	2.50	Good Compatibility with Family Life and Outside Activities
Transportation and Material Moving	2.45	Good Compatibility with Family Life and Outside Activities
Entertainment and Sports	2.25	Fair Compatibility with Family Life and Outside Activities
Military	1.00	Poor Compatibility with Family Life and Outside Activities
Overall Average	2.81	Very Good Compatibility with Family Life and Outside Activities

Figure 15: Average Quality of Work Conditions by Career, Measured by Average of Included Jobs

Judged in the same way, how are the survival and growth prospects for jobs in each occupational group for 2033? Using the same system, except with the five categories (Poor, Fair, Good, Very Good, and Excellent) converted to rankings of 1 to 5, we get the following.

Occupation Group	1 to 5 Scale	Average Result
Community and Social Service	3.60	Very Good
Healthcare	3.44	Good
Building and Grounds Cleaning	3.17	Good
Personal Care and Service	3.16	Good
Life, Physical, and Social Science	2.77	Good
Construction and Extraction	2.58	Good
Installation, Maintenance, and Repair	2.54	Good
Architecture and Engineering	2.43	Fair
Education, Training, and Library	2.29	Fair
Food Preparation and Serving	2.25	Fair
Management	2.07	Fair
Business and Financial	2.00	Fair
Sales	1.94	Fair
Transportation and Material Moving	1.93	Fair
Protective Service	1.93	Fair
Media and Communications	1.90	Fair
Legal	1.83	Fair
Arts and Design	1.80	Fair
Entertainment and Sports	1.63	Fair
Farming, Fishing, and Forestry	1.43	Poor
Math	1.40	Poor
Office and Administrative Support	1.26	Poor
Computer and Information Technology	1.25	Poor
Production	1.14	Poor
Military	1.00	Poor
Overall Average	2.23	Fair

Figure 16: Average Survival and Growth Forecast for 2033 by Career, Measured by Average of Included Jobs

This last chart is a good summary of how careers in general will fare through 2033. Some fields that have been fine in recent decades and still have strong reputations, such as Math, Computer and Information Technology, and Office and Administrative Support, come out near the bottom here, whereas Personal Care and Service and Building and Grounds Cleaning, while usually paying poorly, are among the best otherwise. Lines of work that one might think would end up about the same, such as Installation, Maintenance and Repair, Transportation and Material Moving, and Production, finished widely spaced apart. As we saw in the previous chapter and will see further in the detailed job listings, many of these similar-seeming positions conceal extreme differences in their prospects.

So what are the highest ranking individual jobs within these categories? That is in Chapter 5.

Chapter 5:

The Best Jobs, in Different Ways and in General

They are happy men whose natures sort with their vocations. —*Francis Bacon*[236]

What are the best jobs? What does that mean to you? What positions will come out ahead in the next 20 years?

Of the more than 150,000,000 Americans in the labor force, there are close to 150 million opinions and sets of specific preferences. While this book focuses on whether jobs and careers will be around for decades to come, other factors are meaningful as well. So let us look at the best positions from some different standpoints.

First, we list the jobs with the strongest chances to endure and become more common for Americans throughout the next 20 years. Only 19 of the 506 received forecasts of Excellent. Figure 17 shows them.

Job	Occupation Group
Aerospace Engineering and Operations Technicians	Architecture and Engineering
Animal Care and Service Workers	Personal Care and Service
Audiologists	Healthcare
Bicycle Repairers	Installation, Maintenance, and Repair
Cardiovascular Technologists and Technicians and Vascular Technologists	Healthcare
Civil Engineering Technicians	Architecture and Engineering
EMTs and Paramedics	Healthcare
Home Health and Personal Care Aides	Healthcare
Maids and Housekeeping Cleaners	Building and Grounds Cleaning
Massage Therapists	Healthcare
Medical Scientists	Life, Physical, and Social Science
Mental Health Counselors and Marriage and Family Therapists	Community and Social Service
Nursing Aides, Orderlies, and Attendants	Healthcare
Occupational Therapists	Healthcare
Occupational Therapy Assistants and Aides	Healthcare
Personal Assistants, Personal Organizers, and Task Completers	Personal Care and Service

Physical Therapist Assistants and Aides	Healthcare
Physician Assistants	Healthcare
Residential Advisors	Personal Care and Service

Figure 17: Jobs with Excellent Survival and Growth Forecasts for 2033

An additional 55 were given ratings of Very Good. They are in Figure 18.

Job	Occupation Group
Aerospace Engineers	Architecture and Engineering
Amusement and Recreation Attendants	Personal Care and Service
Barbers, Hairdressers, and Cosmetologists	Personal Care and Service
Biochemists and Biophysicists	Life, Physical, and Social Science
Biological Technicians	Life, Physical, and Social Science
Brickmasons, Blockmasons, and Stonemasons	Construction and Extraction
Career and Technical Education Teachers	Education, Training, and Library
Carpenters	Construction and Extraction
Childcare Workers	Personal Care and Service
Chiropractors	Healthcare
Civil Engineers	Architecture and Engineering
Concierges	Personal Care and Service
Construction Equipment Operators	Construction and Extraction
Construction Managers	Management
Cooks	Food Preparation and Serving
Dental Hygienists	Healthcare
Elementary, Middle, and High School Principals	Management
Elevator Installers and Repairers	Construction and Extraction
Environmental Engineering Technicians	Architecture and Engineering
Environmental Engineers	Architecture and Engineering
Fitness Trainers and Instructors	Personal Care and Service
Glaziers	Construction and Extraction
Health Educators	Community and Social Service
Landscape Architects	Architecture and Engineering
Licensed Practical and Licensed Vocational Nurses	Healthcare
Manicurists and Pedicurists	Personal Care and Service
Market Research Analysts	Business and Financial
Medical Assistants	Healthcare
Medical Equipment Preparers	Healthcare
Medical Equipment Repairers	Installation, Maintenance, and Repair
Medical Roboticists (Khanna and Smith)	Architecture and Engineering
Microbiologists	Life, Physical, and Social Science
Occupational Health and Safety Technicians	Healthcare
Optometrists	Healthcare
Physical Therapists	Healthcare
Physicians and Surgeons	Healthcare
Physicists and Astronomers	Life, Physical, and Social Science

Plumbers, Pipefitters, and Steamfitters	Construction and Extraction
Podiatrists	Healthcare
Probation Officers and Correctional Treatment Specialists	Community and Social Service
Prostitutes (Legal)	Personal Care and Service
Recreational Therapists	Healthcare
Recreational Vehicle Service Technicians	Installation, Maintenance, and Repair
Registered Nurses	Healthcare
Rehabilitation Counselors	Community and Social Service
Respiratory Therapy Technicians	Healthcare
Skincare Specialists	Personal Care and Service
Substance Abuse and Behavioral Disorder Counselors	Community and Social Service
Surgical Technologists	Healthcare
Taxi Drivers and Chauffeurs	Transportation and Material Moving
Teacher Assistants	Education, Training, and Library
Tour Guides and Escorts	Personal Care and Service
Travel Guides	Personal Care and Service
Veterinarians	Healthcare
Veterinary Assistants and Laboratory Animal Caretakers	Healthcare

Figure 18: Jobs with Very Good Survival and Growth Forecasts for 2033

From here, I will take the best scores on other criteria and put them into combinations that may reveal something. Thirty-nine of the Excellent and Very Good-forecasted positions had high chances of providing a reasonably comfortable living wage. They are shown in Figure 19.

Job	Occupation Group	2033 Forecast
Aerospace Engineering and Operations Technicians	Architecture and Engineering	Excellent
Aerospace Engineers	Architecture and Engineering	Very Good
Audiologists	Healthcare	Excellent
Biochemists and Biophysicists	Life, Physical, and Social Science	Very Good
Brickmasons, Blockmasons, and Stonemasons	Construction and Extraction	Very Good
Cardiovascular Technologists and Technicians and Vascular Technologists	Healthcare	Excellent
Career and Technical Education Teachers	Education, Training, and Library	Very Good
Chiropractors	Healthcare	Very Good
Civil Engineering Technicians	Architecture and Engineering	Excellent
Civil Engineers	Architecture and Engineering	Very Good
Construction Managers	Management	Very Good
Dental Hygienists	Healthcare	Very Good
Elementary, Middle, and High School Principals	Management	Very Good
Elevator Installers and Repairers	Construction and Extraction	Very Good
Environmental Engineering Technicians	Architecture and Engineering	Very Good
Environmental Engineers	Architecture and Engineering	Very Good
Health Educators	Community and Social Service	Very Good
Landscape Architects	Architecture and Engineering	Very Good
Market Research Analysts	Business and Financial	Very Good

Medical Equipment Repairers	Installation, Maintenance, and Repair	Very Good
Medical Roboticists (Khanna and Smith)	Architecture and Engineering	Very Good
Medical Scientists	Life, Physical, and Social Science	Excellent
Mental Health Counselors and Marriage and Family Therapists	Community and Social Service	Excellent
Microbiologists	Life, Physical, and Social Science	Very Good
Occupational Health and Safety Technicians	Healthcare	Very Good
Occupational Therapists	Healthcare	Excellent
Occupational Therapy Assistants and Aides	Healthcare	Excellent
Optometrists	Healthcare	Very Good
Physical Therapists	Healthcare	Very Good
Physician Assistants	Healthcare	Excellent
Physicians and Surgeons	Healthcare	Very Good
Physicists and Astronomers	Life, Physical, and Social Science	Very Good
Plumbers, Pipefitters, and Steamfitters	Construction and Extraction	Very Good
Podiatrists	Healthcare	Very Good
Probation Officers and Correctional Treatment Specialists	Community and Social Service	Very Good
Registered Nurses	Healthcare	Very Good
Respiratory Therapy Technicians	Healthcare	Very Good
Surgical Technologists	Healthcare	Very Good
Veterinarians	Healthcare	Very Good

Figure 19: Jobs with Very Good and Excellent Survival and Growth Forecasts for 2033, with a High Chance for a Good Living Wage

There were also 47 with 2033 projections of Good, with similar financial prospects. They are in Figure 20.

Job	Occupation Group
Agents and Business Managers of Artists, Performers, and Athletes	Business and Financial
Aircraft and Avionics Equipment Mechanics and Technicians	Installation, Maintenance, and Repair
Airfield Operations Specialists	Transportation and Material Moving
Art Directors	Arts and Design
Atmospheric Scientists, Including Meteorologists	Life, Physical, and Social Science
Biomedical Engineers	Architecture and Engineering
Boilermakers	Construction and Extraction
Chemists and Materials Scientists	Life, Physical, and Social Science
Conservation Scientists and Foresters	Life, Physical, and Social Science
Construction and Building Inspectors	Construction and Extraction
Dentists	Healthcare
Diagnostic Medical Sonographers	Healthcare
Electricians	Construction and Extraction
Electro-mechanical Technicians	Architecture and Engineering
Environmental Scientists and Specialists	Life, Physical, and Social Science

Epidemiologists	Life, Physical, and Social Science
Film and Video Editors and Camera Operators	Media and Communications
Food Service Managers	Management
Forensic Science Technicians	Life, Physical, and Social Science
Geographers	Life, Physical, and Social Science
Geological and Petroleum Technicians	Life, Physical, and Social Science
Geoscientists	Life, Physical, and Social Science
Hydrologists	Life, Physical, and Social Science
Industrial Machinery Mechanics and Maintenance Workers	Installation, Maintenance, and Repair
Judges, Mediators, and Hearing Officers	Legal
Kindergarten and Elementary School Teachers	Education, Training, and Library
Line Installers and Repairers	Installation, Maintenance, and Repair
Lodging Managers	Management
Management Analysts	Business and Financial
Medical and Clinical Laboratory Technologists and Technicians	Healthcare
Middle School Teachers	Education, Training, and Library
Millwrights	Installation, Maintenance, and Repair
Occupational Health and Safety Specialists	Healthcare
Orthotists and Prosthetists	Healthcare
Police and Detectives	Protective Service
Psychologists	Life, Physical, and Social Science
Purchasing Managers, Buyers, and Purchasing Agents	Business and Financial
Radiation Therapists	Healthcare
Rail-Track Laying and Maintenance Equipment Operators	Construction and Extraction
Respiratory Therapists	Healthcare
Sales Engineers	Sales
School and Career Counselors	Community and Social Service
Social and Community Service Managers	Management
Social Media Managers	Management
Speech-Language Pathologists	Healthcare
Technical Writers	Media and Communications
Water Transportation Occupations	Transportation and Material Moving

Figure 20: Jobs with Good Survival and Growth Forecasts for 2033, with a High Chance for a Good Living Wage

Working environments vary a lot, from places where people do things such as clean toilets, talk with irate customers, and endanger their own lives, to offices where the politics cause the only real discomfort. There are 58 positions with Excellent or Very Good 2033 forecasts that also have generally fine work conditions:

Job	Occupation Group	2033 Forecast
Aerospace Engineering and Operations Technicians	Architecture and Engineering	Excellent
Aerospace Engineers	Architecture and Engineering	Very Good

Amusement and Recreation Attendants	Personal Care and Service	Very Good
Animal Care and Service Workers	Personal Care and Service	Excellent
Audiologists	Healthcare	Excellent
Barbers, Hairdressers, and Cosmetologists	Personal Care and Service	Very Good
Bicycle Repairers	Installation, Maintenance, and Repair	Excellent
Biochemists and Biophysicists	Life, Physical, and Social Science	Very Good
Biological Technicians	Life, Physical, and Social Science	Very Good
Cardiovascular Technologists and Technicians and Vascular Technologists	Healthcare	Excellent
Career and Technical Education Teachers	Education, Training, and Library	Very Good
Childcare Workers	Personal Care and Service	Very Good
Chiropractors	Healthcare	Very Good
Civil Engineering Technicians	Architecture and Engineering	Excellent
Civil Engineers	Architecture and Engineering	Very Good
Concierges	Personal Care and Service	Very Good
Construction Managers	Management	Very Good
Dental Hygienists	Healthcare	Very Good
Elementary, Middle, and High School Principals	Management	Very Good
EMTs and Paramedics	Healthcare	Excellent
Environmental Engineering Technicians	Architecture and Engineering	Very Good
Environmental Engineers	Architecture and Engineering	Very Good
Fitness Trainers and Instructors	Personal Care and Service	Very Good
Health Educators	Community and Social Service	Very Good
Home Health and Personal Care Aides	Healthcare	Excellent
Landscape Architects	Architecture and Engineering	Very Good
Licensed Practical and Licensed Vocational Nurses	Healthcare	Very Good
Manicurists and Pedicurists	Personal Care and Service	Very Good
Market Research Analysts	Business and Financial	Very Good
Medical Assistants	Healthcare	Very Good
Medical Equipment Preparers	Healthcare	Very Good
Medical Equipment Repairers	Installation, Maintenance, and Repair	Very Good
Medical Roboticists (Khanna and Smith)	Architecture and Engineering	Very Good
Medical Scientists	Life, Physical, and Social Science	Excellent
Mental Health Counselors and Marriage and Family Therapists	Community and Social Service	Excellent
Microbiologists	Life, Physical, and Social Science	Very Good
Occupational Health and Safety Technicians	Healthcare	Very Good
Occupational Therapists	Healthcare	Excellent
Occupational Therapy Assistants and Aides	Healthcare	Excellent
Optometrists	Healthcare	Very Good
Personal Assistants, Personal Organizers, and Task Completers	Personal Care and Service	Excellent
Physical Therapist Assistants and Aides	Healthcare	Excellent
Physical Therapists	Healthcare	Very Good
Physician Assistants	Healthcare	Excellent
Physicians and Surgeons	Healthcare	Very Good
Physicists and Astronomers	Life, Physical, and Social Science	Very Good
Podiatrists	Healthcare	Very Good

Recreational Therapists	Healthcare	Very Good
Registered Nurses	Healthcare	Very Good
Rehabilitation Counselors	Community and Social Service	Very Good
Residential Advisors	Personal Care and Service	Excellent
Respiratory Therapy Technicians	Healthcare	Very Good
Skincare Specialists	Personal Care and Service	Very Good
Substance Abuse and Behavioral Disorder Counselors	Community and Social Service	Very Good
Surgical Technologists	Healthcare	Very Good
Teacher Assistants	Education, Training, and Library	Very Good
Tour Guides and Escorts	Personal Care and Service	Very Good
Travel Guides	Personal Care and Service	Very Good

Figure 21: Jobs with Very Good and Excellent Survival and Growth Forecasts for 2033, with High-Quality Work Conditions

Fifty-eight jobs with Good projections also have top environments, as follows:

Job	Occupation Group
Agents and Business Managers of Artists, Performers, and Athletes	Business and Financial
Airfield Operations Specialists	Transportation and Material Moving
Art Directors	Arts and Design
Atmospheric Scientists, Including Meteorologists	Life, Physical, and Social Science
Baggage Porters and Bellhops	Personal Care and Service
Biomedical Engineers	Architecture and Engineering
Chemical Technicians	Life, Physical, and Social Science
Chemists and Materials Scientists	Life, Physical, and Social Science
Clergy	Community and Social Service
Coin, Vending, and Amusement Machine Servicers and Repairers	Installation, Maintenance, and Repair
Conservation Scientists and Foresters	Life, Physical, and Social Science
Construction and Building Inspectors	Construction and Extraction
Craft and Fine Artists	Arts and Design
Credit Counselors	Business and Financial
Curators, Museum Technicians, and Conservators	Education, Training, and Library
Dental Assistants	Healthcare
Dentists	Healthcare
Diagnostic Medical Sonographers	Healthcare
Dietetic Technicians	Healthcare
Directors, Religious Activities and Education	Community and Social Service
Electro-mechanical Technicians	Architecture and Engineering
Environmental Science and Protection Technicians	Life, Physical, and Social Science
Environmental Scientists and Specialists	Life, Physical, and Social Science
Epidemiologists	Life, Physical, and Social Science
Film and Video Editors and Camera Operators	Media and Communications
First-line Supervisors of Landscaping, Lawn Service, and Groundskeeping Workers	Building and Grounds Cleaning
First-line Supervisors of Personal Service Workers	Personal Care and Service
Forest and Conservation Technicians	Life, Physical, and Social Science

Geographers	Life, Physical, and Social Science
Geological and Petroleum Technicians	Life, Physical, and Social Science
Geoscientists	Life, Physical, and Social Science
Hydrologists	Life, Physical, and Social Science
Judges, Mediators, and Hearing Officers	Legal
Kindergarten and Elementary School Teachers	Education, Training, and Library
Lifeguards, Ski Patrol, and Other Recreational Protective Service Workers	Protective Service
Lodging Managers	Management
Management Analysts	Business and Financial
Mechanical Door Repairers	Installation, Maintenance, and Repair
Medical and Clinical Laboratory Technologists and Technicians	Healthcare
Meeting, Convention, and Event Planners	Business and Financial
Middle School Teachers	Education, Training, and Library
Occupational Health and Safety Specialists	Healthcare
Orthotists and Prosthetists	Healthcare
Preschool Teachers	Education, Training, and Library
Psychologists	Life, Physical, and Social Science
Purchasing Managers, Buyers, and Purchasing Agents	Business and Financial
Radiation Therapists	Healthcare
Respiratory Therapists	Healthcare
Sales Engineers	Sales
School and Career Counselors	Community and Social Service
Security and Fire Alarm Systems Installers	Installation, Maintenance, and Repair
Social and Community Service Managers	Management
Social and Human Service Assistants	Community and Social Service
Social Media Managers	Management
Social Workers	Community and Social Service
Speech-Language Pathologists	Healthcare
Tax Preparers	Business and Financial
Technical Writers	Media and Communications

Figure 22: Jobs with Good Survival and Growth Forecasts for 2033, with High-Quality Work Conditions

The next consideration, compatibility with both family life and extensive other involvements, is rated highly on 63 of the jobs with Excellent and Very Good 2033 expectations. They are listed in Figure 23.

Job	Occupation Group	2033 Forecast
Aerospace Engineers	Architecture and Engineering	Very Good
Amusement and Recreation Attendants	Personal Care and Service	Very Good
Animal Care and Service Workers	Personal Care and Service	Excellent
Audiologists	Healthcare	Excellent
Barbers, Hairdressers, and Cosmetologists	Personal Care and Service	Very Good
Bicycle Repairers	Installation, Maintenance, and Repair	Excellent

Biochemists and Biophysicists	Life, Physical, and Social Science	Very Good
Biological Technicians	Life, Physical, and Social Science	Very Good
Brickmasons, Blockmasons, and Stonemasons	Construction and Extraction	Very Good
Cardiovascular Technologists and Technicians and Vascular Technologists	Healthcare	Excellent
Career and Technical Education Teachers	Education, Training, and Library	Very Good
Carpenters	Construction and Extraction	Very Good
Childcare Workers	Personal Care and Service	Very Good
Chiropractors	Healthcare	Very Good
Concierges	Personal Care and Service	Very Good
Construction Equipment Operators	Construction and Extraction	Very Good
Construction Managers	Management	Very Good
Cooks	Food Preparation and Serving	Very Good
Dental Hygienists	Healthcare	Very Good
Elementary, Middle, and High School Principals	Management	Very Good
Elevator Installers and Repairers	Construction and Extraction	Very Good
EMTs and Paramedics	Healthcare	Excellent
Fitness Trainers and Instructors	Personal Care and Service	Very Good
Glaziers	Construction and Extraction	Very Good
Health Educators	Community and Social Service	Very Good
Home Health and Personal Care Aides	Healthcare	Excellent
Landscape Architects	Architecture and Engineering	Very Good
Licensed Practical and Licensed Vocational Nurses	Healthcare	Very Good
Maids and Housekeeping Cleaners	Building and Grounds Cleaning	Excellent
Manicurists and Pedicurists	Personal Care and Service	Very Good
Market Research Analysts	Business and Financial	Very Good
Massage Therapists	Healthcare	Excellent
Medical Assistants	Healthcare	Very Good
Medical Equipment Preparers	Healthcare	Very Good
Medical Roboticists (Khanna and Smith)	Architecture and Engineering	Very Good
Medical Scientists	Life, Physical, and Social Science	Excellent
Mental Health Counselors and Marriage and Family Therapists	Community and Social Service	Excellent
Microbiologists	Life, Physical, and Social Science	Very Good
Nursing Aides, Orderlies, and Attendants	Healthcare	Excellent
Occupational Health and Safety Technicians	Healthcare	Very Good
Occupational Therapists	Healthcare	Excellent
Occupational Therapy Assistants and Aides	Healthcare	Excellent
Optometrists	Healthcare	Very Good
Personal Assistants, Personal Organizers, and Task Completers	Personal Care and Service	Excellent
Physical Therapist Assistants and Aides	Healthcare	Excellent
Physical Therapists	Healthcare	Very Good
Physician Assistants	Healthcare	Excellent
Physicists and Astronomers	Life, Physical, and Social Science	Very Good
Podiatrists	Healthcare	Very Good
Probation Officers and Correctional Treatment Specialists	Community and Social Service	Very Good

Recreational Therapists	Healthcare	Very Good
Recreational Vehicle Service Technicians	Installation, Maintenance, and Repair	Very Good
Registered Nurses	Healthcare	Very Good
Rehabilitation Counselors	Community and Social Service	Very Good
Residential Advisors	Personal Care and Service	Excellent
Respiratory Therapy Technicians	Healthcare	Very Good
Skincare Specialists	Personal Care and Service	Very Good
Substance Abuse and Behavioral Disorder Counselors	Community and Social Service	Very Good
Surgical Technologists	Healthcare	Very Good
Taxi Drivers and Chauffeurs	Transportation and Material Moving	Very Good
Teacher Assistants	Education, Training, and Library	Very Good
Veterinarians	Healthcare	Very Good
Veterinary Assistants and Laboratory Animal Caretakers	Healthcare	Very Good

Figure 23: Jobs with Very Good and Excellent Survival and Growth Forecasts for 2033, with High Compatibility with Family Life and Outside Activities

Eighty-five of the jobs with Good projections also received top ratings for family and other activity suitability. Figure 24 shows them.

Job	Occupation Group
Agents and Business Managers of Artists, Performers, and Athletes	Business and Financial
Aircraft and Avionics Equipment Mechanics and Technicians	Installation, Maintenance, and Repair
Ambulance Drivers and Attendants, Except Emergency Medical Technicians	Transportation and Material Moving
Atmospheric Scientists, Including Meteorologists	Life, Physical, and Social Science
Automotive and Watercraft Service Attendants	Transportation and Material Moving
Automotive Body and Glass Repairers	Installation, Maintenance, and Repair
Automotive Service Technicians and Mechanics	Installation, Maintenance, and Repair
Baggage Porters and Bellhops	Personal Care and Service
Boilermakers	Construction and Extraction
Carpet Installers	Construction and Extraction
Cement Masons and Terrazzo Workers	Construction and Extraction
Chefs and Head Cooks	Food Preparation and Serving
Chemical Technicians	Life, Physical, and Social Science
Chemists and Materials Scientists	Life, Physical, and Social Science
Clergy	Community and Social Service
Coin, Vending, and Amusement Machine Servicers and Repairers	Installation, Maintenance, and Repair
Conservation Scientists and Foresters	Life, Physical, and Social Science
Construction and Building Inspectors	Construction and Extraction
Construction Laborers and Helpers	Construction and Extraction
Couriers and Messengers	Office and Administrative Support
Craft and Fine Artists	Arts and Design
Credit Counselors	Business and Financial
Curators, Museum Technicians, and Conservators	Education, Training, and Library
Dental Assistants	Healthcare

Dentists	Healthcare
Diagnostic Medical Sonographers	Healthcare
Diesel Service Technicians and Mechanics	Installation, Maintenance, and Repair
Dietetic Technicians	Healthcare
Directors, Religious Activities and Education	Community and Social Service
Drywall and Ceiling Tile Installers, and Tapers	Construction and Extraction
Electricians	Construction and Extraction
Epidemiologists	Life, Physical, and Social Science
Fence Erectors	Construction and Extraction
First-line Supervisors of Landscaping, Lawn Service, and Groundskeeping Workers	Building and Grounds Cleaning
First-line Supervisors of Personal Service Workers	Personal Care and Service
Forest and Conservation Technicians	Life, Physical, and Social Science
General Maintenance and Repair Workers	Installation, Maintenance, and Repair
Geographers	Life, Physical, and Social Science
Geological and Petroleum Technicians	Life, Physical, and Social Science
Geoscientists	Life, Physical, and Social Science
Grounds Maintenance Workers	Building and Grounds Cleaning
Heating, Air Conditioning, and Refrigeration Mechanics and Installers	Installation, Maintenance, and Repair
Heavy Vehicle and Mobile Equipment Service Technicians	Installation, Maintenance, and Repair
Highway Maintenance Workers	Construction and Extraction
Hydrologists	Life, Physical, and Social Science
Janitors and Building Cleaners	Building and Grounds Cleaning
Judges, Mediators, and Hearing Officers	Legal
Kindergarten and Elementary School Teachers	Education, Training, and Library
Lifeguards, Ski Patrol, and Other Recreational Protective Service Workers	Protective Service
Mechanical Door Repairers	Installation, Maintenance, and Repair
Medical and Clinical Laboratory Technologists and Technicians	Healthcare
Middle School Teachers	Education, Training, and Library
Occupational Health and Safety Specialists	Healthcare
Orthotists and Prosthetists	Healthcare
Pest Control Workers	Building and Grounds Cleaning
Pipelayers	Construction and Extraction
Plasterers and Stucco Masons	Construction and Extraction
Police and Detectives	Protective Service
Preschool Teachers	Education, Training, and Library
Psychiatric Technicians and Aides	Healthcare
Psychologists	Life, Physical, and Social Science
Radiation Therapists	Healthcare
Rail-Track Laying and Maintenance Equipment Operators	Construction and Extraction
Reinforcing Iron and Rebar Workers	Construction and Extraction
Respiratory Therapists	Healthcare
Retail Sales Workers	Sales
Riggers	Installation, Maintenance, and Repair
Roofers	Construction and Extraction

School and Career Counselors	Community and Social Service
Security and Fire Alarm Systems Installers	Installation, Maintenance, and Repair
Segmental Pavers	Construction and Extraction
Septic Tank Servicers and Sewer Pipe Cleaners	Construction and Extraction
Sheet Metal Workers	Construction and Extraction
Small Engine Mechanics	Installation, Maintenance, and Repair
Social and Community Service Managers	Management
Social and Human Service Assistants	Community and Social Service
Social Media Managers	Management
Social Workers	Community and Social Service
Speech-Language Pathologists	Healthcare
Structural Iron and Steel Workers	Construction and Extraction
Tax Examiners and Collectors, and Revenue Agents	Business and Financial
Tax Preparers	Business and Financial
Technical Writers	Media and Communications
Tile and Marble Setters	Construction and Extraction
Veterinary Technologists and Technicians	Healthcare

Figure 24: Jobs with Good Survival and Growth Forecasts for 2033, with High Compatibility with Family Life and Outside Activities

Combining these elements allows us to see the positions with more than one advantage. If we search for the jobs with high chances for both good living wages and good working conditions, we get 70 in the Good, Very Good, and Excellent 2033 prediction categories:

Job	Occupation Group	2033 Forecast
Aerospace Engineering and Operations Technicians	Architecture and Engineering	Excellent
Aerospace Engineers	Architecture and Engineering	Very Good
Agents and Business Managers of Artists, Performers, and Athletes	Business and Financial	Good
Airfield Operations Specialists	Transportation and Material Moving	Good
Art Directors	Arts and Design	Good
Atmospheric Scientists, Including Meteorologists	Life, Physical, and Social Science	Good
Audiologists	Healthcare	Excellent
Biochemists and Biophysicists	Life, Physical, and Social Science	Very Good
Biomedical Engineers	Architecture and Engineering	Good
Cardiovascular Technologists and Technicians and Vascular Technologists	Healthcare	Excellent
Career and Technical Education Teachers	Education, Training, and Library	Very Good
Chemists and Materials Scientists	Life, Physical, and Social Science	Good
Chiropractors	Healthcare	Very Good
Civil Engineering Technicians	Architecture and Engineering	Excellent
Civil Engineers	Architecture and Engineering	Very Good
Conservation Scientists and Foresters	Life, Physical, and Social Science	Good
Construction and Building Inspectors	Construction and Extraction	Good
Construction Managers	Management	Very Good

Dental Hygienists	Healthcare	Very Good
Dentists	Healthcare	Good
Diagnostic Medical Sonographers	Healthcare	Good
Electro-mechanical Technicians	Architecture and Engineering	Good
Elementary, Middle, and High School Principals	Management	Very Good
Environmental Engineering Technicians	Architecture and Engineering	Very Good
Environmental Engineers	Architecture and Engineering	Very Good
Environmental Scientists and Specialists	Life, Physical, and Social Science	Good
Epidemiologists	Life, Physical, and Social Science	Good
Film and Video Editors and Camera Operators	Media and Communications	Good
Geographers	Life, Physical, and Social Science	Good
Geological and Petroleum Technicians	Life, Physical, and Social Science	Good
Geoscientists	Life, Physical, and Social Science	Good
Health Educators	Community and Social Service	Very Good
Hydrologists	Life, Physical, and Social Science	Good
Judges, Mediators, and Hearing Officers	Legal	Good
Kindergarten and Elementary School Teachers	Education, Training, and Library	Good
Landscape Architects	Architecture and Engineering	Very Good
Lodging Managers	Management	Good
Management Analysts	Business and Financial	Good
Market Research Analysts	Business and Financial	Very Good
Medical and Clinical Laboratory Technologists and Technicians	Healthcare	Good
Medical Equipment Repairers	Installation, Maintenance, and Repair	Very Good
Medical Roboticists (Khanna and Smith)	Architecture and Engineering	Very Good
Medical Scientists	Life, Physical, and Social Science	Excellent
Mental Health Counselors and Marriage and Family Therapists	Community and Social Service	Excellent
Microbiologists	Life, Physical, and Social Science	Very Good
Middle School Teachers	Education, Training, and Library	Good
Occupational Health and Safety Specialists	Healthcare	Good
Occupational Health and Safety Technicians	Healthcare	Very Good
Occupational Therapists	Healthcare	Excellent
Occupational Therapy Assistants and Aides	Healthcare	Excellent
Optometrists	Healthcare	Very Good
Orthotists and Prosthetists	Healthcare	Good
Physical Therapists	Healthcare	Very Good
Physician Assistants	Healthcare	Excellent
Physicians and Surgeons	Healthcare	Very Good
Physicists and Astronomers	Life, Physical, and Social Science	Very Good
Podiatrists	Healthcare	Very Good
Psychologists	Life, Physical, and Social Science	Good
Purchasing Managers, Buyers, and Purchasing Agents	Business and Financial	Good
Radiation Therapists	Healthcare	Good
Registered Nurses	Healthcare	Very Good
Respiratory Therapists	Healthcare	Good

Respiratory Therapy Technicians	Healthcare	Very Good
Sales Engineers	Sales	Good
School and Career Counselors	Community and Social Service	Good
Social and Community Service Managers	Management	Good
Social Media Managers	Management	Good
Speech-Language Pathologists	Healthcare	Good
Surgical Technologists	Healthcare	Very Good
Technical Writers	Media and Communications	Good

Figure 25: Jobs with Good, Very Good and Excellent Survival and Growth Forecasts for 2033, with Both a High Chance for a Good Living Wage and High-Quality Work Conditions

There are 62 positions with projections of Good or better, along with both a high expectation for comfortable wages and great compatibility with family and outside activities, as shown in Figure 26.

Job	Occupation Group	2033 Forecast
Aerospace Engineers	Architecture and Engineering	Very Good
Agents and Business Managers of Artists, Performers, and Athletes	Business and Financial	Good
Aircraft and Avionics Equipment Mechanics and Technicians	Installation, Maintenance, and Repair	Good
Atmospheric Scientists, Including Meteorologists	Life, Physical, and Social Science	Good
Audiologists	Healthcare	Excellent
Biochemists and Biophysicists	Life, Physical, and Social Science	Very Good
Boilermakers	Construction and Extraction	Good
Brickmasons, Blockmasons, and Stonemasons	Construction and Extraction	Very Good
Cardiovascular Technologists and Technicians and Vascular Technologists	Healthcare	Excellent
Career and Technical Education Teachers	Education, Training, and Library	Very Good
Chemists and Materials Scientists	Life, Physical, and Social Science	Good
Chiropractors	Healthcare	Very Good
Conservation Scientists and Foresters	Life, Physical, and Social Science	Good
Construction and Building Inspectors	Construction and Extraction	Good
Construction Managers	Management	Very Good
Dental Hygienists	Healthcare	Very Good
Dentists	Healthcare	Good
Diagnostic Medical Sonographers	Healthcare	Good
Electricians	Construction and Extraction	Good
Elementary, Middle, and High School Principals	Management	Very Good
Elevator Installers and Repairers	Construction and Extraction	Very Good
Epidemiologists	Life, Physical, and Social Science	Good
Geographers	Life, Physical, and Social Science	Good
Geological and Petroleum Technicians	Life, Physical, and Social Science	Good
Geoscientists	Life, Physical, and Social Science	Good
Health Educators	Community and Social Service	Very Good
Hydrologists	Life, Physical, and Social Science	Good

Judges, Mediators, and Hearing Officers	Legal	Good
Kindergarten and Elementary School Teachers	Education, Training, and Library	Good
Landscape Architects	Architecture and Engineering	Very Good
Market Research Analysts	Business and Financial	Very Good
Medical and Clinical Laboratory Technologists and Technicians	Healthcare	Good
Medical Roboticists (Khanna and Smith)	Architecture and Engineering	Very Good
Medical Scientists	Life, Physical, and Social Science	Excellent
Mental Health Counselors and Marriage and Family Therapists	Community and Social Service	Excellent
Microbiologists	Life, Physical, and Social Science	Very Good
Middle School Teachers	Education, Training, and Library	Good
Occupational Health and Safety Specialists	Healthcare	Good
Occupational Health and Safety Technicians	Healthcare	Very Good
Occupational Therapists	Healthcare	Excellent
Occupational Therapy Assistants and Aides	Healthcare	Excellent
Optometrists	Healthcare	Very Good
Orthotists and Prosthetists	Healthcare	Good
Physical Therapists	Healthcare	Very Good
Physician Assistants	Healthcare	Excellent
Physicists and Astronomers	Life, Physical, and Social Science	Very Good
Podiatrists	Healthcare	Very Good
Police and Detectives	Protective Service	Good
Probation Officers and Correctional Treatment Specialists	Community and Social Service	Very Good
Psychologists	Life, Physical, and Social Science	Good
Radiation Therapists	Healthcare	Good
Rail-Track Laying and Maintenance Equipment Operators	Construction and Extraction	Good
Registered Nurses	Healthcare	Very Good
Respiratory Therapists	Healthcare	Good
Respiratory Therapy Technicians	Healthcare	Very Good
School and Career Counselors	Community and Social Service	Good
Social and Community Service Managers	Management	Good
Social Media Managers	Management	Good
Speech-Language Pathologists	Healthcare	Good
Surgical Technologists	Healthcare	Very Good
Technical Writers	Media and Communications	Good
Veterinarians	Healthcare	Very Good

Figure 26: Jobs with Good, Very Good and Excellent Survival and Growth Forecasts for 2033, with Both a High Chance for a Good Living Wage and High Compatibility with Family Life and Outside Activities

Combining prime working conditions with high family and project suitability gives us 95 jobs in the top three 2033 forecast categories, as follows:

Job	Occupation Group	2033 Forecast
Aerospace Engineers	Architecture and Engineering	Very Good
Agents and Business Managers of Artists, Performers, and Athletes	Business and Financial	Good
Amusement and Recreation Attendants	Personal Care and Service	Very Good
Animal Care and Service Workers	Personal Care and Service	Excellent
Atmospheric Scientists, Including Meteorologists	Life, Physical, and Social Science	Good
Audiologists	Healthcare	Excellent
Baggage Porters and Bellhops	Personal Care and Service	Good
Barbers, Hairdressers, and Cosmetologists	Personal Care and Service	Very Good
Bicycle Repairers	Installation, Maintenance, and Repair	Excellent
Biochemists and Biophysicists	Life, Physical, and Social Science	Very Good
Biological Technicians	Life, Physical, and Social Science	Very Good
Cardiovascular Technologists and Technicians and Vascular Technologists	Healthcare	Excellent
Career and Technical Education Teachers	Education, Training, and Library	Very Good
Chemical Technicians	Life, Physical, and Social Science	Good
Chemists and Materials Scientists	Life, Physical, and Social Science	Good
Childcare Workers	Personal Care and Service	Very Good
Chiropractors	Healthcare	Very Good
Clergy	Community and Social Service	Good
Coin, Vending, and Amusement Machine Servicers and Repairers	Installation, Maintenance, and Repair	Good
Concierges	Personal Care and Service	Very Good
Conservation Scientists and Foresters	Life, Physical, and Social Science	Good
Construction and Building Inspectors	Construction and Extraction	Good
Construction Managers	Management	Very Good
Craft and Fine Artists	Arts and Design	Good
Credit Counselors	Business and Financial	Good
Curators, Museum Technicians, and Conservators	Education, Training, and Library	Good
Dental Assistants	Healthcare	Good
Dental Hygienists	Healthcare	Very Good
Dentists	Healthcare	Good
Diagnostic Medical Sonographers	Healthcare	Good
Dietetic Technicians	Healthcare	Good
Directors, Religious Activities and Education	Community and Social Service	Good
Elementary, Middle, and High School Principals	Management	Very Good
EMTs and Paramedics	Healthcare	Excellent
Epidemiologists	Life, Physical, and Social Science	Good
First-line Supervisors of Landscaping, Lawn Service, and Groundskeeping Workers	Building and Grounds Cleaning	Good
First-line Supervisors of Personal Service Workers	Personal Care and Service	Good
Fitness Trainers and Instructors	Personal Care and Service	Very Good
Forest and Conservation Technicians	Life, Physical, and Social Science	Good
Geographers	Life, Physical, and Social Science	Good
Geological and Petroleum Technicians	Life, Physical, and Social Science	Good
Geoscientists	Life, Physical, and Social Science	Good
Health Educators	Community and Social Service	Very Good

Home Health and Personal Care Aides	Healthcare	Excellent
Hydrologists	Life, Physical, and Social Science	Good
Judges, Mediators, and Hearing Officers	Legal	Good
Kindergarten and Elementary School Teachers	Education, Training, and Library	Good
Landscape Architects	Architecture and Engineering	Very Good
Licensed Practical and Licensed Vocational Nurses	Healthcare	Very Good
Lifeguards, Ski Patrol, and Other Recreational Protective Service Workers	Protective Service	Good
Manicurists and Pedicurists	Personal Care and Service	Very Good
Market Research Analysts	Business and Financial	Very Good
Mechanical Door Repairers	Installation, Maintenance, and Repair	Good
Medical and Clinical Laboratory Technologists and Technicians	Healthcare	Good
Medical Assistants	Healthcare	Very Good
Medical Equipment Preparers	Healthcare	Very Good
Medical Roboticists (Khanna and Smith)	Architecture and Engineering	Very Good
Medical Scientists	Life, Physical, and Social Science	Excellent
Mental Health Counselors and Marriage and Family Therapists	Community and Social Service	Excellent
Microbiologists	Life, Physical, and Social Science	Very Good
Middle School Teachers	Education, Training, and Library	Good
Occupational Health and Safety Specialists	Healthcare	Good
Occupational Health and Safety Technicians	Healthcare	Very Good
Occupational Therapists	Healthcare	Excellent
Occupational Therapy Assistants and Aides	Healthcare	Excellent
Optometrists	Healthcare	Very Good
Orthotists and Prosthetists	Healthcare	Good
Personal Assistants, Personal Organizers, and Task Completers	Personal Care and Service	Excellent
Physical Therapist Assistants and Aides	Healthcare	Excellent
Physical Therapists	Healthcare	Very Good
Physician Assistants	Healthcare	Excellent
Physicists and Astronomers	Life, Physical, and Social Science	Very Good
Podiatrists	Healthcare	Very Good
Preschool Teachers	Education, Training, and Library	Good
Psychologists	Life, Physical, and Social Science	Good
Radiation Therapists	Healthcare	Good
Recreational Therapists	Healthcare	Very Good
Registered Nurses	Healthcare	Very Good
Rehabilitation Counselors	Community and Social Service	Very Good
Residential Advisors	Personal Care and Service	Excellent
Respiratory Therapists	Healthcare	Good
Respiratory Therapy Technicians	Healthcare	Very Good
School and Career Counselors	Community and Social Service	Good
Security and Fire Alarm Systems Installers	Installation, Maintenance, and Repair	Good
Skincare Specialists	Personal Care and Service	Very Good
Social and Community Service Managers	Management	Good
Social and Human Service Assistants	Community and Social Service	Good
Social Media Managers	Management	Good

Social Workers	Community and Social Service	Good
Speech-Language Pathologists	Healthcare	Good
Substance Abuse and Behavioral Disorder Counselors	Community and Social Service	Very Good
Surgical Technologists	Healthcare	Very Good
Tax Preparers	Business and Financial	Good
Teacher Assistants	Education, Training, and Library	Very Good
Technical Writers	Media and Communications	Good

Figure 27: Jobs with Good, Very Good and Excellent Survival and Growth Forecasts for 2033, with Both High-Quality Work Conditions and High Compatibility with Family Life and Outside Activities

Requiring top ratings in all three of the factors just discussed—chance for a good living wage, work environments, and compatibility with family life and other activities—precipitates a list of 53 positions, all with Good or better 2033 projections. They are listed in Figure 28.

Job	Occupation Group	2033 Forecast
Aerospace Engineers	Architecture and Engineering	Very Good
Agents and Business Managers of Artists, Performers, and Athletes	Business and Financial	Good
Atmospheric Scientists, Including Meteorologists	Life, Physical, and Social Science	Good
Audiologists	Healthcare	Excellent
Biochemists and Biophysicists	Life, Physical, and Social Science	Very Good
Cardiovascular Technologists and Technicians and Vascular Technologists	Healthcare	Excellent
Career and Technical Education Teachers	Education, Training, and Library	Very Good
Chemists and Materials Scientists	Life, Physical, and Social Science	Good
Chiropractors	Healthcare	Very Good
Conservation Scientists and Foresters	Life, Physical, and Social Science	Good
Construction and Building Inspectors	Construction and Extraction	Good
Construction Managers	Management	Very Good
Dental Hygienists	Healthcare	Very Good
Dentists	Healthcare	Good
Diagnostic Medical Sonographers	Healthcare	Good
Elementary, Middle, and High School Principals	Management	Very Good
Epidemiologists	Life, Physical, and Social Science	Good
Geographers	Life, Physical, and Social Science	Good
Geological and Petroleum Technicians	Life, Physical, and Social Science	Good
Geoscientists	Life, Physical, and Social Science	Good
Health Educators	Community and Social Service	Very Good
Hydrologists	Life, Physical, and Social Science	Good
Judges, Mediators, and Hearing Officers	Legal	Good
Kindergarten and Elementary School Teachers	Education, Training, and Library	Good
Landscape Architects	Architecture and Engineering	Very Good
Market Research Analysts	Business and Financial	Very Good
Medical and Clinical Laboratory Technologists and Technicians	Healthcare	Good

Medical Roboticists (Khanna and Smith)	Architecture and Engineering	Very Good
Medical Scientists	Life, Physical, and Social Science	Excellent
Mental Health Counselors and Marriage and Family Therapists	Community and Social Service	Excellent
Microbiologists	Life, Physical, and Social Science	Very Good
Middle School Teachers	Education, Training, and Library	Good
Occupational Health and Safety Specialists	Healthcare	Good
Occupational Health and Safety Technicians	Healthcare	Very Good
Occupational Therapists	Healthcare	Excellent
Occupational Therapy Assistants and Aides	Healthcare	Excellent
Optometrists	Healthcare	Very Good
Orthotists and Prosthetists	Healthcare	Good
Physical Therapists	Healthcare	Very Good
Physician Assistants	Healthcare	Excellent
Physicists and Astronomers	Life, Physical, and Social Science	Very Good
Podiatrists	Healthcare	Very Good
Psychologists	Life, Physical, and Social Science	Good
Radiation Therapists	Healthcare	Good
Registered Nurses	Healthcare	Very Good
Respiratory Therapists	Healthcare	Good
Respiratory Therapy Technicians	Healthcare	Very Good
School and Career Counselors	Community and Social Service	Good
Social and Community Service Managers	Management	Good
Social Media Managers	Management	Good
Speech-Language Pathologists	Healthcare	Good
Surgical Technologists	Healthcare	Very Good
Technical Writers	Media and Communications	Good

Figure 28: Jobs with Good, Very Good and Excellent Survival and Growth Forecasts for 2033, with a High Chance for a Good Living Wage, High-Quality Work Conditions, and High Compatibility with Family Life and Outside Activities

To thin the above listing out, if we add the requirement that each have median compensation of $80,000 or more,[237] we reduce it to only 12 positions. This, along with Figure 17, which contains those with excellent 2033 prospects, becomes a possible "best jobs" compilation. Note that there is only one position, Physician Assistants, on both lists.

Job	Occupation Group	2033 Forecast
Aerospace Engineers	Architecture and Engineering	Very Good
Atmospheric Scientists, Including Meteorologists	Life, Physical, and Social Science	Good
Construction Managers	Management	Very Good
Dentists	Healthcare	Good
Elementary, Middle, and High School Principals	Management	Very Good
Geoscientists	Life, Physical, and Social Science	Good
Judges, Mediators, and Hearing Officers	Legal	Good

Optometrists	Healthcare	Very Good
Physician Assistants	Healthcare	Excellent
Physicists and Astronomers	Life, Physical, and Social Science	Very Good
Podiatrists	Healthcare	Very Good
Social Media Managers	Management	Good

Figure 29: Jobs with Good, Very Good and Excellent Survival and Growth Forecasts for 2033, with a High Chance of a Good Living Wage, High-Quality Work Conditions, and High Compatibility with Family Life and Outside Activities, and with 2010 Median Annual Compensation Over $80,000

So there we are. These are not those likely to be the most plentiful in 2033, but the best from perhaps the most meaningful perspectives. They are the jobs I recommend the most for careers expected to last at least 15 or 20 years into the future.

What about self-employment? Chapter 6 addresses that possibility, to be followed by the complete catalogue of 506 positions, with detailed information, in Chapter 7.

Chapter 6:

Self-Employment: What's the Real Story?

Everybody I've ever heard of who makes big money, unless it was inherited, works extremely hard for it—at a pace that a lot of people can't match. —Bruce Williams[238]

Throughout American history, there have been many ways for people to work for themselves. As business writer and educator Peter Drucker put it, "whenever you see a successful business, someone once made a courageous decision."[239] The highest incomes belong to entrepreneurs, not employees. So what does it really take to be your own boss, what issues are there with small business as a widespread choice, and what possibilities are good and bad?

What Working for Yourself Really Requires

Running a serious enterprise is a challenge. Radio talk-show host and long-time entrepreneur Bruce Williams described it as "more difficult than it looks"[240] and pointed out that owners are "not really free" in acting with customers.[241] Those working for themselves will also often find that their new supervisor is tougher than others could be.[242]

Not many people, especially those who have been only narrowly specialized before,[243] can succeed. Small ventures typically require proprietors to take on many roles, such as dealing with difficult customers,[244] sales, accounting, buying, marketing, management, and even janitorial work,[245] along with hiring, firing, training and motivating employees, doing payroll and budgeting, and dealing with lawyers and bankers.[246] Owners must be greatly self-motivated and should expect to work long hours.[247] In *Small Business for Dummies,* authors Eric Tyson and Jim Schell presented a fitness quiz for running one's own venture. It indicates their valued qualities were interest in the business, persistence under adversity, high energy, ability to research and implement difficult decisions, a positive attitude, preference for action over inactivity, related work experience, creativity, recovering from failure, natural leadership, and discipline—a list which many or most prospective full-time proprietors would match poorly. They also refer to confidence, intuition, drive, and passion.[248] Bruce Williams said that if people wanted a lot of time with their families, sought the security of working for others, needed a boss to tell them to be at work on time, would stop working if they won the lottery, or had a low tolerance for risk,[249] they would not be well suited for entrepreneurship. A further consideration is whether a businessperson is more compatible with running an existing venture or starting a new one, which often require very different skill and disposition sets.[250] As well, if an enterprise has no reasonable chance of becoming profitable, it should be discontinued without regard for the owner's vanity[251] or sunk costs, a decision hard for many to make.

Some advantages of having a company are personal satisfaction, independence, more scheduling control, and potential income.[252] However, the drawbacks are also extensive and include great responsibility, dealing with competition and change, managing many random factors, conforming to government requirements, and the chance of losing one's entire, possibly large, investment in a failure.[253] It is almost mandatory for potential business owners to pay off all of their consumer-related debt before starting and then minimize their personal expenses.[254] Proprietors must also obtain any benefits they want themselves, which can be costly without an employer providing them,[255] especially when considering many must be paid for with after-tax dollars.

For these and other reasons, remarkably few Americans run their own businesses full time. Although Robert J. Samuelson stated that "the entrepreneurial instinct seems deeply ingrained in the nation's economic culture,"[256] and numerous others have agreed, much data supports the opposite. A 2007 study showed that only 7.2% of Americans were self-employed, trailing Canada, Australia, New Zealand, and 16 countries in Western Europe, ahead of only Luxembourg. Most differences were large, with most other developed nations between 10.6% and 14.4%, and some were enormous: Ireland, New Zealand, Spain, Portugal, and Italy had 16.8% to 26.4%, while Greece, with 35.9% self-employed even before its financial crisis, reported almost five times America's rate.[257]

In all, regardless of the independence in American national character, the great majority want, and are better suited, to work for others. That is not so bad, as about half of all new businesses fail.[258] Therefore, while self-employment possibilities are still around and may be the best choices for those with the drive and the skills, they are, as they always have been in the United States, a proposition for only a minority.

Problems with Wide-Scale Self-Employment

One deterrent to full-time startups has been health insurance. In 2009, studies implied that losing work-connected health coverage deterred many from leaving work to start businesses,[259] making a great deal of self-employment part time, and entrepreneurial professor Scott Shane contended that "the health care mess is clearly weighing down entrepreneurship in this country."[260]

New businesses have also often been credited with a lot of American jobs. Per senior research fellow Tim Kane, firms in their first 12 months typically create about three million positions a year, while all other companies together end more than they start. Ben Bernanke said in July 2010 that small ventures started since 2008 had 10% of all people working but 25% of all new jobs,[261] which is misleading, as *small* businesses, also often recognized with originating positions, are different from *new* businesses, and of companies of the same age there is no connection between job creation and firm size.[262] Startups also perforce generate jobs, since before they had none at all.

New ventures have widely varying effects on their proprietors and on the economy. Some entrepreneurs stop working for others and put in hundred-hour weeks, some are financially secure and start businesses for pleasure, and some keep their jobs and sell the likes of Amway or Mary Kay products. Some enterprises are sole proprietorships employing nobody else, while others are 20-worker corporations. New concerns may add zero, one, or many more new full-time positions, yet all count in the numbers.[263] Even many full-time entrepreneurial efforts, retroactively, were never even jobs in an economic sense; almost nobody working for others loses money from his or her labors, but if a million people start businesses and half are never profitable, the effect on employment is the same as if only 500,000 worked and the others spent the time and money they lost on other things.[264]

Startups are certainly worthwhile but often do not provide lasting jobs. Even in the better times of around 1990, 80% of small businesses failed, most within three or four years.[265] Buying successful existing enterprises can be better, but one must consider the investment income foregone from their costs, which may indicate the purchaser is in effect only buying a job.[266] If the overwhelming majority of 2014 new ventures' positions will be gone by 2018, then we have to wonder if the emphasis on them we have seen is truly justified.[267]

Entrepreneurial Opportunities: The Good, the Bad, and the Ugly

Eric Tyson and Jim Schell named four categories of business: retailing, service, manufacturing, and wholesaling.[268] What can we say about these, from a Work's New Age standpoint?

While the same economic realities apply to being an owner and being an employee, one spot may be better than the other. American manufacturing jobs may continue to shrink, but prospects are brighter for companies with at least the option of making products overseas. However, manufacturing concerns here, even if having production done elsewhere, must compete with foreign-only enterprises, which, by keeping everything together, have extra economies of scale and efficiencies of production.[269] Manufacturing startups are the most capital-intensive of the four types, and can become very large if successful,[270] so choosing that is usually, for better or worse, playing for higher stakes than the other possibilities.

The second most expensive form of new business is wholesaling. It may seem surprising that initial capital requirements are high, but they are, since inventories are generally large,[271] and at the beginning it may be difficult for an owner to acquire goods on credit. Opportunities with foreign manufactured products can be excellent, as makers elsewhere may offer the best prices, along with large quantity discounts, when shipping to only one address and company. Wholesaling, in general, should still be a solid area by 2033.

Retail ventures are the most visible small businesses. They often appear in storefronts, with startup costs ranging from moderate to remarkably large; for example, a McDonald's franchise generally requires a minimum of $750,000 in non-borrowed money.[272] With lower but still high inventory requirements, and the prospect of getting sales more quickly, the initial cost is generally less than for either wholesaling or manufacturing, though the risk of undercapitalizing remains considerable. Bruce Williams often recommended that anyone opening a retail business have enough cash to cover the startup and six months of expenses after that, assuming no incoming revenue at all. Retail success can range from nonexistent to the beginning of a multi-thousand-outlet brand name. The value of such ventures in the Work's New Age climate of the next two decades will depend on what they are selling, what advantages they offer customers over big-box stores and other existing sources, and what value they can get from being locally bound or at least based in America. If you have an idea for a retail effort and cannot decisively and convincingly answer those questions, you should not follow through with it.

The cheapest small businesses to start are those offering services. These can be invisible from the street, with work done from private homes and advertising not pointing to physical addresses. They often also have the least need to be local, which, as discussed in the chapters about jobs, is a real exposure. There is an enormous variety of possible services, and the best areas will require in-person providers; if not, foreign companies will probably outcompete them.

The bilge of the metaphorical small-business boat is schemes which aren't really businesses at all. When money is transferred without differential goods and services, such as taking in each other's laundry for the same amount, there is no true business activity. Selling possessions, as more than a stopgap, may be a money source but is not indefinitely ongoing, and pyramid-related ventures such as multilevel marketing are often even worse.[273] Although the very rare person can net significant money at these, I do not recommend them.

Outside more conventional ideas, what are some specific businesses that could succeed? Let us look at some of the trends in Chapter 3. One with extensive significance for self-employment is the concentration of work hours and work income into fewer people, who will be longer on money than on time to obtain many things with it. Some services they will be willing to purchase, if convenient and comprehensively provided enough, are the following:

- Giving counseling and advice, if high-quality, specific to American situations, backed by appropriate credentials, and especially if available over the phone or electronically.
- Errand running, and help researching and completing many tasks, possibly by personal assistants,[274] secretaries, or concierges.
- Street vending of top-quality food, even simple fare such as hot dogs.[275]
- Dog walking[276] and performing other pet-related tasks.
- Windshield washing[277] and other chores once performed by full-service gas stations.
- Pedicab and bicycle rickshaw transportation.[278]
- Providing any commonly used resource which becomes time-consuming or difficult to get. One example, "proxy gas-getting" from the early 1970s energy crisis, was paid remarkably highly.
- Information compiling, using efficiency, knowledge, and judgment to sort through the facts on almost anything, thereby imparting understanding instead of only data.
- Finding, obtaining, and delivering high-end personal products of all kinds.
- Arranging exotic, first-class, and custom travel.
- Gift shopping, gift wrapping, and gift basket assembly and delivery.[279]
- Catering high-end meals, at homes or in scenic locations.[280]
- Performing services once done by home servants: cleaning, cooking, driving, maintaining cars, gardening, other yard work and small-scale landscaping,[281] and related modern tasks such as answering emails.
- Completing real-estate-related projects, such as buying it, selling it, remodeling, decorating, and so on.
- Locating and purchasing goods and services for wealthy tourists.

Another development will be more people living together, sharing smaller home areas. That could provide increased opportunities for such ventures as these:

- Public living rooms, private video watching areas (as now popular in Korea, where home space is often tight), game rooms, and coffee shops where people are under no pressure to leave quickly (as in Italy)
- "PC rooms" filled with state-of-the-art computers loaded with current gaming software. These are also widespread, actually ubiquitous, in Korea and could also be used socially, though people there seemed to keep their eyes forward rather consistently.

Over the next two decades, there will be more interest in experiences, even when not expensive. That could lead to good opportunities in such things as the following:

- Modeling for artists or photographers.[282]
- Enhancing parties with such things as doing lipstick reading, doing face painting, making twisted balloon animals and other things, coordinating treasure hunts,[283] and providing services yet to be publicized or invented.
- Running low-priced but exotic restaurants.
- Providing partial or simulated travel-related adventures.
- If legal, offering a variety of sexual services and fantasy-fulfilling experiences.
- Facilitating other exotic in-person involvements, to be determined.

Some manufacturing, gathering, and farming activities with potential include the following:

- Beekeeping and chicken raising.[284]
- Breeding and selling Betta fish[285] or other tropical fish.
- Growing and marketing plants of various sorts.[286]
- Collecting and selling Hawaiian kahelelani shells.[287]
- Making and selling soap,[288] candles, or jewelry.[289]
- When legal, growing and marketing high-end marijuana, which will generate interest similar to that in microbrew beer.

Any of these could be added to more typical entrepreneurial ideas, and, if personal and financial considerations are in order, are worthy of attention. All ventures should be well studied and planned before implementation. An excellent quick summary of typical problems overlooked by entrepreneurs, "12 Reasons Why New Businesses Fail," is available online.[290] The proper preparation time will save any owner tremendous amounts of grief later.

Onondaga County Public Library
Syracuse, New York

Chapter 7:
The Outlook, Job by Job

There's no labor a man can do that's undignified, if he does it right. —Bill Cosby[291]

Job Name	Accountants and Auditors	Actors	Actuaries	Adhesive Bonding Machine Operators and Tenders
Occupation Group	Business and Financial	Entertainment and Sports	Math	Production
Local-Boundness	Low	Medium	Low	Medium
Resistance to Robotics	High	High	High	Medium
Resistance to Computing and Connectivity	Low	Medium	High	High
Pertinent Principles (Good)			1	
Pertinent Principles (Maybe Good)	14			
Pertinent Principles (Bad)				17
2010 Number of Workers	1,216,900	66,500	21,700	15,100
Chance for Good Living Wage	Medium	Low	High	Low
2010 Median Pay	Medium	Low	High	Low
Median Quality of Work Conditions	High	High	High	Medium
Family and Outside Activities Compatibility	Medium	Medium	High	High
Forecast for 2010-2020 Change	16%	4%	27%	5%
Forecast for 2033	Poor	Poor	Poor	Fair
Comments	Very automatable and not at all necessary to be done in the United States.	Along with sports, singing, and other entertainment careers, a pyramid, at which remarkably few people world wide can fit at the top, and not many with less ability can get others to pay to see them, when the best are so available through mass media, including the Internet. Part-time and seasonal positions also exist.[292]	High pay, lack of need to be local, and information available from other sources mean that by 2033 they will rarely work for individual companies, and few will be needed.	More will be tenders than operators, as machines get more automated, though these functions will stay common enough for these local-only jobs to continue.

Job Name	Administrative Service Managers	Adult Literacy and GED Teachers	Advertising Sales Agents	Advertising, Promotion, and Marketing Managers
Occupation Group	Management	Education, Training, and Library	Sales	Management
Local-Boundness	High	Medium	Medium	Medium
Resistance to Robotics	High	High	High	High
Resistance to Computing and Connectivity	Medium	Medium	Medium	High
Pertinent Principles (Good)	3			1
Pertinent Principles (Maybe Good)	5, 14	14	14	
Pertinent Principles (Bad)				
2010 Number of Workers	254,300	86,900	160,400	216,800
Chance for Good Living Wage	High	Medium	High	High
2010 Median Pay	Medium	Medium	Medium	High
Median Quality of Work Conditions	High	High	Medium	High
Family and Outside Activities Compatibility	High	High	Medium	High
Forecast for 2010-2020 Change	15%	15%	13%	14%
Forecast for 2033	Poor	Fair	Fair	Fair
Comments	The number of clerical employees has been dropping, and so will the number of their managers. Can be combined with other functions in larger offices, leaving the smaller ones, which pay less.	May be hurt by cost-cutting and by the growing knowledge that GEDs are not as good for getting hired for many jobs as original high school diplomas. Can also be done remotely.	Historically an in-person job even when selling to businesses, which may change within the next generation. However, they will still be needed to work out the details of advertising, in ways that will not be easily automatable.	Many people work in these positions and will be vulnerable to outsourcing, especially in the larger organizations.

Job Name	Aerospace Engineering and Operations Technicians	Aerospace Engineers	Agents and Business Managers of Artists, Performers, and Athletes	Agricultural and Food Science Technicians
Occupation Group	Architecture and Engineering	Architecture and Engineering	Business and Financial	Life, Physical, and Social Science
Local-Boundness	Medium	Low	Low	High
Resistance to Robotics	High	High	High	High
Resistance to Computing and Connectivity	Medium	Low	High	High
Pertinent Principles (Good)	7	7	1	1, 3
Pertinent Principles (Maybe Good)	9	9, 10		
Pertinent Principles (Bad)				
2010 Number of Workers	8,700	81,000	24,100	21,300
Chance for Good Living Wage	High	High	High	Low
2010 Median Pay	Medium	High	Medium	Low
Median Quality of Work Conditions	High	High	High	High
Family and Outside Activities Compatibility	Medium	High	High	High
Forecast for 2010-2020 Change	-2%	5%	14%	7%
Forecast for 2033	Excellent	Very Good	Good	Fair
Comments	Very strong in the decades to come, as commercial and recreational space travel become more viable and much more common.	Robust for the same reasons as technicians, but will still face competition from both international workers and computers.	These jobs require working with potential employers, knowing their quirks, and getting American bookings, a set of skills not suited to anything automated or foreign, even by 2033.	Needed to test food through due diligence. Will substitute for the scientists in some ways and continue to help them in others.

Job Name	Agricultural Engineers	Agricultural Inspectors	Agricultural Workers	Agriculture and Food Scientists
Occupation Group	Architecture and Engineering	Farming, Fishing, and Forestry	Farming, Fishing, and Forestry	Life, Physical, and Social Science
Local-Boundness	Low	Medium	High	High
Resistance to Robotics	High	High	High	High
Resistance to Computing and Connectivity	Medium	High	High	High
Pertinent Principles (Good)		1	1, 3	1, 3
Pertinent Principles (Maybe Good)		5	5	
Pertinent Principles (Bad)	16		16	
2010 Number of Workers	2,700	19,300	757,900	33,500
Chance for Good Living Wage	High	Medium	Low	High
2010 Median Pay	Medium	Medium	Low	Medium
Median Quality of Work Conditions	High	Medium	Low	High
Family and Outside Activities Compatibility	High	Medium	High	High
Forecast for 2010-2020 Change	9%	1%	-3%	10%
Forecast for 2033	Poor	Poor	Fair	Fair
Comments	Some will still be required, but accumulated knowledge will enable many to be replaced by lower-paid technicians.	Even without considering technical improvements, their number will fall with that of farms.	Employment here has dropped for about 100 years, but it may be leveling off, and technology, for something this physical, can only go so far.	Will be needed mainly for agricultural research, which will continue in significant amounts, especially if farm subsidies are diminished.

Job Name	Air Traffic Controllers	Aircraft and Avionics Equipment Mechanics and Technicians	Aircraft Cargo-Handling Supervisors	Airfield Operations Specialists
Occupation Group	Transportation and Material Moving	Installation, Maintenance, and Repair	Transportation and Material Moving	Transportation and Material Moving
Local-Boundness	Low	Medium	Medium	High
Resistance to Robotics	Medium	Medium	High	High
Resistance to Computing and Connectivity	Low	High	Medium	Medium
Pertinent Principles (Good)				3
Pertinent Principles (Maybe Good)	9, 10	5, 9		9, 13
Pertinent Principles (Bad)				
2010 Number of Workers	27,000	142,300	6,300	6,900
Chance for Good Living Wage	High	High	High	High
2010 Median Pay	High	Medium	Medium	Medium
Median Quality of Work Conditions	Medium	Medium	High	High
Family and Outside Activities Compatibility	Medium	High	Medium	Medium
Forecast for 2010-2020 Change	-3%	6%	20%	8%
Forecast for 2033	Poor	Good	Fair	Good
Comments	A position with extreme accuracy requirements, high pay, and algorithmic thinking is one that will be taken over by computers—in this case, years before 2033.	Airplane safety and, by extension, maintenance will stay highly valued, and in 20 years many of the planes now in use will still be flying.	Air freight will have good business through at least 2033, but more efficient and automated processes will limit the number of new jobs.	Many airports will be enlarged or built over the next two decades, and people to run the logistics on the ground, doing things that will stay too physical and interconnected for computers or robots, will be in demand.

Job Name	Airline and Commercial Pilots	Ambulance Drivers and Attendants, Except Emergency Medical Technicians	Amusement and Recreation Attendants	Animal Care and Service Workers
Occupation Group	Transportation and Material Moving	Transportation and Material Moving	Personal Care and Service	Personal Care and Service
Local-Boundness	Medium	High	High	High
Resistance to Robotics	Medium	High	High	High
Resistance to Computing and Connectivity	Medium	High	High	High
Pertinent Principles (Good)	7	1, 3	1, 3, 4	1, 3, 4, 8
Pertinent Principles (Maybe Good)	9, 10, 11	5, 19, 20	5, 14	5, 14, 19
Pertinent Principles (Bad)				
2010 Number of Workers	103,500	19,600	261,300	234,900
Chance for Good Living Wage	High	Low	Low	Low
2010 Median Pay	High	Low	Low	Low
Median Quality of Work Conditions	High	Medium	High	High
Family and Outside Activities Compatibility	Low	High	High	High
Forecast for 2010-2020 Change	11%	32%	14%	23%
Forecast for 2033	Fair	Good	Very Good	Excellent
Comments	In or near the 2020s, we will find out if airline passengers will accept robot-controlled aircraft. They probably will not, but that is the clear direction of the industry sooner or later.	Ambulance service is plainly a growth area, and drivers are needed and low paid. In many cases, though, EMTs, who can do more on the scenes, will end up driving instead.	Amusement facilities still require a human touch. Even the next generation probably won't want to ride, say, a completely unattended Ferris wheel. Low pay and a variable environment also mean little opportunity for robotics, and sales skills can play a role as well.	An in-person, non-automatable job with low pay which won't go away. The only disadvantage is that some will regard pet services as unaffordable luxuries.

Job Name	Animal Control Workers	Announcers	Anthropologists and Archaeologists	Appraisers and Assessors of Real Estate
Occupation Group	Protective Service	Media and Communications	Life, Physical, and Social Science	Business and Financial
Local-Boundness	High	Low	Medium	Medium
Resistance to Robotics	High	Medium	High	High
Resistance to Computing and Connectivity	High	High	High	Low
Pertinent Principles (Good)	1, 3		1	
Pertinent Principles (Maybe Good)	5			
Pertinent Principles (Bad)				
2010 Number of Workers	15,500	61,900	6,100	77,800
Chance for Good Living Wage	Low	Low	High	Medium
2010 Median Pay	Low	Low	Medium	Medium
Median Quality of Work Conditions	Medium	High	High	High
Family and Outside Activities Compatibility	High	High	Medium	High
Forecast for 2010-2020 Change	12%	7%	21%	7%
Forecast for 2033	Fair	Poor	Fair	Poor
Comments	A steady area without much growth, but, as a face-to-face job, not endangered by mechanization. No reason for decline, either.	Human-sounding virtual announcers should be common on the airwaves of 2033. In addition, the consolidation of radio and TV into fewer and fewer ownership groups means much programming, such as feature items on news broadcasts, can be used on multiple stations.	They are still almost exclusively in academics if in the field at all, which most are not.	Algorithmic, algorithmic, algorithmic—and even the photographs won't long need to be taken in person.

Job Name	Architects	Architectural and Engineering Managers	Archivists	Art Directors
Occupation Group	Architecture and Engineering	Management	Education, Training, and Library	Arts and Design
Local-Boundness	Low	Low	Low	Low
Resistance to Robotics	High	High	High	High
Resistance to Computing and Connectivity	Medium	High	Medium	High
Pertinent Principles (Good)		1		1
Pertinent Principles (Maybe Good)	13		5	14
Pertinent Principles (Bad)				
2010 Number of Workers	113,700	176,800	6,100	73,900
Chance for Good Living Wage	High	High	High	High
2010 Median Pay	Medium	High	Medium	High
Median Quality of Work Conditions	High	High	High	High
Family and Outside Activities Compatibility	High	High	High	Medium
Forecast for 2010-2020 Change	24%	9%	12%	9%
Forecast for 2033	Fair	Poor	Fair	Good
Comments	Some vulnerability to efficiency and automation. One area good for them will be airport design.	Very high pay and little need to be on site means Americans with these jobs may be replaced by cheaper foreigners.	Much material is not archived properly. Improving technology and efficiency, though, may keep the number of people in this field low.	A rare area where technology mostly provides options instead of making work easier. Companies and other organizations will often not want cookie-cutter solutions here, even if they are "the best."

Job Name	Assemblers and Fabricators	Athletes and Sports Competitors	Athletic Trainers	Atmospheric Scientists, Including Meteorologists
Occupation Group	Production	Entertainment and Sports	Healthcare	Life, Physical, and Social Science
Local-Boundness	Low	Medium	High	Low
Resistance to Robotics	Low	High	High	High
Resistance to Computing and Connectivity	High	High	High	Medium
Pertinent Principles (Good)		1	1, 3	
Pertinent Principles (Maybe Good)			5, 14, 20	
Pertinent Principles (Bad)	17			
2010 Number of Workers	1,626,500	16,500	18,200	9,500
Chance for Good Living Wage	Low	Low	Medium	High
2010 Median Pay	Low	Low	Medium	High
Median Quality of Work Conditions	Medium	Medium	High	High
Family and Outside Activities Compatibility	High	Medium	High	High
Forecast for 2010-2020 Change	5%	22%	30%	11%
Forecast for 2033	Poor	Poor	Fair	Good
Comments	Mainline manufacturing activities susceptible to automation, globalization, and efficiency—three main factors of Work's New Age.	Many will and should try for careers here, as the top of the pyramid is very high indeed, but the time of local athletes making good money is long gone, as millions of people watch only hundreds or even dozens.	A lot of sports are being played, but how necessary are the trainers? Will be hurt by falling college enrollment.	Weather measurements, models, and predictions are getting better and better, and research in the field is valued, even outside universities.

Job Name	Audiologists	Audio-Visual and Multimedia Collections Specialists	Automotive and Watercraft Service Attendants	Automotive Body and Glass Repairers
Occupation Group	Healthcare	Education, Training, and Library	Transportation and Material Moving	Installation, Maintenance, and Repair
Local-Boundness	High	High	High	High
Resistance to Robotics	High	High	High	Medium
Resistance to Computing and Connectivity	High	High	High	High
Pertinent Principles (Good)	1, 3	1, 3	1, 3	3
Pertinent Principles (Maybe Good)	5, 11, 14, 19, 20	14	5, 9	5, 9
Pertinent Principles (Bad)				
2010 Number of Workers	13,000	8,400	86,300	170,900
Chance for Good Living Wage	High	High	Low	Medium
2010 Median Pay	Medium	Medium	Low	Low
Median Quality of Work Conditions	High	High	Medium	Medium
Family and Outside Activities Compatibility	High	High	High	High
Forecast for 2010-2020 Change	37%	13%	22%	19%
Forecast for 2033	Excellent	Poor	Good	Good
Comments	Any health-related position with duties similar to those of physicians but paying substantially less is a strong proposition, and catering to those over 65 makes this one even better.	A set of specialty tasks that will, in most places, end up combined with those of librarians or handled by teachers themselves, as most AV material is now electronic.	A personal service once commonplace, and could come back in some form, as people, especially those older, will appreciate those pumping gas, adding oil, or doing other small car- and boat-related tasks.	As automobiles become longer-lasting and costlier, more will be repaired instead of junked. The work may be reduced by subassemblies but still must be done locally, as transporting cars is expensive.

Job Name	Automotive Service Technicians and Mechanics	Baggage Porters and Bellhops	Bakers	Barbers, Hairdressers, and Cosmetologists
Occupation Group	Installation, Maintenance, and Repair	Personal Care and Service	Production	Personal Care and Service
Local-Boundness	High	High	Medium	High
Resistance to Robotics	Medium	Medium	Low	High
Resistance to Computing and Connectivity	High	High	High	High
Pertinent Principles (Good)	3	3, 4, 7		1, 3, 4
Pertinent Principles (Maybe Good)	5, 9	5, 9		5, 14
Pertinent Principles (Bad)				
2010 Number of Workers	723,400	5,700	149,800	712,200
Chance for Good Living Wage	Medium	Low	Low	Low
2010 Median Pay	Low	Low	Low	Low
Median Quality of Work Conditions	Medium	High	Medium	High
Family and Outside Activities Compatibility	High	High	High	High
Forecast for 2010-2020 Change	17%	12%	2%	14%
Forecast for 2033	Good	Good	Poor	Very Good
Comments	Cars need less maintenance and fewer repairs than in the past, but they are on the road longer, and work on them must be done one at a time.	With travelers getting older, this field may get a resurgence. It's not hard to imagine robot bellhops, but since much of their pay comes from tips, management will have less incentive to try them.	Must be done somewhere reasonably close to the customers, but even that could change. Susceptible to further automation.	In one study, barbers stayed with their jobs longer than any others. In these three nonautomatable, local-only positions, workers may be able to do that for decades more.

Job Name	Bartenders	Bicycle Repairers	Bill and Account Collectors	Biochemists and Biophysicists
Occupation Group	Food Preparation and Serving	Installation, Maintenance, and Repair	Office and Administrative Support	Life, Physical, and Social Science
Local-Boundness	High	High	Low	Low
Resistance to Robotics	Medium	High	High	High
Resistance to Computing and Connectivity	High	High	Medium	High
Pertinent Principles (Good)	3, 4	1, 3		1
Pertinent Principles (Maybe Good)	5	5, 9	5, 14	11
Pertinent Principles (Bad)				
2010 Number of Workers	503,200	9,900	401,700	25,100
Chance for Good Living Wage	Low	Low	Low	High
2010 Median Pay	Low	Low	Low	Medium
Median Quality of Work Conditions	Medium	High	Low	High
Family and Outside Activities Compatibility	High	High	High	High
Forecast for 2010-2020 Change	9%	38%	14%	31%
Forecast for 2033	Fair	Excellent	Fair	Very Good
Comments	A classic in-person, food-service-related position, but susceptible to automation, which not only saves labor but cuts legal liability. A thorougly automated bar will have arrived well before 2033, but will customers accept it?	A lot of room for growth, as the number of American bicycle riders will increase, maybe dramatically, and rates for repairs, to be needed indefinitely, are low.	Much of their work can be done without human involvement, but some will require it. Lower employment levels will mean more bills and accounts in default, providing security for this occupation.	Connects with genetic study, a particularly strong area, and medical research, which should be at least steady. Numbers could greatly increase.

Job Name	Biological Technicians	Biomedical Engineers	Boilermakers	Bookkeeping, Accounting, and Auditing Clerks
Occupation Group	Life, Physical, and Social Science	Architecture and Engineering	Construction and Extraction	Office and Administrative Support
Local-Boundness	Medium	Medium	High	Low
Resistance to Robotics	High	High	Medium	High
Resistance to Computing and Connectivity	High	Medium	High	Low
Pertinent Principles (Good)	1		3	
Pertinent Principles (Maybe Good)	5	20	5, 12	14
Pertinent Principles (Bad)				2
2010 Number of Workers	80,200	15,700	19,800	1,898,300
Chance for Good Living Wage	Medium	High	High	Low
2010 Median Pay	Low	High	Medium	Low
Median Quality of Work Conditions	High	High	Medium	High
Family and Outside Activities Compatibility	High	Medium	High	High
Forecast for 2010-2020 Change	14%	62%	21%	14%
Forecast for 2033	Very Good	Good	Good	Poor
Comments	Are doing many of the full scientists' tasks already, so don't have as much area to grow into. However, genetics and other related areas will be superb over the next 20 years.	Very good now, but knowledge accumulating will hurt. Still has prospects well above average.	Although more and more liquid- and gas-holding containers may be prefabricated, this work must still be done in person, and there may not be remote solutions to such things as leaks.	A field waiting for end-to-end automated answers, which will remove the need for the great majority of accounting entries for routine transactions. These workers will go the way of payroll clerks, who were very common before computerization.

Job Name	Brickmasons, Blockmasons, and Stonemasons	Bridge and Lock Tenders	Broadcast and Sound Engineering Technicians	Budget Analysts
Occupation Group	Construction and Extraction	Transportation and Material Moving	Media and Communications	Business and Financial
Local-Boundness	High	Medium	Medium	Low
Resistance to Robotics	Medium	Medium	High	High
Resistance to Computing and Connectivity	High	Low	Medium	Medium
Pertinent Principles (Good)	3			
Pertinent Principles (Maybe Good)	5, 12			
Pertinent Principles (Bad)				
2010 Number of Workers	104,800	3,500	116,900	62,100
Chance for Good Living Wage	High	Medium	Medium	High
2010 Median Pay	Medium	Medium	Medium	Medium
Median Quality of Work Conditions	Medium	High	High	High
Family and Outside Activities Compatibility	High	High	High	High
Forecast for 2010-2020 Change	40%	-1%	10%	10%
Forecast for 2033	Very Good	Poor	Fair	Fair
Comments	With land being developed, they will have plenty of tasks, which must be done right there.	Some people will still be needed, but many more can work remotely or be replaced by automated systems.	Sound systems requiring less human intervention will hurt this field, which otherwise fills a need sometimes urgent and will not go away.	Not as easy to mechanize as accounting, but has no need to be done in person. When people in cheaper-labor countries pile up related experience, they will get the work.

Job Name	Bus Drivers	Camera and Photographic Equipment Repairers	Cardiovascular Technologists and Technicians and Vascular Technologists	Career and Technical Education Teachers
Occupation Group	Transportation and Material Moving	Installation, Maintenance, and Repair	Healthcare	Education, Training, and Library
Local-Boundness	Medium	Medium	High	High
Resistance to Robotics	Low	High	High	High
Resistance to Computing and Connectivity	High	High	High	High
Pertinent Principles (Good)		1	1, 3	1, 3
Pertinent Principles (Maybe Good)	9	5	5, 14, 19, 20	
Pertinent Principles (Bad)				
2010 Number of Workers	647,200	3,300	49,400	103,000
Chance for Good Living Wage	Low	Medium	High	High
2010 Median Pay	Low	Low	Medium	Medium
Median Quality of Work Conditions	Medium	High	High	High
Family and Outside Activities Compatibility	Medium	High	High	High
Forecast for 2010-2020 Change	13%	10%	29%	2%
Forecast for 2033	Good	Fair	Excellent	Very Good
Comments	Automated buses will take longer to arrive than automated airplanes, and bus travel may become more common as fewer people own cars.	Digital cameras, now the standard, are dropping in price to the point where repairs to most are not cost effective. There will still be opportunities on the high end, with both cameras and related equipment.	As with audiologists, will take over an increasing number of tasks from physicians, in this case cardiologists, who are paid much higher.	There is a real chance that more high school students will choose vocational tracks, swelling enrollments in areas not compatible with large class sizes. As the subject is hands on, much technical material cannot be taught online.

Job Name	Cargo and Freight Agents	Carpenters	Carpet Installers	Cartographers and Photogrammetrists
Occupation Group	Office and Administrative Support	Construction and Extraction	Construction and Extraction	Architecture and Engineering
Local-Boundness	High	High	High	Low
Resistance to Robotics	Medium	High	Medium	High
Resistance to Computing and Connectivity	Low	High	High	Medium
Pertinent Principles (Good)	3	1, 3	3	
Pertinent Principles (Maybe Good)	5	5, 12	5, 13	
Pertinent Principles (Bad)				
2010 Number of Workers	82,200	1,001,700	47,500	13,800
Chance for Good Living Wage	Medium	Medium	Medium	High
2010 Median Pay	Low	Medium	Low	Medium
Median Quality of Work Conditions	High	Medium	Medium	High
Family and Outside Activities Compatibility	High	High	High	High
Forecast for 2010-2020 Change	29%	20%	10%	22%
Forecast for 2033	Fair	Very Good	Good	Fair
Comments	By 2033, the higher need for in-person activity here will have roughly offset greater automation, of such things as form preparation, within the job.	Much of their work involves on-site assessment and adjustment of items for which mechanization will have done little by 2033.	Some tasks here may be automatable, but not all, and new buildings require new carpets.	Mapping is necessary, but much of it has already been done, so the field will move to changing existing charts, which will not require as much work or as many people.

Job Name	Cashiers	Cement Masons and Terrazzo Workers	Chefs and Head Cooks	Chemical Engineers
Occupation Group	Sales	Construction and Extraction	Food Preparation and Serving	Architecture and Engineering
Local-Boundness	High	High	High	Low
Resistance to Robotics	Low	Medium	High	High
Resistance to Computing and Connectivity	Medium	High	High	Medium
Pertinent Principles (Good)	3, 4	3	1, 3, 7	
Pertinent Principles (Maybe Good)	5, 14	5, 12	5, 14	
Pertinent Principles (Bad)				
2010 Number of Workers	3,362,000	148,400	100,600	30,200
Chance for Good Living Wage	Low	Medium	Medium	High
2010 Median Pay	Low	Low	Medium	High
Median Quality of Work Conditions	High	Medium	Medium	High
Family and Outside Activities Compatibility	High	High	High	High
Forecast for 2010-2020 Change	7%	34%	-1%	6%
Forecast for 2033	Poor	Good	Good	Fair
Comments	Automated checkout lines have thus far met real customer resistance, but that will not always be the case. Before 2033, most retail establishments will have lost most of these employees.	Partially automatable through robotics, but still a lot of work that must be done in person and will continue.	Job listings increased 34% from August 2011 to August 2012.[293] Opportunities will be at the highest-end restaurants, which are generally in expensive-living areas. Fewer places with high but not top-end check ranges (about $40 to $60 per person in 2013) will have well-paid cooks.	Rapidly accumulating knowledge in this field will be roughly offset by the ongoing need for new, improved products.

Job Name	Chemical Equipment Operators and Tenders	Chemical Plant and System Operators	Chemical Technicians	Chemists and Materials Scientists
Occupation Group	Production	Production	Life, Physical, and Social Science	Life, Physical, and Social Science
Local-Boundness	Medium	Medium	Medium	Low
Resistance to Robotics	Low	Low	High	High
Resistance to Computing and Connectivity	High	High	High	High
Pertinent Principles (Good)			1	1
Pertinent Principles (Maybe Good)			5	
Pertinent Principles (Bad)	17	17		
2010 Number of Workers	47,400	43,300	61,000	90,900
Chance for Good Living Wage	Medium	High	Medium	High
2010 Median Pay	Medium	Medium	Medium	Medium
Median Quality of Work Conditions	Medium	Medium	High	High
Family and Outside Activities Compatibility	High	High	High	High
Forecast for 2010-2020 Change	-7%	-12%	7%	4%
Forecast for 2033	Poor	Poor	Good	Good
Comments	A machine operating duty tied to manufacturing, which means its jobs will be shrunk by automation, foreign competition, or, most likely, both.	Calls for a lot of skill, but that will not help its possible replacement by robots and the ongoing shift to manufacturing elsewhere.	Chemical research will continue, though it lacks a specific area expected to be tremendous for the next two decades, such as genetics. Technicians are already acting as scientists.	Dependent on funding, which may be erratic, but with strong ties to companies which can always use discoveries for a competitive advantage.

Job Name	Childcare Workers	Chiropractors	Civil Engineering Technicians	Civil Engineers
Occupation Group	Personal Care and Service	Healthcare	Architecture and Engineering	Architecture and Engineering
Local-Boundness	High	High	High	Medium
Resistance to Robotics	High	High	High	High
Resistance to Computing and Connectivity	High	High	Medium	Medium
Pertinent Principles (Good)	1, 3, 4, 6, 8	1, 3	3	
Pertinent Principles (Maybe Good)	5, 14	5, 11, 20	13	13
Pertinent Principles (Bad)				
2010 Number of Workers	1,282,300	52,600	79,000	262,800
Chance for Good Living Wage	Low	High	High	High
2010 Median Pay	Low	Medium	Medium	Medium
Median Quality of Work Conditions	High	High	High	High
Family and Outside Activities Compatibility	High	High	Medium	Medium
Forecast for 2010-2020 Change	20%	28%	12%	19%
Forecast for 2033	Very Good	Very Good	Excellent	Very Good
Comments	A low-paid, in-person, female-dominated position that won't go away and may well end up paying more. The disadvantage is that when fewer people work, fewer need childcare services, but the greater needs of the 1% will help with that.	Lacking the connection with older people, but still a high-skilled, health-related job not done by medical doctors.	Superbly positioned to take advantage of the need for infrastructure rebuilding and repair. Will take over much work from civil engineers.	Will be involved in upcoming infrastructure work, though will be replaced in many spots by technicians.

Job Name	Claims Adjusters, Appraisers, Examiners, and Investigators	Cleaning, Washing, and Metal Pickling Equipment Operators and Tenders	Clergy	Coaches and Scouts
Occupation Group	Business and Financial	Production	Community and Social Service	Entertainment and Sports
Local-Boundness	Low	Medium	High	High
Resistance to Robotics	High	Low	High	High
Resistance to Computing and Connectivity	Medium	High	High	High
Pertinent Principles (Good)			1, 3, 18	1, 3
Pertinent Principles (Maybe Good)				
Pertinent Principles (Bad)				
2010 Number of Workers	290,700	17,700	230,800	242,900
Chance for Good Living Wage	High	Low	Medium	Low
2010 Median Pay	Medium	Low	Medium	Low
Median Quality of Work Conditions	High	Medium	High	High
Family and Outside Activities Compatibility	High	High	High	High
Forecast for 2010-2020 Change	3%	1%	18%	29%
Forecast for 2033	Fair	Poor	Good	Fair
Comments	The need for judgment on many insurance matters will see that humans have some of these duties through at least 2033.	People will be needed to watch over these increasingly reliable machines, but their numbers will drop.	Religion will stay important to many, who will want at least the possibility of in-person guidance. Pay may get lower as parishioners have less money to contribute.	More people are playing sports, but the share of girls and women may be peaking. A pyramid, though better for people at the bottom than athletics itself.

Job Name	Coin, Vending, and Amusement Machine Servicers and Repairers	Commercial Divers	Compensation and Benefits Managers	Compensation, Benefits, and Job Analysis Specialists
Occupation Group	Installation, Maintenance, and Repair	Installation, Maintenance, and Repair	Management	Business and Financial
Local-Boundness	High	High	Low	Low
Resistance to Robotics	Medium	Low	High	High
Resistance to Computing and Connectivity	High	High	High	Medium
Pertinent Principles (Good)	3	3	1	
Pertinent Principles (Maybe Good)	5	5	14	14
Pertinent Principles (Bad)				
2010 Number of Workers	39,100	3,800	31,800	5,500
Chance for Good Living Wage	Low	High	High	High
2010 Median Pay	Low	Medium	High	Medium
Median Quality of Work Conditions	High	Low	High	High
Family and Outside Activities Compatibility	High	Medium	High	High
Forecast for 2010-2020 Change	22%	16%	3%	5%
Forecast for 2033	Good	Poor	Poor	Poor
Comments	Vending machines, which will become even more common, will still require a lot of work, though those accepting only credit cards will need less.	A fine application for remote-controlled robots, to avoid great dangers. The only advantage is the low number employed now.	Only the largest companies will need someone dedicated full time here, and those people need not do the job from the same office or even the same country.	A human resources area and bound to the same problems with that field. A perpetual employer's market means reduced attention paid to workers.

Job Name	Compliance Officers	Computer and Information Research Scientists	Computer and Information Systems Managers	Computer Hardware Engineers
Occupation Group	Business and Financial	Computer and Information Technology	Management	Architecture and Engineering
Local-Boundness	Low	Low	Low	Low
Resistance to Robotics	High	High	High	High
Resistance to Computing and Connectivity	Medium	Medium	High	Low
Pertinent Principles (Good)			1	
Pertinent Principles (Maybe Good)		10		
Pertinent Principles (Bad)				
2010 Number of Workers	32,400	28,200	307,900	70,000
Chance for Good Living Wage	High	High	High	High
2010 Median Pay	Medium	High	High	High
Median Quality of Work Conditions	High	High	High	High
Family and Outside Activities Compatibility	High	High	High	High
Forecast for 2010-2020 Change	15%	19%	18%	9%
Forecast for 2033	Poor	Fair	Fair	Poor
Comments	A business specialty ripe for consolidation with others, though some organizations will justify having someone dedicated to these general areas of compliance.	Computing technology will march on, in fundamental as well as incremental ways, but American workers have no monopoly on designing it.	A highly paid management position that need not be done on site, but the level of change means more IT managers will be needed, and involved, than those of other departments.	A few people will be required to design computers based on nanotechnology and quantum mechanics, but there is every reason for Americans employed in this field to drastically shrink in numbers.

Job Name	Computer Operators	Computer Programmers	Computer Support Specialists	Computer Systems Analysts
Occupation Group	Office and Administrative Support	Computer and Information Technology	Computer and Information Technology	Computer and Information Technology
Local-Boundness	Low	Low	Low	Low
Resistance to Robotics	High	High	High	High
Resistance to Computing and Connectivity	Low	Medium	Low	Low
Pertinent Principles (Good)				
Pertinent Principles (Maybe Good)				
Pertinent Principles (Bad)	2			
2010 Number of Workers	86,400	363,100	607,100	544,400
Chance for Good Living Wage	Low	High	Low	High
2010 Median Pay	Low	Medium	Medium	Medium
Median Quality of Work Conditions	High	High	High	High
Family and Outside Activities Compatibility	High	High	High	High
Forecast for 2010-2020 Change	-9%	12%	18%	22%
Forecast for 2033	Poor	Poor	Poor	Fair
Comments	Once a much larger occupation, it has been automated by the computers themselves, and when people are needed they can be anywhere on the planet.	Two major problems: the ability of programming to be done from anywhere and the continuing trend of computer languages becoming more and more powerful, thereby cutting work.	This job can be, and often is, done from anywhere by anyone with the ability.	The requirement of knowing the businesses and cultures involved will keep much true systems analysis out of the easily-outsourced category.

Job Name	Computer, ATM, and Office Machine Repairers	Concierges	Conservation Scientists and Foresters	Construction and Building Inspectors
Occupation Group	Installation, Maintenance, and Repair	Personal Care and Service	Life, Physical, and Social Science	Construction and Extraction
Local-Boundness	High	High	Medium	High
Resistance to Robotics	Medium	Medium	High	High
Resistance to Computing and Connectivity	High	High	Medium	Medium
Pertinent Principles (Good)	3	3, 7, 8		3
Pertinent Principles (Maybe Good)	5	5, 9, 14		5, 12
Pertinent Principles (Bad)				
2010 Number of Workers	146,200	20,300	34,900	102,400
Chance for Good Living Wage	Medium	Low	High	High
2010 Median Pay	Low	Low	Medium	Medium
Median Quality of Work Conditions	Medium	High	High	High
Family and Outside Activities Compatibility	High	High	High	High
Forecast for 2010-2020 Change	7%	12%	5%	18%
Forecast for 2033	Fair	Very Good	Good	Good
Comments	As with automobiles, office machines need fewer repairs, but many will continue to be replaced, necessitating workers' knowledge, as they get obsolete.	Strong from many perspectives. Will be increasingly valued to provide clear information and to get hotel guests, and others, the assistance they need.	Trees cut down are crops, and the best opportunities for foresters may be with private industry maximizing long-term profitability, which goes with maintaining land. In effect an agricultural position that will not require large numbers of people but will still call for some.	May thin out, through preapproval or automated compliance assessment systems, but a lot of work will remain necessary for people on site.

Job Name	Construction Equipment Operators	Construction Laborers and Helpers	Construction Managers	Continuous Mining Machine Operators
Occupation Group	Construction and Extraction	Construction and Extraction	Management	Construction and Extraction
Local-Boundness	High	High	High	High
Resistance to Robotics	Medium	Medium	High	Low
Resistance to Computing and Connectivity	High	High	High	High
Pertinent Principles (Good)	3	3	1, 3	3
Pertinent Principles (Maybe Good)	5, 12, 13	5, 13	13	5
Pertinent Principles (Bad)				16
2010 Number of Workers	404,900	1,250,200	523,100	13,900
Chance for Good Living Wage	Medium	Low	High	Medium
2010 Median Pay	Medium	Low	High	Medium
Median Quality of Work Conditions	Medium	Low	High	Low
Family and Outside Activities Compatibility	High	High	High	High
Forecast for 2010-2020 Change	23%	25%	17%	0%
Forecast for 2033	Very Good	Good	Very Good	Poor
Comments	Construction machines will grow in complexity, and while some will be remotely controlled or replaced by robots, most will not, and the need for human operators will be greater than ever.	As with the higher-level construction jobs, robotics and more efficient processes will cut some opportunities, but most will remain for lack of alternatives.	Construction, especially that of roads, bridges, and airports, will be a fine area, and managers in that field need to be onsite more than others. Automated products will shorten building times, but the work will still need to be coordinated.	A front-line extraction job, and, as such, a physically dangerous field, so particularly subject to robotics.

Job Name	Control and Valve Installers and Repairers, Except Mechanical Door	Cooks	Cooling and Freezing Equipment Operators and Tenders	Correctional Officers
Occupation Group	Installation, Maintenance, and Repair	Food Preparation and Serving	Production	Protective Service
Local-Boundness	High	High	Medium	High
Resistance to Robotics	High	High	Low	Medium
Resistance to Computing and Connectivity	High	High	High	High
Pertinent Principles (Good)	1, 3	1, 3, 4		3
Pertinent Principles (Maybe Good)	5	5		
Pertinent Principles (Bad)				
2010 Number of Workers	43,800	2,050,800	8,900	493,100
Chance for Good Living Wage	High	Low	Low	Medium
2010 Median Pay	Medium	Low	Low	Low
Median Quality of Work Conditions	High	Medium	Medium	Medium
Family and Outside Activities Compatibility	High	High	High	High
Forecast for 2010-2020 Change	0%	8%	1%	5%
Forecast for 2033	Fair	Very Good	Poor	Poor
Comments	The need for these controls will stay, and robots won't help in either repair or installation, though remote systems are likely to replace some jobs.	Pay is low enough so this position, already dependent on many time- and labor-saving practices and devices, will get little robotics attention.	Cooling and freezing machines, with few moving parts, require even less involvement than many others, so large numbers of them, even at multiple locations, can be tended by few workers.	The incarcerated population may go up or down. If down, there will be a real drop in the number of corrections officers needed. In either case, prisons will have increasing use for remote supervision and will use many robotic guards.

Job Name	Cost Estimators	Costume Attendants	Counter and Rental Clerks	Couriers and Messengers
Occupation Group	Business and Financial	Personal Care and Service	Sales	Office and Administrative Support
Local-Boundness	Low	High	High	High
Resistance to Robotics	High	High	Medium	Medium
Resistance to Computing and Connectivity	Medium	High	Medium	Medium
Pertinent Principles (Good)		1, 3	3, 4	3, 8
Pertinent Principles (Maybe Good)		5, 14	5, 14	5
Pertinent Principles (Bad)				
2010 Number of Workers	185,400	5,500	419,500	116,200
Chance for Good Living Wage	High	Low	Low	Low
2010 Median Pay	Medium	Low	Low	Low
Median Quality of Work Conditions	High	High	Medium	Medium
Family and Outside Activities Compatibility	High	High	High	High
Forecast for 2010-2020 Change	36%	10%	12%	13%
Forecast for 2033	Fair	Fair	Fair	Good
Comments	Most of these positions will require little or no travel and thus can be done from anywhere. May still, though, remain too complex for computers.	Should continue about as it is, with more complicated costumes and a similar number of productions needing them offset by general efficiency.	Parts of their jobs will be automated that aren't yet, but the main task, including face-to-face customer contact, will remain.	Must be done in person, and most common in large cities such as New York. They need to be cheaper or faster than taxicabs to get business, which they can often accomplish.

Job Name	Court Reporters	Craft and Fine Artists	Credit Analysts	Credit Counselors
Occupation Group	Legal	Arts and Design	Business and Financial	Business and Financial
Local-Boundness	Medium	Low	Low	Low
Resistance to Robotics	High	High	High	High
Resistance to Computing and Connectivity	Medium	High	Low	High
Pertinent Principles (Good)		1, 7		1
Pertinent Principles (Maybe Good)	5, 14	14		14
Pertinent Principles (Bad)				
2010 Number of Workers	22,000	56,900	63,300	33,100
Chance for Good Living Wage	Medium	Medium	High	Medium
2010 Median Pay	Medium	Medium	Medium	Low
Median Quality of Work Conditions	High	High	High	High
Family and Outside Activities Compatibility	High	High	High	High
Forecast for 2010-2020 Change	14%	5%	20%	20%
Forecast for 2033	Fair	Good	Poor	Good
Comments	Voice recognition software may make this work feasible without as much technical ability, and potentially it could also be done remotely. Only the laws, which may change, keep this field as viable as it is.	There will always be significant demand for handmade craft art, as people want at least some things physical as opposed to virtual. Fine art, though, is a pyramid, and most of its practitioners will not earn enough for a full-time living.	By 2033, credit analysis will be a completely computerized task requiring no more than brief concurrence from a general manager.	A nonalgorithmic job valuable to explain things to people in financial trouble, who will become increasingly common. A growing social service.

Job Name	Crossing Guards	Crushing, Grinding, and Polishing Machine Setters, Operators, and Tenders	Curators, Museum Technicians, and Conservators	Customer Service Representatives
Occupation Group	Protective Service	Production	Education, Training, and Library	Office and Administrative Support
Local-Boundness	High	Medium	High	Low
Resistance to Robotics	Medium	Low	High	Medium
Resistance to Computing and Connectivity	High	High	High	Medium
Pertinent Principles (Good)	3		1, 3, 7	
Pertinent Principles (Maybe Good)	14		5	14
Pertinent Principles (Bad)		17		
2010 Number of Workers	69,300	33,400	23,800	2,187,300
Chance for Good Living Wage	Low	Low	Medium	Low
2010 Median Pay	Low	Low	Medium	Low
Median Quality of Work Conditions	Medium	Medium	High	Medium
Family and Outside Activities Compatibility	High	High	High	High
Forecast for 2010-2020 Change	1%	5%	16%	15%
Forecast for 2033	Fair	Poor	Good	Poor
Comments	Will still be needed, probably in similar numbers to today. Many will be volunteers, but automated systems that make them seem unnecessary will meet with resistance.	Machine operation for manufacturing, in almost all cases, will employ far fewer Americans in 2033 than now. No exception here.	Must be done locally and won't be automated, but museums are dependent on private donations and government money, either or both of which may shrink.	Job listings increased 50% from August 2011 to August 2012.[294] One of the most common employment categories in 2010, it will be devastated before 2033 by foreign competition and robotic voice systems. Many Americans will still be needed, but no more than a few hundred thousand.

Job Name	Cutters and Trimmers, Hand	Cutting and Slicing Machine Setters, Operators, and Tenders	Dancers and Choreographers	Data Entry Keyers
Occupation Group	Production	Production	Entertainment and Sports	Office and Administrative Support
Local-Boundness	High	Medium	High	Low
Resistance to Robotics	Low	Low	High	High
Resistance to Computing and Connectivity	High	High	High	Low
Pertinent Principles (Good)	3		1, 3	
Pertinent Principles (Maybe Good)			14	5, 14
Pertinent Principles (Bad)	17	17		2
2010 Number of Workers	17,400	61,400	25,600	234,700
Chance for Good Living Wage	Low	Low	Low	Low
2010 Median Pay	Low	Low	Low	Low
Median Quality of Work Conditions	Medium	Medium	Medium	High
Family and Outside Activities Compatibility	High	High	Medium	High
Forecast for 2010-2020 Change	-6%	0%	18%	-7%
Forecast for 2033	Poor	Poor	Poor	Poor
Comments	Not many items need to be cut or trimmed by humans now, and that number will only decrease with more sensitive robotics technology.	Will have their scope of tasks greatly reduced by robots long before 2033.	Some required in person for such as theme-park shows, but few will have steady work, far fewer at good pay. Part-time and seasonal positions, such as dance host and motivational dancer, will also exist.[295]	Another once-common job going obsolete, in this case because of computer-to-computer connectivity making humans unnecessary.

Job Name	Database Administrators	Delivery Truck Drivers and Driver/Sales Workers	Demonstrators and Product Promoters	Dental Assistants
Occupation Group	Computer and Information Technology	Transportation and Material Moving	Sales	Healthcare
Local-Boundness	Low	Medium	High	High
Resistance to Robotics	High	Low	High	Medium
Resistance to Computing and Connectivity	Low	High	High	High
Pertinent Principles (Good)			1, 3, 4	3
Pertinent Principles (Maybe Good)		5		5, 14, 19, 20
Pertinent Principles (Bad)				
2010 Number of Workers	110,800	1,262,600	90,100	297,200
Chance for Good Living Wage	High	Low	Low	Low
2010 Median Pay	Medium	Low	Low	Low
Median Quality of Work Conditions	High	Medium	Medium	High
Family and Outside Activities Compatibility	High	High	High	High
Forecast for 2010-2020 Change	31%	13%	18%	31%
Forecast for 2033	Poor	Fair	Fair	Good
Comments	No need for it to be done locally or to be performed in ways specialized to organizations or cultures. Fewer people can oversee more databases.	Many kinds of commerce require deliveries of packages, which will generally continue, despite some automation and electronic alternatives being implemented.	Will remain an in-person sales proposition resistant to both mechanization and remote workers. The disadvantage is that fewer possible customers will pay attention.	A necessary, female-dominated health care job, but susceptible to streamlined procedures, and pay is high enough to provide incentive for the number of workers to be reduced.

Job Name	Dental Hygienists	Dental Laboratory Technicians	Dentists	Desktop Publishers
Occupation Group	Healthcare	Production	Healthcare	Office and Administrative Support
Local-Boundness	High	Low	High	Low
Resistance to Robotics	High	Medium	High	Medium
Resistance to Computing and Connectivity	High	High	High	Medium
Pertinent Principles (Good)	1, 3		1, 3	
Pertinent Principles (Maybe Good)	5, 14, 19, 20	19, 20	5, 11, 19, 20	14
Pertinent Principles (Bad)				2
2010 Number of Workers	181,800	40,900	155,700	22,600
Chance for Good Living Wage	High	Medium	High	Low
2010 Median Pay	Medium	Low	High	Low
Median Quality of Work Conditions	High	High	High	High
Family and Outside Activities Compatibility	High	High	High	High
Forecast for 2010-2020 Change	38%	1%	21%	-15%
Forecast for 2033	Very Good	Fair	Good	Poor
Comments	Have far more face time with patients than do dentists, and that may even increase. The only downsides are a chance for fewer Americans getting dental care, and high salaries spurring replacements.	More of a craft than manufacturing. Further automation, while possible, will eliminate few of these healthcare workers in a steady field.	As the most highly paid people in dental offices, they are vulnerable, and as these workplaces get larger, efficiencies may cut the number of their jobs. Still a lot of strengths.	With advances in software making it easy for other professionals to do their work themselves, they are going the way of 1980s word processing clerks and will be all but extinct before 2033.

Job Name	Diagnostic Medical Sonographers	Diesel Service Technicians and Mechanics	Dietetic Technicians	Dieticians and Nutritionists
Occupation Group	Healthcare	Installation, Maintenance, and Repair	Healthcare	Healthcare
Local-Boundness	High	High	High	Low
Resistance to Robotics	High	Medium	Medium	High
Resistance to Computing and Connectivity	High	High	High	Low
Pertinent Principles (Good)	1, 3	3	3	
Pertinent Principles (Maybe Good)	5, 14, 20	5	14, 20	14, 20
Pertinent Principles (Bad)				
2010 Number of Workers	53,700	242,200	24,200	64,400
Chance for Good Living Wage	High	Medium	Low	High
2010 Median Pay	Medium	Medium	Low	Medium
Median Quality of Work Conditions	High	Medium	High	High
Family and Outside Activities Compatibility	High	High	High	High
Forecast for 2010-2020 Change	44%	15%	16%	20%
Forecast for 2033	Good	Good	Good	Fair
Comments	The share of pregnant women getting ultrasounds keeps rising, but will the technology be replaced by 2033? Good prospects for those who can readily convert to using other ones, if they require as much human involvement.	Diesel trucks and buses are expensive and last a long time, so they will continue to be maintained and repaired, though will need work less often.	As in-person faces for many dietiticians, these technicians will cover many of their duties with patients.	A health-related job but one that can be done remotely, is algorithmic, and may suffer from budget cuts.

Job Name	Directors, Religious Activities and Education	Dishwashers	Dispatchers, Except Fire, Police, and Ambulance	Door-to-Door Sales workers, News and Street Vendors, and Related Workers
Occupation Group	Community and Social Service	Food Preparation and Serving	Office and Administrative Support	Sales
Local-Boundness	Medium	High	Low	High
Resistance to Robotics	High	Low	High	Medium
Resistance to Computing and Connectivity	High	High	Low	High
Pertinent Principles (Good)	1, 18	3, 4		3, 4
Pertinent Principles (Maybe Good)	14		5	5
Pertinent Principles (Bad)				
2010 Number of Workers	126,000	510,200	185,200	153,800
Chance for Good Living Wage	Low	Low	Low	Low
2010 Median Pay	Low	Low	Low	Low
Median Quality of Work Conditions	High	Medium	High	Medium
Family and Outside Activities Compatibility	High	High	High	High
Forecast for 2010-2020 Change	17%	7%	19%	-7%
Forecast for 2033	Good	Poor	Poor	Fair
Comments	More people will get social services from churches, which will be squeezed further by declining contributions. Pay may decrease, and some employees will be replaced by volunteers.	For a long time, they have used fast-running machines. By 2033, systems that also load and unload should be in place in most restaurants.	Except for a few settings where back-and-forth voice conversations are truly necessary, there is no reason why most dispatching cannot be handled through computers or by cheaper workers overseas in 2013, let alone in 2033.	Door-to-door sales is much diminished in America, but street sales, if more people do not have cars, could have a real upswing.

Job Name	Drafters	Drywall and Ceiling Tile Installers, and Tapers	Earth Drillers, Except Oil and Gas	Economists
Occupation Group	Architecture and Engineering	Construction and Extraction	Construction and Extraction	Life, Physical, and Social Science
Local-Boundness	Low	High	High	Low
Resistance to Robotics	High	Medium	Low	High
Resistance to Computing and Connectivity	Low	High	High	Medium
Pertinent Principles (Good)		3	3	
Pertinent Principles (Maybe Good)	13	5, 12	5	
Pertinent Principles (Bad)			16	
2010 Number of Workers	205,100	129,600	17,800	15,400
Chance for Good Living Wage	Medium	Medium	Medium	High
2010 Median Pay	Medium	Low	Medium	High
Median Quality of Work Conditions	High	Medium	Medium	High
Family and Outside Activities Compatibility	High	High	High	High
Forecast for 2010-2020 Change	6%	29%	14%	6%
Forecast for 2033	Poor	Good	Poor	Fair
Comments	Infrastructure projects offer some hope, but as CADD (computer-aided design and drafting) software becomes more and more powerful, drafters, a.k.a. CADD operators, will shrink in number, and most will be from other countries.	Automation will remove a few jobs, but the bulk of their work, which should be substantial, will continue to be done by onsite humans.	This extraction position is subject to takeover by robots, who should be doing almost all such things in the United States by 2033.	Most work for governments, where their efforts help drive monetary and other policy. Vulnerable to reductions in their positions, and opportunities could be cut way down.

Job Name	Editors	Electrical and Electronic Engineering Technicians	Electrical and Electronics Engineers	Electrical and Electronics Installers and Repairers
Occupation Group	Media and Communications	Architecture and Engineering	Architecture and Engineering	Installation, Maintenance, and Repair
Local-Boundness	Low	Medium	Medium	High
Resistance to Robotics	Medium	High	High	Medium
Resistance to Computing and Connectivity	Medium	Medium	Medium	High
Pertinent Principles (Good)				3
Pertinent Principles (Maybe Good)	14, 15			5
Pertinent Principles (Bad)				
2010 Number of Workers	127,200	151,100	294,000	141,100
Chance for Good Living Wage	High	High	High	Medium
2010 Median Pay	Medium	Medium	High	Medium
Median Quality of Work Conditions	High	High	High	Medium
Family and Outside Activities Compatibility	High	High	High	High
Forecast for 2010-2020 Change	1%	2%	6%	3%
Forecast for 2033	Fair	Fair	Fair	Fair
Comments	Good ones are now superior to anything computer-generated, but will that be true in 2033? Although it can be done completely remotely, the need for proficiency in American English excludes almost all foreigners. Expect some consolidation of related jobs, and requirements to write as well.	Should continue along, with growing ability to take over work from engineers being offset by equipment needing less attention.	Many people in this field are relatively young and have little chance of retiring soon, balancing work provided by ever-continuing innovation.	The increasing amount of electronic equipment will roughly offset its improved durability.

Job Name	Electricians	Electro-mechanical Technicians	Elementary, Middle, and High School Principals	Elevator Installers and Repairers
Occupation Group	Construction and Extraction	Architecture and Engineering	Management	Construction and Extraction
Local-Boundness	High	Low	High	High
Resistance to Robotics	Medium	High	High	Medium
Resistance to Computing and Connectivity	High	High	High	High
Pertinent Principles (Good)	3	1	1, 3	3
Pertinent Principles (Maybe Good)	5, 12, 13		14	5, 12, 13
Pertinent Principles (Bad)				
2010 Number of Workers	577,000	16,400	236,100	19,900
Chance for Good Living Wage	High	High	High	High
2010 Median Pay	Medium	Medium	High	Medium
Median Quality of Work Conditions	Medium	High	High	Medium
Family and Outside Activities Compatibility	High	Low	High	High
Forecast for 2010-2020 Change	23%	1%	10%	11%
Forecast for 2033	Good	Good	Very Good	Very Good
Comments	The connection with highway, airport, and tower construction will mean more for them to do, but concern with safety may precipitate more robotic solutions.	As the machines they use require less in-person maintenance, they will often need to live on the road, but the work will still be there for some.	Schools, which will not be consolidated much more, will continue needing principals to run them, a need not at all endangered by automation, globalization, or efficiency.	Pay, unusually high in this field, may come down, but the in-person requirement, connecting with airport construction as well as with taller and more modern buildings, means solid prospects.

Job Name	Embalmers	Emergency Management Directors	EMTs and Paramedics	Environmental Engineering Technicians
Occupation Group	Personal Care and Service	Management	Healthcare	Architecture and Engineering
Local-Boundness	High	Low	High	Low
Resistance to Robotics	High	High	High	High
Resistance to Computing and Connectivity	High	Medium	High	High
Pertinent Principles (Good)	1, 3		1, 3	1
Pertinent Principles (Maybe Good)	5		5, 19, 20	
Pertinent Principles (Bad)				
2010 Number of Workers	7,100	12,100	226,500	18,800
Chance for Good Living Wage	Medium	High	Medium	High
2010 Median Pay	Medium	Medium	Low	Medium
Median Quality of Work Conditions	Low	High	High	High
Family and Outside Activities Compatibility	High	High	High	Low
Forecast for 2010-2020 Change	5%	13%	33%	24%
Forecast for 2033	Fair	Fair	Excellent	Very Good
Comments	This position figures to decline as less expensive ways of dealing with the dead take hold. Yet few will want to do this job.	Disaster recovery, also called "continuity services," is a necessary planning area, especially for large companies, though efficiency gains will limit growth in its number of dedicated managers.	They seem very underpaid, especially considering skyrocketing ambulance charges, and they are better than doctors in many situations. This occupation could expand to include house call service, and if the average worker still earns less than $15 per hour, that could be a huge success. Very strong, and could get even stronger.	As long as Democrats control the House, Senate, or White House, there will be increasing environmental work activity, most done by technicians.

Job Name	Environmental Engineers	Environmental Science and Protection Technicians	Environmental Scientists and Specialists	Epidemiologists
Occupation Group	Architecture and Engineering	Life, Physical, and Social Science	Life, Physical, and Social Science	Life, Physical, and Social Science
Local-Boundness	Low	Medium	Medium	Low
Resistance to Robotics	High	High	High	High
Resistance to Computing and Connectivity	High	High	High	Medium
Pertinent Principles (Good)	1	1	1	
Pertinent Principles (Maybe Good)		5		20
Pertinent Principles (Bad)				
2010 Number of Workers	51,400	29,600	89,400	5,000
Chance for Good Living Wage	High	Medium	High	High
2010 Median Pay	Medium	Medium	Medium	Medium
Median Quality of Work Conditions	High	High	High	High
Family and Outside Activities Compatibility	Medium	Medium	Medium	High
Forecast for 2010-2020 Change	22%	24%	19%	24%
Forecast for 2033	Very Good	Good	Good	Good
Comments	The need for green projects, as opposed to processes, will jump with the passage of new laws, which will probably happen often. The field is new enough that more engineers, as well as technicians, will be required.	Environmental monitoring is well established but will change over time. These positions are also strengthened by chances to take over work now done by the scientists themselves.	The field will continue to evolve, so routines will not stay in place. Expect a lot of opportunities for those on the front edge.	Not many people work in this area, and few in absolute numbers will be added, but it will remain necessary.

Job Name	Etchers and Engravers	Explosives Workers, Ordnance Handling Experts, and Blasters	Extruding and Forming Machine Setters, Operators, and Tenders, Synthetic and Glass Fibers	Extruding, Forming, Pressing, and Compacting Machine Setters, Operators, and Tenders
Occupation Group	Production	Construction and Extraction	Production	Production
Local-Boundness	Medium	High	Medium	Medium
Resistance to Robotics	Low	Low	Low	Low
Resistance to Computing and Connectivity	High	High	High	High
Pertinent Principles (Good)		3		
Pertinent Principles (Maybe Good)		5, 13		
Pertinent Principles (Bad)	17	16	17	17
2010 Number of Workers	10,900	6,800	14,700	65,400
Chance for Good Living Wage	Low	High	Low	Low
2010 Median Pay	Low	Medium	Low	Low
Median Quality of Work Conditions	Medium	Low	Medium	Medium
Family and Outside Activities Compatibility	High	High	High	High
Forecast for 2010-2020 Change	-3%	0%	-2%	2%
Forecast for 2033	Poor	Poor	Poor	Poor
Comments	Another manufacturing field to be hurt even more by efficiency, automation, and reduced American activity in general.	Both the extraction and construction side of explosive handling should, in 2033, be the province of robots.	No exception to the rule that jobs operating manufacturing machines, because of robotics and further efficiency, have poor prospects.	Robots, or remote workers, will be running these machines by 2033, leaving only a small staff of humans on site.

Job Name	Fabric and Apparel Patternmakers	Fabric Menders, Except Garment	Farm and Home Management Advisors	Farm Labor Contractors
Occupation Group	Production	Installation, Maintenance, and Repair	Education, Training, and Library	Business and Financial
Local-Boundness	Low	Medium	Medium	High
Resistance to Robotics	Medium	High	High	High
Resistance to Computing and Connectivity	Low	High	Medium	Medium
Pertinent Principles (Good)		1		3
Pertinent Principles (Maybe Good)		5	5, 14	
Pertinent Principles (Bad)	17			
2010 Number of Workers	6,000	800	13,000	300
Chance for Good Living Wage	Low	Low	High	Low
2010 Median Pay	Low	Low	Medium	Low
Median Quality of Work Conditions	Medium	High	High	High
Family and Outside Activities Compatibility	High	High	High	High
Forecast for 2010-2020 Change	-36%	-6%	17%	-1%
Forecast for 2033	Poor	Poor	Poor	Fair
Comments	Can be done through computer interfaces, from anywhere in the world.	Some fabric repair will give way to replacement, and more can be done in batch mode overseas. A necessary function in some cases, but not worth many entire American positions.	A service mainly for small farms, which are becoming rarer and rarer. The tasks can be covered by others in addition to the rest of their work.	Many farm workers, documented or not, speak little English, so these contractors can help find them when online and print venues might not. Should provide jobs for a few, maybe more, in 2033.

Job Name	Farmers, Ranchers, and Other Agricultural Managers	Fashion Designers	Fence Erectors	Film and Video Editors and Camera Operators
Occupation Group	Management	Arts and Design	Construction and Extraction	Media and Communications
Local-Boundness	High	Low	High	High
Resistance to Robotics	High	High	Medium	Medium
Resistance to Computing and Connectivity	High	Medium	High	High
Pertinent Principles (Good)	1, 3	7	3	3
Pertinent Principles (Maybe Good)	5	14	5, 13	
Pertinent Principles (Bad)	16			
2010 Number of Workers	1,202,500	21,500	32,100	58,300
Chance for Good Living Wage	High	High	Low	High
2010 Median Pay	Medium	Medium	Low	Medium
Median Quality of Work Conditions	Medium	High	Medium	High
Family and Outside Activities Compatibility	Medium	High	High	Medium
Forecast for 2010-2020 Change	-8%	0%	24%	4%
Forecast for 2033	Fair	Fair	Good	Good
Comments	Consolidation may reach a limit, and farm management with little actual physical work may become more common. In the meantime, though, the number of farms is still shrinking.	The artistic side is a pyramid, and the technical side can be facilitated through automation. Either can be done from anywhere in the world.	Fences will need to be built, and seem beyond the horizon for robots, especially when pay is relatively low.	For video editors, job listings increased 36% from August 2011 to August 2012.[296] Given that there are tens of billions of videos available, professionals at making them are not abundant. Videos are still getting new applications, so there will be plenty of work for Americans as well as for others.

Job Name	Financial Analysts	Financial Clerks	Financial Examiners	Financial Managers
Occupation Group	Business and Financial	Office and Administrative Support	Business and Financial	Management
Local-Boundness	Low	Medium	Low	Low
Resistance to Robotics	High	Low	High	High
Resistance to Computing and Connectivity	Low	Medium	Medium	High
Pertinent Principles (Good)				1
Pertinent Principles (Maybe Good)		14		
Pertinent Principles (Bad)				
2010 Number of Workers	236,000	1,395,500	29,300	527,100
Chance for Good Living Wage	Medium	Low	High	High
2010 Median Pay	Medium	Low	Medium	High
Median Quality of Work Conditions	High	High	High	Medium
Family and Outside Activities Compatibility	Medium	High	Medium	Medium
Forecast for 2010-2020 Change	23%	11%	27%	9%
Forecast for 2033	Poor	Poor	Fair	Fair
Comments	Job listings increased 39% from August 2011 to August 2012.[297] The need will continue, but automated financial advisers, who don't miss any public information, seem completely possible, as are foreigners.	Another common job headed for automation near-extinction. Even casino gaming cage workers, included here, will be replaced by robotic systems. Why will we need humans to buy or sell chips, when machinery is almost 100% reliable, not to mention needing no monitoring?	Better than many other financial positions, as the work requires being skeptical, not a strength for computers or software.	Will still be needed, but no more of them, as automated and streamlined financial procedures will mean they have fewer employees to supervise and less work to oversee.

Job Name	Fire Inspectors and Investigators	Firefighters	First-line Supervisors of Construction Trades and Extraction Workers	First-line Supervisors of Correctional Officers
Occupation Group	Protective Service	Protective Service	Construction and Extraction	Protective Service
Local-Boundness	High	High	High	Medium
Resistance to Robotics	High	Medium	High	High
Resistance to Computing and Connectivity	High	High	High	High
Pertinent Principles (Good)	1, 3	3	1, 3	1
Pertinent Principles (Maybe Good)	5	5, 15	5, 13	
Pertinent Principles (Bad)				
2010 Number of Workers	13,600	310,400	558,500	41,500
Chance for Good Living Wage	High	High	High	High
2010 Median Pay	Medium	Medium	Medium	Medium
Median Quality of Work Conditions	High	Low	High	Medium
Family and Outside Activities Compatibility	Medium	High	High	High
Forecast for 2010-2020 Change	9%	9%	23%	6%
Forecast for 2033	Fair	Fair	Fair	Poor
Comments	Efficiency will limit growth in their numbers, but they will continue to be required on site and with little notice.	With the great drop in fires, this field is merging with emergency medical care, possibly resulting in one title and similar duties for both. Clearly necessary, though, and resistant to most job-cutting trends.	Extraction is a weak area, and while construction is much stronger, most of these foremen work with skilled tradesmen, who will eventually be perceived to need less supervision.	The prison industry will probably become more streamlined, with less need for supervisors as well as for correctional officers themselves.

Job Name	First-line Supervisors of Farming, Fishing, and Forestry Workers	First-line Supervisors of Fire Fighting and Prevention Officers	First-line Supervisors of Food Preparation and Serving Workers	First-line Supervisors of Helpers, Laborers, and Material Movers, Hand
Occupation Group	Farming, Fishing, and Forestry	Protective Service	Food Preparation and Serving	Transportation and Material Moving
Local-Boundness	High	Medium	High	High
Resistance to Robotics	High	High	High	Medium
Resistance to Computing and Connectivity	High	High	High	High
Pertinent Principles (Good)	1, 3	1	1, 3	3
Pertinent Principles (Maybe Good)	5	5	5, 14	5
Pertinent Principles (Bad)	16, 17			
2010 Number of Workers	47,000	60,100	801,100	167,400
Chance for Good Living Wage	Medium	High	Low	High
2010 Median Pay	Medium	Medium	Low	Medium
Median Quality of Work Conditions	High	High	Medium	High
Family and Outside Activities Compatibility	High	High	High	High
Forecast for 2010-2020 Change	-1%	8%	10%	27%
Forecast for 2033	Poor	Fair	Fair	Fair
Comments	With declining numbers of workers in these extraction fields, the number of their bosses will drop as well.	May become more physically remote but still necessary in numbers proportional to those of firefighters.	Some demand will continue, but many of their charges will be automated away, and others may not require supervision as direct, allowing one person to manage multiple sites.	Not all of their employees will be needed by 2033, but most will be, and supervisors have enough day-to-day exception reqirements to keep them human and on site.

Job Name	First-line Supervisors of Housekeeping and Janitorial Workers	First-line Supervisors of Landscaping, Lawn Service, and Groundskeeping Workers	First-line Supervisors of Mechanics, Installers, and Repairers	First-line Supervisors of Non-retail Sales Workers
Occupation Group	Building and Grounds Cleaning	Building and Grounds Cleaning	Installation, Maintenance, and Repair	Sales
Local-Boundness	High	High	Medium	Medium
Resistance to Robotics	Medium	Medium	High	High
Resistance to Computing and Connectivity	High	High	High	High
Pertinent Principles (Good)	3	3	1	1
Pertinent Principles (Maybe Good)	5	5	5	5
Pertinent Principles (Bad)				
2010 Number of Workers	226,700	202,900	431,200	422,900
Chance for Good Living Wage	Medium	Medium	High	High
2010 Median Pay	Low	Medium	Medium	Medium
Median Quality of Work Conditions	High	High	High	High
Family and Outside Activities Compatibility	High	High	High	High
Forecast for 2010-2020 Change	1%	15%	12%	4%
Forecast for 2033	Fair	Good	Fair	Fair
Comments	Much of the janitorial field may end up with robots. Otherwise managers will be necessary, but may end up with more workers apiece.	More of a customer-service-related position than managing the likes of janitors, so they will have tasks that cannot easily be automated or sourced elsewhere.	The work of installers and repairers is generally where supervisors will not follow, meaning they will be remote and thus can work from anywhere, contacting customers as needed. Managers of mechanics have better prospects.	Demand for non-retail sales workers will continue, as will the need for people to supervise them, although reporting groups may get larger.

Job Name	First-line Supervisors of Office and Administrative Support Workers	First-line Supervisors of Personal Service Workers	First-line Supervisors of Police and Detectives	First-line Supervisors of Production and Operating Workers
Occupation Group	Office and Administrative Support	Personal Care and Service	Protective Service	Production
Local-Boundness	Medium	High	Medium	Low
Resistance to Robotics	High	High	High	Medium
Resistance to Computing and Connectivity	High	High	High	High
Pertinent Principles (Good)	1	1, 3	1	
Pertinent Principles (Maybe Good)	5, 14	5, 14	5	
Pertinent Principles (Bad)				17
2010 Number of Workers	1,424,400	218,900	106,100	588,500
Chance for Good Living Wage	Medium	Medium	High	High
2010 Median Pay	Medium	Low	Medium	High
Median Quality of Work Conditions	High	High	High	High
Family and Outside Activities Compatibility	High	High	High	High
Forecast for 2010-2020 Change	14%	14%	2%	2%
Forecast for 2033	Poor	Good	Fair	Poor
Comments	Many will be required, but with all the clerical positions facing obsolescence, managers will often only rarely need to be on site, so their numbers must drop.	Personal services will be a good vocational area for 2033 and before, and while supervisors will become less hands-on, a lot will still be needed.	There may be adjustments in the number required to manage and where, but demand generally will continue.	Will be reduced in number along with the production workers themselves, with the added liability of more viable remote supervision.

Job Name	First-line Supervisors of Retail Sales Workers	First-line Supervisors of Transportation and Material-Moving Machine and Vehicle Operators	Fishers and Related Fishing Workers	Fitness Trainers and Instructors
Occupation Group	Sales	Transportation and Material Moving	Farming, Fishing, and Forestry	Personal Care and Service
Local-Boundness	High	Medium	High	High
Resistance to Robotics	High	Medium	High	High
Resistance to Computing and Connectivity	High	High	High	High
Pertinent Principles (Good)	1, 3		1, 3	1, 3, 7
Pertinent Principles (Maybe Good)	5, 14		5	14
Pertinent Principles (Bad)		17	16	
2010 Number of Workers	1,619,500	198,700	32,000	251,400
Chance for Good Living Wage	Medium	High	Low	Low
2010 Median Pay	Low	Medium	Low	Low
Median Quality of Work Conditions	High	High	Low	High
Family and Outside Activities Compatibility	High	High	Medium	High
Forecast for 2010-2020 Change	8%	14%	-6%	24%
Forecast for 2033	Fair	Poor	Poor	Very Good
Comments	There are enough exceptions needing management attention, and enough retail sales workers themselves, to keep supervising them a steady job.	Dependent on having workers moving heavy or bulky materials, which will be cut by robotics and declining manufacturing.	Fishing has a tension between environmental concerns and more efficient practices, but both lower workers' numbers.	Indicators are positive, as people struggling with obesity look for personal help.

Job Name	Flight Attendants	Floor Layers, Except Carpet, Wood, and Hard Tiles	Floor Sanders and Finishers	Floral Designers
Occupation Group	Transportation and Material Moving	Construction and Extraction	Construction and Extraction	Arts and Design
Local-Boundness	Medium	High	High	Medium
Resistance to Robotics	Medium	Medium	Low	Medium
Resistance to Computing and Connectivity	High	High	High	Medium
Pertinent Principles (Good)	7	3	3	4, 6
Pertinent Principles (Maybe Good)	9, 14	5, 12	5	14
Pertinent Principles (Bad)				
2010 Number of Workers	90,500	17,600	10,700	66,500
Chance for Good Living Wage	Medium	Medium	Low	Low
2010 Median Pay	Medium	Low	Low	Low
Median Quality of Work Conditions	High	Medium	Medium	Medium
Family and Outside Activities Compatibility	Medium	High	High	High
Forecast for 2010-2020 Change	0%	7%	18%	-9%
Forecast for 2033	Fair	Fair	Poor	Poor
Comments	Could be automated away, but the safety component of their jobs makes that unlikely by 2033. Airlines could go even more to part-timers, reducing pay.	Robotics threatens it more than other skilled trades, though the takeover may not happen soon. In any event, a job that needs to be done.	Waiting for further developments in cost-effective use of robots to unemploy most in this field.	Already into mass local production, and market prices have crashed. Some humans will be needed, as flowers may not be easy to handle robotically, and if that proves true at least the field won't get much worse.

Job Name	Food and Beverage Serving and Related Workers	Food Preparation Workers	Food Processing Occupations	Food Processing Operators
Occupation Group	Food Preparation and Serving	Food Preparation and Serving	Production	Production
Local-Boundness	High	High	Medium	Low
Resistance to Robotics	High	High	Low	Low
Resistance to Computing and Connectivity	High	High	High	High
Pertinent Principles (Good)	1, 3, 4	1, 3, 4		
Pertinent Principles (Maybe Good)	5, 14	5		
Pertinent Principles (Bad)				
2010 Number of Workers	4,110,400	813,700	311,300	131,000
Chance for Good Living Wage	Low	Low	Low	Low
2010 Median Pay	Low	Low	Low	Low
Median Quality of Work Conditions	Medium	Medium	Medium	Medium
Family and Outside Activities Compatibility	High	High	High	High
Forecast for 2010-2020 Change	12%	10%	12%	2%
Forecast for 2033	Fair	Fair	Poor	Poor
Comments	Needed in person for now, but the sheer number of general restaurant workers will gather automation attention, which may succeed if customers accept it.	Will still be in demand, but the multi-decade trend toward pre-prepared food will limit their numbers. Can easily be combined with other restaurant positions.	Robots should, by 2033, be able to commandeer most of this field, through devices which determine the dimensions of pieces of meat, fish, or other foods.	More effective food processing machines will make fewer workers necessary.

Job Name	Food Service Managers	Forensic Science Technicians	Forest and Conservation Technicians	Forest and Conservation Workers
Occupation Group	Management	Life, Physical, and Social Science	Life, Physical, and Social Science	Farming, Fishing, and Forestry
Local-Boundness	High	Medium	Medium	High
Resistance to Robotics	High	High	High	High
Resistance to Computing and Connectivity	High	Medium	High	High
Pertinent Principles (Good)	1, 3		1	1, 3
Pertinent Principles (Maybe Good)		5	5	5
Pertinent Principles (Bad)				
2010 Number of Workers	320,600	13,000	36,500	13,700
Chance for Good Living Wage	High	High	Low	Low
2010 Median Pay	Medium	Medium	Low	Low
Median Quality of Work Conditions	Medium	Medium	High	Medium
Family and Outside Activities Compatibility	Medium	Medium	High	High
Forecast for 2010-2020 Change	-3%	19%	-1%	1%
Forecast for 2033	Good	Good	Good	Fair
Comments	Restaurant management will become easier and less physical with automated procedures, but will still call for a strong presence in person. The number of food outlets should increase with time.	This area has progressed a great deal and will continue to be valued. More in this job may be on call, working over wider areas and traveling a lot, with their services in demand.	The need will continue, and they may replace conservation scientists for some duties.	Forest work is on the side of the environmentalists, so has better prospects than otherwise related farming and fishing positions. It may get some boost as more forests, often economically weak places anyway, are preserved.

Job Name	Forest Fire Inspectors and Prevention Specialists	Funeral Attendants	Funeral Directors	Furnace, Kiln, Oven, Drier, and Kettle Operators and Tenders
Occupation Group	Protective Service	Personal Care and Service	Personal Care and Service	Production
Local-Boundness	Medium	High	High	Medium
Resistance to Robotics	High	High	High	Low
Resistance to Computing and Connectivity	High	High	High	High
Pertinent Principles (Good)	1	1, 3, 4	1, 3	
Pertinent Principles (Maybe Good)		5	5	
Pertinent Principles (Bad)				17
2010 Number of Workers	1,600	31,000	29,300	20,400
Chance for Good Living Wage	Low	Low	High	Low
2010 Median Pay	Low	Low	Medium	Low
Median Quality of Work Conditions	High	Medium	Medium	Medium
Family and Outside Activities Compatibility	Medium	High	High	High
Forecast for 2010-2020 Change	6%	5%	18%	1%
Forecast for 2033	Fair	Fair	Fair	Poor
Comments	Not many are here given the extent of American forest land, and this job's numbers should grow slightly, as it has little to fear from automation.	Funerals may be on a slow decline, but people, who will not be mechanized away, will still be needed to do various tasks at funeral homes.	Will need to adapt to changing times, with Americans having increasingly diverse opinions about how deaths should be handled. Cheaper alternatives will hurt.	The dangers of heating have made these workers more valued than other machine operators, but they are susceptible to both robotics and remote operations.

Job Name	Gaming Change Persons and Booth Cashiers	Gaming Services Occupations	Gas Compressor and Gas Pumping Station Operators	Gas Plant Operators
Occupation Group	Sales	Personal Care and Service	Transportation and Material Moving	Production
Local-Boundness	High	High	Medium	Low
Resistance to Robotics	Low	High	Medium	Low
Resistance to Computing and Connectivity	Low	High	High	Medium
Pertinent Principles (Good)	3, 4	1, 3		
Pertinent Principles (Maybe Good)	5, 14	14		
Pertinent Principles (Bad)	2		17	
2010 Number of Workers	20,100	177,100	4,500	13,700
Chance for Good Living Wage	Low	Medium	High	High
2010 Median Pay	Low	Low	Medium	Medium
Median Quality of Work Conditions	High	Medium	Medium	High
Family and Outside Activities Compatibility	High	High	High	High
Forecast for 2010-2020 Change	-12%	13%	-10%	-6%
Forecast for 2033	Poor	Fair	Poor	Poor
Comments	Demand for humans to provide change at casinos would be very low, even if slot machines still took coins.	Casino dealers cannot be replaced by robots—at least not for customers of this generation—so they will be around for much longer, even if legal gambling stops spreading.	Robotics, other automation, and remote foreign workers will all play a role in the decline of opportunities here.	A high-responsibility, high-attention job, but largely algorithmic and can be done remotely.

Job Name	General Maintenance and Repair Workers	General Office Clerks	Geographers	Geological and Petroleum Technicians
Occupation Group	Installation, Maintenance, and Repair	Office and Administrative Support	Life, Physical, and Social Science	Life, Physical, and Social Science
Local-Boundness	High	High	Low	High
Resistance to Robotics	High	Medium	High	High
Resistance to Computing and Connectivity	High	Medium	Medium	High
Pertinent Principles (Good)	1, 3	3		1, 3
Pertinent Principles (Maybe Good)	5	5, 14		5
Pertinent Principles (Bad)				
2010 Number of Workers	1,289,000	2,950,700	1,600	14,400
Chance for Good Living Wage	Medium	Low	High	High
2010 Median Pay	Low	Low	Medium	Medium
Median Quality of Work Conditions	Medium	High	High	High
Family and Outside Activities Compatibility	High	High	High	High
Forecast for 2010-2020 Change	11%	17%	35%	15%
Forecast for 2033	Good	Poor	Good	Good
Comments	This field contains many different positions, most of which have opportunities increasing faster than more reliable equipment takes them away.	Many will be needed to do in-person functions, but nowhere near three million, as many of their tasks will either be automated or moved to end users and others in offices.	The overwhelming majority, teaching, are not included here. With the rise of GPS technology, more will be needed to oversee it at a high level. The absolute number of working geographers can only go up.	Well paid but still much less than geoscientists, these technicians will take on tasks. As oil rises in value, pressure to drill it will increase, though depending on politics that may or may not be authorized.

Job Name	Geoscientists	Glaziers	Graders and Sorters, Agricultural Products	Graphic Designers
Occupation Group	Life, Physical, and Social Science	Construction and Extraction	Farming, Fishing, and Forestry	Arts and Design
Local-Boundness	Medium	High	High	Low
Resistance to Robotics	High	Medium	Medium	High
Resistance to Computing and Connectivity	High	High	High	Medium
Pertinent Principles (Good)	1	3	3	
Pertinent Principles (Maybe Good)		5, 12, 13	5, 14	14
Pertinent Principles (Bad)			16	
2010 Number of Workers	33,800	41,900	48,200	279,200
Chance for Good Living Wage	High	Medium	Low	Low
2010 Median Pay	High	Low	Low	Medium
Median Quality of Work Conditions	High	Medium	Medium	High
Family and Outside Activities Compatibility	High	High	High	High
Forecast for 2010-2020 Change	21%	42%	1%	13%
Forecast for 2033	Good	Very Good	Poor	Poor
Comments	The connection with oil makes this a more practical field than other natural sciences and will keep job opportunities and pay higher than others as well.	Skyscrapers and airport terminals need lots of glass, as do other buildings, though future designs may call for easier installation. Protected by relatively low pay.	Some will be required, but the number of farms is still dropping, and streamlining is probable.	Most organizations will want their own publicly visible designs, but one person, who need not be American, can do many. The share of women in the field could still help it.

Job Name	Grinding and Polishing Workers, Hand	Grounds Maintenance Workers	Hand Laborers and Material Movers	Hazardous Materials Removal Workers
Occupation Group	Production	Building and Grounds Cleaning	Transportation and Material Moving	Construction and Extraction
Local-Boundness	High	High	High	High
Resistance to Robotics	Low	Medium	Low	Low
Resistance to Computing and Connectivity	High	High	High	High
Pertinent Principles (Good)	3	3, 4	3	3
Pertinent Principles (Maybe Good)		5	5	5
Pertinent Principles (Bad)	17			
2010 Number of Workers	27,900	1,249,700	3,315,400	38,100
Chance for Good Living Wage	Low	Low	Low	Medium
2010 Median Pay	Low	Low	Low	Low
Median Quality of Work Conditions	Medium	Low	Medium	Low
Family and Outside Activities Compatibility	High	High	High	High
Forecast for 2010-2020 Change	8%	20%	14%	23%
Forecast for 2033	Poor	Good	Fair	Fair
Comments	Robots should be able to take over this job by 2033, though they haven't made as much progress here as in other fields.	Some vulnerability to robotics; otherwise must be done in person and locally, with many locations needing maintenance.	Large warehouses will be much more automated by decade's end, and completely by 2033, but the total volume of items that must be dealt with by hand will stay high.	A job this dangerous will be a target for robots. On the other side, more materials are likely to be designated as hazardous, and there will be increasing removal requirements and efforts.

Job Name	Health and Safety Engineers	Health Educators	Heating, Air Conditioning, and Refrigeration Mechanics and Installers	Heavy and Tractor-trailer Truck Drivers
Occupation Group	Architecture and Engineering	Community and Social Service	Installation, Maintenance, and Repair	Transportation and Material Moving
Local-Boundness	Low	High	High	Medium
Resistance to Robotics	High	High	Medium	High
Resistance to Computing and Connectivity	High	High	High	High
Pertinent Principles (Good)	1	1, 3	3	1
Pertinent Principles (Maybe Good)	20	14, 20	5	
Pertinent Principles (Bad)				
2010 Number of Workers	23,700	63,400	267,800	1,604,800
Chance for Good Living Wage	High	High	Medium	Medium
2010 Median Pay	Medium	Medium	Medium	Low
Median Quality of Work Conditions	High	High	Medium	Medium
Family and Outside Activities Compatibility	High	High	High	Low
Forecast for 2010-2020 Change	13%	37%	34%	21%
Forecast for 2033	Fair	Very Good	Good	Good
Comments	Health and safety regulations march on, requiring engineering solutions, yet much of this work can be done remotely.	Very strong. The only concern is that hiring such people will often be seen as optional, so can suffer from budget cuts.	A good area for work opportunity, but systems will become more robust, so these jobs will be no better in the long term than most other repair and maintenance positions.	Job listings increased 45% from August 2011 to August 2012.[298] Large trucks are still efficient ways of moving many goods, and, though eventually they will be remotely controlled, most will not be by 2033.

Job Name	Heavy Vehicle and Mobile Equipment Service Technicians	Helpers - Extraction Workers	Helpers - Installation, Maintenance, and Repair Workers	Helpers - Production Workers
Occupation Group	Installation, Maintenance, and Repair	Construction and Extraction	Installation, Maintenance, and Repair	Production
Local-Boundness	High	High	High	High
Resistance to Robotics	High	Medium	High	Medium
Resistance to Computing and Connectivity	High	High	High	High
Pertinent Principles (Good)	1, 3	3	1, 3	3
Pertinent Principles (Maybe Good)	5	5	5	
Pertinent Principles (Bad)		16		17
2010 Number of Workers	179,200	24,600	125,000	395,100
Chance for Good Living Wage	Medium	Low	Low	Low
2010 Median Pay	Medium	Low	Low	Low
Median Quality of Work Conditions	Medium	Low	Medium	Low
Family and Outside Activities Compatibility	High	High	High	High
Forecast for 2010-2020 Change	16%	5%	18%	9%
Forecast for 2033	Good	Fair	Fair	Poor
Comments	The scope and complexity of heavy equipment will increase, meaning the range of repairs and required maintenance will rise as well, although individual pieces will need less.	Will fare better than more skilled extraction workers, and may even take over their jobs, if robotic equipment monitoring is added to their duties.	Provide a cheaper alternative for labor such as cleaning machines at larger locations, but at smaller ones they won't be able to justify themselves.	May last longer than some machine operators, but factories are increasingly designed for minimum human involvement, and American manufacturing will continue to decline.

Job Name	High School Teachers	Highway Maintenance Workers	Historians	Home Appliance Repairers
Occupation Group	Education, Training, and Library	Construction and Extraction	Life, Physical, and Social Science	Installation, Maintenance, and Repair
Local-Boundness	Medium	High	Low	High
Resistance to Robotics	High	Medium	High	High
Resistance to Computing and Connectivity	Medium	High	High	High
Pertinent Principles (Good)		3	1	1, 3
Pertinent Principles (Maybe Good)	14, 15	5, 13	11	5
Pertinent Principles (Bad)				
2010 Number of Workers	1,037,600	148,500	4,000	47,700
Chance for Good Living Wage	High	Medium	High	Medium
2010 Median Pay	Medium	Low	Medium	Low
Median Quality of Work Conditions	High	Medium	High	High
Family and Outside Activities Compatibility	High	High	High	High
Forecast for 2010-2020 Change	7%	8%	18%	7%
Forecast for 2033	Fair	Good	Fair	Fair
Comments	Both political sides talk about better education, but the outcomes have been weak, and teachers as a group are no longer underpaid. High school will borrow tactics from colleges: namely, online instruction and the use of lower-paid alternatives.	Have a strong connection with the extensive infrastructure work likely to take place before 2033. Robotics will be a factor, but will not replace many workers.	Another academic area with few working in the field. Most now are with the government, and more may find jobs in private industry as well.	A job that generally must be done on location, though subject to appliances becoming increasingly dependable.

Job Name	Home Entertainment Equipment Installers and Repairers	Home Health and Personal Care Aides	Human Resources Managers	Human Resources Specialists
Occupation Group	Installation, Maintenance, and Repair	Healthcare	Management	Business and Financial
Local-Boundness	High	High	Medium	Low
Resistance to Robotics	High	Medium	High	High
Resistance to Computing and Connectivity	High	High	High	Medium
Pertinent Principles (Good)	1, 3	3, 4	1	
Pertinent Principles (Maybe Good)	5	5, 14, 19, 20	14	14
Pertinent Principles (Bad)				
2010 Number of Workers	36,800	1,878,700	71,800	442,200
Chance for Good Living Wage	Medium	Low	High	High
2010 Median Pay	Low	Low	High	Medium
Median Quality of Work Conditions	High	High	High	High
Family and Outside Activities Compatibility	High	High	High	High
Forecast for 2010-2020 Change	14%	70%	13%	21%
Forecast for 2033	Fair	Excellent	Fair	Poor
Comments	Home entertainment is still growing, and many in the 1% will pay for concierge service, but electronics are very reliable without many recurring issues.	With the aging population, ever more will be needed. Expect a range of certifications which will increase pay for those who have them. Will Americans, though, accept robotic caretakers as many Japanese have?	A classic female-dominated field, but with negative indicators: high pay, less attention to workers given their oversupply, and a good chance of a stable period in government regulations.	Their departments will be less valued as employees are. Have been hurt by highly flexible and changing job requirements, which reduce their ability to understand what is needed and what good and bad performance is or is not, so much of their work will be done within functional divisions.

Job Name	Hydrologists	Industrial Designers	Industrial Engineering Technicians	Industrial Engineers
Occupation Group	Life, Physical, and Social Science	Arts and Design	Architecture and Engineering	Architecture and Engineering
Local-Boundness	Medium	Low	Low	Low
Resistance to Robotics	High	High	High	High
Resistance to Computing and Connectivity	High	Low	Medium	Low
Pertinent Principles (Good)	1			
Pertinent Principles (Maybe Good)				
Pertinent Principles (Bad)			17	17
2010 Number of Workers	7,600	40,800	62,500	203,900
Chance for Good Living Wage	High	Medium	High	High
2010 Median Pay	Medium	Medium	Medium	Medium
Median Quality of Work Conditions	High	High	High	High
Family and Outside Activities Compatibility	High	High	Low	Medium
Forecast for 2010-2020 Change	18%	10%	4%	6%
Forecast for 2033	Good	Poor	Poor	Poor
Comments	As population continues to increase in the West and other places where water is scarce, they will have knowledge more people can use.	The sort of job made for contractors, who will work for design firms, agencies, or themselves, if they are American at all. If you need a toaster designed once every three years, why keep someone on the payroll?	Information is piling up in this field, and by 2033 the principles, and the tools to solve it, should be part of general plant management.	Any position this dependent on abstract rules is almost certain to be primarily lost to software long before 2033.

Job Name	Industrial Machinery Mechanics and Maintenance Workers	Industrial Production Managers	Information Clerks	Information Security Analysts, Web Developers, and Computer Network Architects
Occupation Group	Installation, Maintenance, and Repair	Management	Office and Administrative Support	Computer and Information Technology
Local-Boundness	High	High	Medium	Low
Resistance to Robotics	High	High	Medium	High
Resistance to Computing and Connectivity	High	High	Medium	Low
Pertinent Principles (Good)	1, 3	1, 3		
Pertinent Principles (Maybe Good)	5		5, 14	
Pertinent Principles (Bad)				
2010 Number of Workers	357,000	150,300	1,605,300	302,300
Chance for Good Living Wage	High	High	Low	High
2010 Median Pay	Medium	High	Low	Medium
Median Quality of Work Conditions	Medium	High	High	High
Family and Outside Activities Compatibility	Medium	High	High	High
Forecast for 2010-2020 Change	19%	9%	7%	22%
Forecast for 2033	Good	Fair	Poor	Poor
Comments	Industrial machinery is getting more varied and complicated, and, although increasingly reliable, it is critical that it have minimal downtime, which calls for someone with specialized knowledge to maintain and repair it.	Manufacturing is shrinking, but what will remain will need financial and logistical monitoring and action taken when necessary. Could drop in pay or numbers as automated processes call for fewer decisions.	As with office clerks, they will still be common in 2033 but without nearly the number as today. Many of their functions can be automated or sourced to different countries, and even the likes of hotel and motel desk clerks may be replaced by cameras and remote voices, or even eliminated.	Require communication with users, but that need not be done in person, so Americans will prove too expensive.

Job Name	Instructional Coordinators	Insulation Workers	Insurance Sales Agents	Insurance Underwriters
Occupation Group	Education, Training, and Library	Construction and Extraction	Sales	Business and Financial
Local-Boundness	Low	High	Low	Low
Resistance to Robotics	High	Low	High	High
Resistance to Computing and Connectivity	Medium	High	Medium	Low
Pertinent Principles (Good)		3		
Pertinent Principles (Maybe Good)	14	5	5	14
Pertinent Principles (Bad)				
2010 Number of Workers	139,700	51,400	411,500	101,800
Chance for Good Living Wage	High	Low	Medium	High
2010 Median Pay	Medium	Low	Medium	Medium
Median Quality of Work Conditions	High	Medium	Medium	High
Family and Outside Activities Compatibility	High	High	High	High
Forecast for 2010-2020 Change	20%	28%	22%	6%
Forecast for 2033	Fair	Fair	Fair	Poor
Comments	A lasting educational need, but there is a good chance that coordination duties will move more to the teachers themselves or will be done remotely.	Construction requires insulation, but this field seems more susceptible to robotics and other automation than most.	The easiest of their work, selling policies that people seek to buy, such as auto coverage, will earn them little in the future. They will need to focus on optional products and providing top service when something goes wrong. Both will see that people are still needed in this field.	Just too algorithmic to require humans. Although intuition and currently undefinable considerations play a part, they will not be sufficient to save this job.

Job Name	Interior Designers	Interpreters and Translators	Janitors and Building Cleaners	Jewelers and Precious Stone and Metal Workers
Occupation Group	Arts and Design	Media and Communications	Building and Grounds Cleaning	Production
Local-Boundness	Low	Medium	High	Low
Resistance to Robotics	High	High	Medium	Medium
Resistance to Computing and Connectivity	Medium	Low	High	High
Pertinent Principles (Good)	7		3, 4	7
Pertinent Principles (Maybe Good)	14		5	5
Pertinent Principles (Bad)				
2010 Number of Workers	56,500	58,400	2,310,400	39,200
Chance for Good Living Wage	Medium	Medium	Low	Medium
2010 Median Pay	Medium	Medium	Low	Low
Median Quality of Work Conditions	High	High	Low	High
Family and Outside Activities Compatibility	High	High	High	High
Forecast for 2010-2020 Change	19%	42%	11%	-2%
Forecast for 2033	Poor	Poor	Good	Fair
Comments	When organizations can get predesigned space plans for a fraction of a custom design, almost all will do that. Those in the 1%, though, will use a few for their homes.	The years 2013 to 2025 may be their peak time. After that, voice recognition and translating software should limit professionals to the most important and sensitive applications.	As with maintenance, has some vulnerability to robotics; otherwise, must be done in person and locally, with many locations needing it.	Jewelry need not be made in America, and when robots deal better with sensitive touch, this field will be more automated. However, fine jewelry has lasting appeal, people will continue to prefer to see it before buying, and in-person, craft-level work will be valued.

Job Name	Judges, Mediators, and Hearing Officers	Judicial Law Clerks	Kindergarten and Elementary School Teachers	Landscape Architects
Occupation Group	Legal	Legal	Education, Training, and Library	Architecture and Engineering
Local-Boundness	High	Medium	High	Medium
Resistance to Robotics	High	High	High	High
Resistance to Computing and Connectivity	High	Medium	Medium	Medium
Pertinent Principles (Good)	1, 3		3, 6	
Pertinent Principles (Maybe Good)	5, 11, 15	5, 11	14, 15	13
Pertinent Principles (Bad)				
2010 Number of Workers	62,700	29,800	1,655,800	21,600
Chance for Good Living Wage	High	Medium	High	High
2010 Median Pay	High	Medium	Medium	Medium
Median Quality of Work Conditions	High	High	High	High
Family and Outside Activities Compatibility	High	Medium	High	High
Forecast for 2010-2020 Change	7%	8%	17%	16%
Forecast for 2033	Good	Fair	Good	Very Good
Comments	Will be needed indefinitely, even in person, but lower-paid assistants may increasingly be used at preliminary levels to save money. Will not be automated or globalized away.	Traditionally a short-term job for good law school graduates, and many judges will want the assistance at current bargain rates, even if software is much cheaper for legal research now.	More locally bound than middle school or high school teachers. A good area, but well paid and full, and will be further crowded when more and more men get into it.	Landforms, local preferences, and environmental considerations make this a field unsuited to consistent rules. One of the best architectural or engineering opportunities.

Job Name	Laundry and Dry-cleaning Workers	Lawyers	Layout Workers, Metal and Plastic	Legislators
Occupation Group	Production	Legal	Production	Management
Local-Boundness	High	Low	High	Medium
Resistance to Robotics	Low	High	Medium	High
Resistance to Computing and Connectivity	High	Medium	Medium	High
Pertinent Principles (Good)	3, 7, 8		3	1
Pertinent Principles (Maybe Good)	14	5, 11		
Pertinent Principles (Bad)			17	
2010 Number of Workers	225,200	728,200	8,900	67,700
Chance for Good Living Wage	Low	High	Medium	Low
2010 Median Pay	Low	High	Low	Low
Median Quality of Work Conditions	Low	High	Medium	High
Family and Outside Activities Compatibility	High	Low	High	High
Forecast for 2010-2020 Change	1%	10%	14%	0%
Forecast for 2033	Fair	Poor	Poor	Fair
Comments	The drycleaning industry was badly damaged by lower office dress standards, and it will be hurt further by automation. Some shops in smaller towns will survive, and others will specialize in caring for high-end garments, but the easy quantity business, such as cleaning men's shirts, will continue to shrink.	There is an oversupply of law school graduates, and in some specialties, especially research, software is savaging jobs. As with physicians, the tasks lawyers instead of paralegals and other well-trained assistants do may continue to dwindle, and they may end up "blessing" other people's work more than doing it themselves.	More of a thinking job than a manufacturing one, but will largely be replaced by electronic communication and robotics by 2033.	Perforce, the number of legislators who work for domestic governments stays the same. Federal lawmakers are well paid, and, unlike most local and state ones, are often under pressure about that.

Job Name	Librarians	Library Technicians and Assistants	Licensed Practical and Licensed Vocational Nurses	Lifeguards, Ski Patrol, and Other Recreational Protective Service Workers
Occupation Group	Education, Training, and Library	Education, Training, and Library	Healthcare	Protective Service
Local-Boundness	Medium	Medium	High	High
Resistance to Robotics	High	High	High	Medium
Resistance to Computing and Connectivity	Medium	Medium	High	High
Pertinent Principles (Good)			1, 3	3
Pertinent Principles (Maybe Good)	5, 14	5, 14	5, 14, 19, 20	
Pertinent Principles (Bad)				
2010 Number of Workers	156,100	231,500	752,300	121,500
Chance for Good Living Wage	High	Low	Medium	Low
2010 Median Pay	Medium	Low	Medium	Low
Median Quality of Work Conditions	High	High	High	High
Family and Outside Activities Compatibility	High	High	High	High
Forecast for 2010-2020 Change	7%	10%	22%	12%
Forecast for 2033	Poor	Fair	Very Good	Good
Comments	The archetypal, largely female-populated field, with excellent working conditions and pay now higher than its reputation would indicate. Ripe for lots of male competition and for some loss of duties to technicians.	Will replace even more librarians, but their overall workload won't increase much, especially as their bosses are dependent on funding that is hardly guaranteed.	All indicators are positive. The only concern is possible consolidation of positions, with home health care aides and registered nurses taking their work.	As the American population continues to age and older people take part more often in outdoor recreation, the safety factor will become more important, and the numbers of these low-paid employees will grow.

Job Name	Line Installers and Repairers	Loan Officers	Locker Room, Coatroom, and Dressing Room Attendants	Locksmiths and Safe Repairers
Occupation Group	Installation, Maintenance, and Repair	Business and Financial	Personal Care and Service	Installation, Maintenance, and Repair
Local-Boundness	High	Low	High	High
Resistance to Robotics	High	High	Low	Medium
Resistance to Computing and Connectivity	High	Low	High	High
Pertinent Principles (Good)	1, 3		3, 4	3
Pertinent Principles (Maybe Good)	5		5	5
Pertinent Principles (Bad)				
2010 Number of Workers	269,100	289,400	17,600	25,700
Chance for Good Living Wage	High	Medium	Low	Medium
2010 Median Pay	Medium	Medium	Low	Low
Median Quality of Work Conditions	Medium	High	High	High
Family and Outside Activities Compatibility	Medium	High	High	Medium
Forecast for 2010-2020 Change	13%	14%	15%	18%
Forecast for 2033	Good	Poor	Fair	Fair
Comments	As with industrial machinery, lines can go down at any time, calling for someone to be at the site quickly. Storms and other causes of power outages will happen even if the equipment is robust.	Almost completely algorithmic; in fact, the linear processes not being followed may in itself constitute illegal discrimination. Why keep humans around for that?	Coatroom attendants will still be needed, and so will many in locker and dressing rooms as well. Their numerical increases will be held off by general efficiency.	Locks cause problems, but less so for computer-controlled ones, which may not be the province of locksmiths. Still, as long as people have cars, they will find ways of locking themselves out of them.

Job Name	Lodging Managers	Logging Workers	Logisticians	Machinists and Tool and Die Makers
Occupation Group	Management	Farming, Fishing, and Forestry	Business and Financial	Production
Local-Boundness	High	High	Low	Low
Resistance to Robotics	High	Medium	High	Low
Resistance to Computing and Connectivity	High	High	Medium	Medium
Pertinent Principles (Good)	1, 3	3		
Pertinent Principles (Maybe Good)	9	5		
Pertinent Principles (Bad)		16		17
2010 Number of Workers	51,400	53,200	108,900	438,100
Chance for Good Living Wage	High	Low	High	Medium
2010 Median Pay	Medium	Low	Medium	Medium
Median Quality of Work Conditions	High	Low	High	Medium
Family and Outside Activities Compatibility	Medium	Medium	High	High
Forecast for 2010-2020 Change	8%	4%	26%	7%
Forecast for 2033	Good	Fair	Fair	Poor
Comments	Along with travel, lodging is a growth area. A hands-on job, and will continue to be.	Extraction, but a lot of wood is needed. That will not be reduced, as people come to understand the difference between cutting down trees which are replanted and destroying forests altogether.	Can be done from anywhere, in theory, but the need for contacts with people with different functions means it will do better than many.	Continued automation will give them less to do as robots take over their preparation tasks. The manufacturing connection is also a large disadvantage.

Job Name	Maids and Housekeeping Cleaners	Mail Clerks and Mail Machine Operators, Except Post Office	Makeup Artists, Theatrical and Performance	Management Analysts
Occupation Group	Building and Grounds Cleaning	Office and Administrative Support	Personal Care and Service	Business and Financial
Local-Boundness	High	High	High	Low
Resistance to Robotics	High	Low	High	High
Resistance to Computing and Connectivity	High	High	High	Medium
Pertinent Principles (Good)	1, 3, 4, 7, 8	3	1, 3	
Pertinent Principles (Maybe Good)	5, 14, 19	5	14	
Pertinent Principles (Bad)				
2010 Number of Workers	1,427,300	126,300	3,500	718,800
Chance for Good Living Wage	Low	Low	High	High
2010 Median Pay	Low	Low	Medium	Medium
Median Quality of Work Conditions	Low	High	High	High
Family and Outside Activities Compatibility	High	High	High	Low
Forecast for 2010-2020 Change	8%	12%	3%	22%
Forecast for 2033	Excellent	Poor	Fair	Good
Comments	Although pay is now lower than for janitors and building maintenance people, these positions have two advantages: lower susceptibility to automation and the high proportion of female workers. No job has more than the eight positive markers here.	Robotics, and the still-dropping amount of physical business mail, including bills paid by check, mean that far fewer will be needed.	Theatrical and other performances and, along with them, the players' need for makeup, will stay strong but will not grow much.	Long popular as a way of getting objective outside assessments without political problems between departments, they may become more valuable as further automation and globalization makes company managers more hands-off than ever.

Job Name	Manicurists and Pedicurists	Manufactured Building and Mobile Home Installers	Marine Engineers and Naval Architects	Market Research Analysts
Occupation Group	Personal Care and Service	Installation, Maintenance, and Repair	Architecture and Engineering	Business and Financial
Local-Boundness	High	High	Low	Low
Resistance to Robotics	High	Medium	High	High
Resistance to Computing and Connectivity	High	High	Medium	Medium
Pertinent Principles (Good)	1, 3, 4, 7	3		
Pertinent Principles (Maybe Good)	5, 14	5	9	15
Pertinent Principles (Bad)				
2010 Number of Workers	81,700	7,800	5,900	282,700
Chance for Good Living Wage	Low	Low	High	High
2010 Median Pay	Low	Low	High	Medium
Median Quality of Work Conditions	High	Medium	High	High
Family and Outside Activities Compatibility	High	High	High	High
Forecast for 2010-2020 Change	17%	14%	17%	41%
Forecast for 2033	Very Good	Fair	Fair	Very Good
Comments	In-person, low paid enough to hold off other ways of providing manicures and pedicures, and customers wouldn't accept robots anyway. These occupations will last.	Simply too large for most to be delivered intact, buildings will increasingly be assembled from prefabricated parts. Potential for growth as more people seek out cheaper housing solutions.	Ships, especially cruise vessels or industrial ones with huge potential for cost cutting, will offer continuing opportunity for design improvements. Foreign competition, though, will hurt.	A rare area compatible with remote work in which Americans will always have the advantage, as cultural knowledge from living in the USA cannot viably be replicated. May give way to predictive data analysts, though, who examine data patterns.[299]

Job Name	Massage Therapists	Material Moving Machine Operators	Material Recording Clerks	Materials Engineers
Occupation Group	Healthcare	Transportation and Material Moving	Office and Administrative Support	Architecture and Engineering
Local-Boundness	High	High	High	Low
Resistance to Robotics	High	Low	Low	High
Resistance to Computing and Connectivity	High	High	Low	Medium
Pertinent Principles (Good)	1, 3, 6, 7	3	3	
Pertinent Principles (Maybe Good)	5, 14, 19, 20		5	
Pertinent Principles (Bad)		16, 17		
2010 Number of Workers	153,700	669,000	2,812,900	22,300
Chance for Good Living Wage	Medium	Low	Low	High
2010 Median Pay	Low	Low	Low	High
Median Quality of Work Conditions	Medium	Medium	High	High
Family and Outside Activities Compatibility	High	High	High	High
Forecast for 2010-2020 Change	20%	12%	2%	9%
Forecast for 2033	Excellent	Poor	Poor	Fair
Comments	This usually optional health care service will increase among the 1% and connects with other physical therapy. Pay should get higher. Tied for the most positive indicators, with no negatives, of any job.	Two large disadvantages: they can be replaced by robots, and most of their tasks are dependent on extraction or manufacturing, both in decline.	Another administrative field to be severely reduced in number by automation and computer-to-computer communication.	Great and continuing potential for innovations, but those can be developed anywhere and have a way of becoming the norm quickly, shrinking the number of people needed.

Job Name	Mathematical Technicians	Mathematicians	Mechanical Door Repairers	Mechanical Engineering Technicians
Occupation Group	Math	Math	Installation, Maintenance, and Repair	Architecture and Engineering
Local-Boundness	Low	Low	High	Low
Resistance to Robotics	High	High	High	High
Resistance to Computing and Connectivity	Low	High	High	Medium
Pertinent Principles (Good)		1	1, 3	
Pertinent Principles (Maybe Good)		10	5	
Pertinent Principles (Bad)				
2010 Number of Workers	1,100	3,100	12,800	44,900
Chance for Good Living Wage	Low	High	Medium	High
2010 Median Pay	Medium	High	Low	High
Median Quality of Work Conditions	High	High	High	High
Family and Outside Activities Compatibility	High	High	High	High
Forecast for 2010-2020 Change	6%	16%	25%	4%
Forecast for 2033	Poor	Poor	Good	Fair
Comments	Between remote work possibilities, the position's algorithmic nature, and students willing to do the work for less, few will be required.	A high share of mathematics experts are teaching it instead of working it, and many more are in the information technology field. Any growth, even at a lower rate of pay, would thus be absorbed immediately.	Mechanical doors, including for garages, have become the norm throughout commercial buildings. They should need little service by 2033 but will still malfunction and then will require a human on site.	Ever more machines will be designed, but, unlike others, almost everything these technicians do can be done from the likes of Mumbai or Sofia.

Job Name	Mechanical Engineers	Medical and Clinical Laboratory Technologists and Technicians	Medical and Health Services Managers	Medical Appliance Technicians
Occupation Group	Architecture and Engineering	Healthcare	Management	Production
Local-Boundness	Low	Medium	Medium	Low
Resistance to Robotics	High	Medium	High	Low
Resistance to Computing and Connectivity	Medium	High	High	Medium
Pertinent Principles (Good)			1	
Pertinent Principles (Maybe Good)		14, 19, 20	14, 19, 20	20
Pertinent Principles (Bad)				17
2010 Number of Workers	243,200	330,600	303,000	14,200
Chance for Good Living Wage	High	High	High	Low
2010 Median Pay	High	Medium	High	Low
Median Quality of Work Conditions	High	High	High	Medium
Family and Outside Activities Compatibility	High	High	High	High
Forecast for 2010-2020 Change	9%	13%	22%	4%
Forecast for 2033	Fair	Good	Fair	Poor
Comments	The indefinitely growing set of mechanisms are now designed by engineers, but by 2033 many will be designed by other machines.	Emergency and urgent assessments will grow and need to be done on site. Analysis of specimens, however, is already highly automated, and other processes in this area will be also, making much laboratory work one of the few medical areas that may be done remotely.	In the health field, but there are many hospital administrators and the like, and often they are blamed for high costs. Their numbers will probably be thinned out.	The health connection aside, almost a blueprint of an occupation endangered by current trends: manufacturing-based, outsourceable, susceptible to robotics improvement.

Job Name	Medical Assistants	Medical Equipment Preparers	Medical Equipment Repairers	Medical Records and Health Information Technicians
Occupation Group	Healthcare	Healthcare	Installation, Maintenance, and Repair	Healthcare
Local-Boundness	High	High	High	Low
Resistance to Robotics	Medium	Medium	High	High
Resistance to Computing and Connectivity	High	High	High	Low
Pertinent Principles (Good)	3	3	1, 3	
Pertinent Principles (Maybe Good)	5, 14, 19, 20	5, 14, 19, 20	5, 19, 20	14, 19, 20
Pertinent Principles (Bad)				2
2010 Number of Workers	527,600	49,200	37,900	179,500
Chance for Good Living Wage	Low	Low	High	Low
2010 Median Pay	Low	Low	Medium	Low
Median Quality of Work Conditions	High	High	High	High
Family and Outside Activities Compatibility	High	High	Medium	High
Forecast for 2010-2020 Change	31%	17%	31%	21%
Forecast for 2033	Very Good	Very Good	Very Good	Poor
Comments	In addition to having several indicators in their favor, they may take over more LPN and even RN territory.	Much of this work, such as cleaning, will remain outside the realm of robotics or even more efficient devices, so this occupation will last.	As medical equipment increases in quantity and complexity, people are increasingly dependent on keeping it running, and repairs are often urgent and critical.	Medical records are suitable for computerization, and decisions can be made algorithmically, giving this job poor prospects after this decade, even without a single-payer national health plan to slash insurance-related office activity.

Job Name	Medical Roboticists [300]	Medical Scientists	Medical Transcriptionists	Meeting, Convention, and Event Planners
Occupation Group	Architecture and Engineering	Life, Physical, and Social Science	Healthcare	Business and Financial
Local-Boundness	Medium	Low	Low	Low
Resistance to Robotics	High	High	High	High
Resistance to Computing and Connectivity	High	High	Low	Medium
Pertinent Principles (Good)	1	1		
Pertinent Principles (Maybe Good)	19, 20	11, 19, 20	5, 14, 19, 20	14
Pertinent Principles (Bad)			2	
2010 Number of Workers	NA	100,000	95,100	71,600
Chance for Good Living Wage	High	High	Low	Medium
2010 Median Pay	Medium	Medium	Low	Medium
Median Quality of Work Conditions	High	High	High	High
Family and Outside Activities Compatibility	High	High	High	Low
Forecast for 2010-2020 Change	NA	36%	6%	44%
Forecast for 2033	Very Good	Excellent	Poor	Good
Comments	Will design robots to care for patients. Could be an excellent growth area, depending on cost, effectiveness, and acceptance.	Serious research into human aging and longevity, including the role played by nanotechnology, could multiply their number. Pay is much lower than for practicing physicians, which reduces incentive for their numbers to be cut.	Speech recognition software will replace the overwhelming majority long before 2033.	Systems allowing quick comparison of alternatives will shrink workloads, but the job still involves enough human coordination and travel to keep most automation and globalization at bay.

Job Name	Mental Health Counselors and Marriage and Family Therapists	Merchandise Displayers and Window Trimmers	Metal and Plastic Machine Workers	Meter Readers, Utilities
Occupation Group	Community and Social Service	Arts and Design	Production	Office and Administrative Support
Local-Boundness	High	High	Low	High
Resistance to Robotics	High	Medium	Low	Low
Resistance to Computing and Connectivity	High	High	Medium	Low
Pertinent Principles (Good)	1, 3	3		3
Pertinent Principles (Maybe Good)	5, 11, 14, 15, 20	5, 14		5
Pertinent Principles (Bad)			17	2
2010 Number of Workers	156,300	91,200	939,700	40,500
Chance for Good Living Wage	High	Low	Low	Low
2010 Median Pay	Medium	Low	Low	Low
Median Quality of Work Conditions	High	High	Medium	Medium
Family and Outside Activities Compatibility	High	High	High	High
Forecast for 2010-2020 Change	37%	13%	6%	1%
Forecast for 2033	Excellent	Fair	Poor	Poor
Comments	A need that won't disappear and can't be covered through mechanization or foreign workers. Expect compensation, now at the bottom of the Medium range, to improve.	These tasks need to be done in person, yet in many cases will be completed by other employees without anyone dedicated on the payroll.	Another manufacturing job that will have its number of workers truncated by more robotics and cheaper foreign competition.	There is little reason in 2013 for meters not to be read by computers, or remotely, and there will be almost none of these employees in 2033.

Job Name	Microbiologists	Middle School Teachers	Military Personnel	Millwrights
Occupation Group	Life, Physical, and Social Science	Education, Training, and Library	Military	Installation, Maintenance, and Repair
Local-Boundness	Low	Medium	Low	High
Resistance to Robotics	High	High	Medium	High
Resistance to Computing and Connectivity	High	Medium	High	High
Pertinent Principles (Good)	1			1, 3
Pertinent Principles (Maybe Good)	20	14, 15	5, 15	5
Pertinent Principles (Bad)				
2010 Number of Workers	20,300	641,700	1,211,575	36,500
Chance for Good Living Wage	High	High	Medium	High
2010 Median Pay	Medium	Medium	Medium	Medium
Median Quality of Work Conditions	High	High	Low	Medium
Family and Outside Activities Compatibility	High	High	Low	Medium
Forecast for 2010-2020 Change	13%	17%	NA	-5%
Forecast for 2033	Very Good	Good	Poor	Good
Comments	Another area that will grow more in the next two decades than recently, it has great potential to reduce disease and improve health. Understanding of microorganisms, especially viruses, has a long way to go.	Not as susceptible to substitutes and online replacements as high school teachers, and demand otherwise will stay much the same.	As war becomes more automated and technology-driven, the armed services will need fewer participants. Many in absolute numbers will still be required, with emphasis on those with specific technical aptitudes.	A lot in common with industrial machinery repairers, and the jobs in many places are the same. A necessary function, whether under this label or the other, and moving around and reassembling are important when factories have limited space.

Job Name	Mine Cutting and Channeling Machine Operators	Mine Shuttle Car Operators	Mining and Geological Engineers	Mixing and Blending Machine Setters, Operators, and Tenders
Occupation Group	Construction and Extraction	Transportation and Material Moving	Architecture and Engineering	Production
Local-Boundness	High	High	Low	Medium
Resistance to Robotics	Low	Low	High	Low
Resistance to Computing and Connectivity	High	High	High	High
Pertinent Principles (Good)	3	3	1	
Pertinent Principles (Maybe Good)	5			
Pertinent Principles (Bad)	16	16	16	17
2010 Number of Workers	7,000	3,100	6,400	124,600
Chance for Good Living Wage	High	High	High	Low
2010 Median Pay	Medium	Medium	High	Low
Median Quality of Work Conditions	Low	Low	High	Medium
Family and Outside Activities Compatibility	High	High	High	High
Forecast for 2010-2020 Change	2%	-6%	10%	-2%
Forecast for 2033	Poor	Poor	Fair	Poor
Comments	Almost all American mine tasks will be done robotically before 2033.	Very few mining workers in general will be needed, and vehicles will be operated by robots.	The earth has vast stocks of unmined resources, but environmental considerations often join logistical ones in preventing their harvesting. Mining on the moon and asteroids may have started by 2033.	Machine-running jobs are susceptible, as are most of the others, to both robots and remote operation.

Job Name	Model Makers, Wood	Models	Molders, Shapers, and Casters, except Metal and Plastic	Motion Picture Projectionists
Occupation Group	Production	Sales	Production	Personal Care and Service
Local-Boundness	Medium	Low	Medium	Medium
Resistance to Robotics	Low	High	Low	Low
Resistance to Computing and Connectivity	Low	High	High	High
Pertinent Principles (Good)		1, 4, 7		4
Pertinent Principles (Maybe Good)		11, 14		
Pertinent Principles (Bad)	2		17	2
2010 Number of Workers	1,600	1,400	43,400	10,400
Chance for Good Living Wage	Low	Low	Low	Low
2010 Median Pay	Low	Low	Low	Low
Median Quality of Work Conditions	High	Medium	Medium	High
Family and Outside Activities Compatibility	High	Medium	High	High
Forecast for 2010-2020 Change	11%	14%	8%	-11%
Forecast for 2033	Poor	Good	Poor	Poor
Comments	Long before 2033, CAD technology and 3D printing will generate almost all physical models.	Some real prospects here, buoyed by the interests of the 1%, for the small minority physically suitable, but an extreme pyramid and a hard field to break into full time. Also opportunities with artists, art classes, or photographers.[301]	Robots should be able to handle these machines, which need not have operators in person, by 2033.	Simply not needed much any more, though at multiplexes it may help to have a few around if any problems require manual solutions.

Job Name	Multimedia Artists and Animators	Music Directors and Composers	Musical Instrument Repairers and Tuners	Musicians and Singers
Occupation Group	Arts and Design	Entertainment and Sports	Installation, Maintenance, and Repair	Entertainment and Sports
Local-Boundness	Low	Medium	Medium	Medium
Resistance to Robotics	High	High	High	High
Resistance to Computing and Connectivity	Medium	Medium	High	Medium
Pertinent Principles (Good)		7	1, 7	7
Pertinent Principles (Maybe Good)	14		5	14
Pertinent Principles (Bad)				
2010 Number of Workers	66,500	93,200	6,300	176,200
Chance for Good Living Wage	Medium	Medium	Low	Low
2010 Median Pay	Medium	Medium	Low	Low
Median Quality of Work Conditions	High	High	High	High
Family and Outside Activities Compatibility	High	High	High	Medium
Forecast for 2010-2020 Change	8%	10%	2%	10%
Forecast for 2033	Fair	Fair	Fair	Fair
Comments	Software will continue to make less work for animators, who can of course be anywhere. The redeeming feature may be that video game players can consume prodigious numbers of games, each of which must be designed in some form.	This field employs a remarkable number of people. Susceptible to lack of funding, though much of their music is popular among the 1%, who may end up supporting it almost completely.	Little chance for large growth, but musical instruments are common analog devices not compatible with robotic tuning and service solutions.	Symphony orchestras, supported by the 1%, will continue to employ a substantial number. Other areas of music are a pyramid, with millions of fans interested only in a few hundred very well-compensated performers.

Job Name	Natural Sciences Managers	Network and Computer Systems Administrators	Nuclear Engineers	Nuclear Medicine Technologists
Occupation Group	Management	Computer and Information Technology	Architecture and Engineering	Healthcare
Local-Boundness	Low	Low	Low	Medium
Resistance to Robotics	High	High	High	Medium
Resistance to Computing and Connectivity	High	Low	Medium	Medium
Pertinent Principles (Good)	1			
Pertinent Principles (Maybe Good)			10	5, 14, 19, 20
Pertinent Principles (Bad)			2	
2010 Number of Workers	49,300	347,200	19,100	21,900
Chance for Good Living Wage	High	High	High	High
2010 Median Pay	High	Medium	High	Medium
Median Quality of Work Conditions	High	High	High	High
Family and Outside Activities Compatibility	High	High	High	High
Forecast for 2010-2020 Change	8%	28%	10%	19%
Forecast for 2033	Poor	Poor	Fair	Fair
Comments	Can be done remotely and pays enough that Americans will be overpriced. It is much too easy to hire highly qualified foreigners instead.	Over the next five to ten years demand may be good, but after that, system and network control will be too automated and of course can be done from elsewhere.	Nuclear power in America may not go much further, especially in Democratic administrations. The best prospects, on the moon, may be in design by 2033.	Demand will continue, but as the technology ages it will be less mystifying and either less feared or administered more remotely, which will cut pay, the number of jobs, or both.

Job Name	Nuclear Technicians	Nursing Aides, Orderlies, and Attendants	Occupational Health and Safety Specialists	Occupational Health and Safety Technicians
Occupation Group	Life, Physical, and Social Science	Healthcare	Healthcare	Healthcare
Local-Boundness	Medium	High	Medium	High
Resistance to Robotics	High	High	High	High
Resistance to Computing and Connectivity	High	High	High	High
Pertinent Principles (Good)	1	1, 3, 4	1	1, 3
Pertinent Principles (Maybe Good)	5	5, 14, 19, 20	14, 20	5, 14, 20
Pertinent Principles (Bad)				
2010 Number of Workers	7,100	1,505,300	58,700	10,600
Chance for Good Living Wage	High	Low	High	High
2010 Median Pay	Medium	Low	Medium	Medium
Median Quality of Work Conditions	Medium	Low	High	High
Family and Outside Activities Compatibility	High	High	High	High
Forecast for 2010-2020 Change	14%	20%	9%	13%
Forecast for 2033	Fair	Excellent	Good	Very Good
Comments	A small field with potential to enlarge but only if many more nuclear power plants are built, which is questionable.	At the bottom of the medical hierarchy, they will get little competition from automation or other workers. Their only disadvantage is that many work in large hospitals, where their numbers can often be trimmed.	Not as many positive markers as other health-related areas, but the trends toward greater workplace safety and changes in perception of settings once considered safe will keep it above average.	A growing lower-paid alternative to occupational specialists, its numbers will continue to increase, maybe greatly.

Job Name	Occupational Therapists	Occupational Therapy Assistants and Aides	Office Machine Operators, Except Computer	Oil and Gas Workers
Occupation Group	Healthcare	Healthcare	Office and Administrative Support	Construction and Extraction
Local-Boundness	High	High	High	High
Resistance to Robotics	High	High	Low	Low
Resistance to Computing and Connectivity	High	High	Low	High
Pertinent Principles (Good)	1, 3	1, 3	3	3
Pertinent Principles (Maybe Good)	5, 14, 19, 20	5, 14, 19, 20	14	5
Pertinent Principles (Bad)				16
2010 Number of Workers	108,800	36,000	69,800	134,800
Chance for Good Living Wage	High	High	Low	Low
2010 Median Pay	Medium	Medium	Low	Medium
Median Quality of Work Conditions	High	High	High	Low
Family and Outside Activities Compatibility	High	High	High	Medium
Forecast for 2010-2020 Change	33%	41%	-10%	8%
Forecast for 2033	Excellent	Excellent	Poor	Poor
Comments	A field continuing to expand and will have even more opportunities as aging people increasingly want to do things they did when they were younger and will have the potential.	All the advantages of occupational therapists and more protected by lower pay. One of the best areas anywhere for the next two decades.	Easier-to-use office machines, the continuing trend for managers to operate machines themselves, and paper consumption expected to slightly drop mean this job will keep getting rarer.	Transportation problems require many to be on site for much more time than they have chores, raising their per-task cost high enough for serious robotics attention. As well, oil drilling may be reduced greatly.

Job Name	Operations Research Analysts	Ophthalmic Laboratory Technicians	Opticians, Dispensing	Optometrists
Occupation Group	Math	Production	Healthcare	Healthcare
Local-Boundness	Low	Low	Medium	High
Resistance to Robotics	High	Low	High	High
Resistance to Computing and Connectivity	High	Medium	Low	High
Pertinent Principles (Good)	1		4	1, 3
Pertinent Principles (Maybe Good)		20	5, 14, 20	5, 11, 20
Pertinent Principles (Bad)		17		
2010 Number of Workers	64,600	29,800	62,600	34,200
Chance for Good Living Wage	High	Low	Low	High
2010 Median Pay	Medium	Low	Low	High
Median Quality of Work Conditions	High	High	High	High
Family and Outside Activities Compatibility	High	High	High	High
Forecast for 2010-2020 Change	15%	13%	29%	33%
Forecast for 2033	Fair	Poor	Poor	Very Good
Comments	Similar to systems analysts, they need to talk with many people but not in person. Their functions will likely be combined with those of others.	Health related or not, the machines make the lenses, and the tasks the workers do will soon be taken over by robots, foreigners, or both.	A field just waiting for automation. Relaying optical prescriptions is better done by computers, and prices of lenses and frames will come way down. Most opticians will be in big-box stores by 2020, and their work will be coverable by other sales clerks before 2033.	Alternatives to opthalmologists for many, and they aren't far behind in knowledge. Yet some of their work, such as explaining how to wear contact lenses, will diminish, and cheaper substitutes, such as prescription determination at optician's offices, will become the norm in America, as they already are elsewhere.

Job Name	Orthotists and Prosthetists	Packaging and Filling Machine Operators and Tenders	Painters, Construction and Maintenance	Painting and Coating Workers
Occupation Group	Healthcare	Production	Construction and Extraction	Production
Local-Boundness	Medium	Medium	High	Low
Resistance to Robotics	High	Low	Low	Low
Resistance to Computing and Connectivity	Medium	High	High	Medium
Pertinent Principles (Good)			3	
Pertinent Principles (Maybe Good)	5, 19, 20		5	
Pertinent Principles (Bad)		17		17
2010 Number of Workers	6,300	337,200	390,500	155,200
Chance for Good Living Wage	High	Low	Low	Low
2010 Median Pay	Medium	Low	Low	Low
Median Quality of Work Conditions	High	Medium	Low	Medium
Family and Outside Activities Compatibility	High	High	High	High
Forecast for 2010-2020 Change	12%	4%	18%	9%
Forecast for 2033	Good	Poor	Fair	Poor
Comments	The number of extra-body devices will increase with the share of those needing them, and in-person consultations, though shorter due to more automated production, will still be needed.	The same story as with much other machine operation: can be done by robots, can be done by foreigners, and suffers from the decline of manufacturing in general.	The work is routine enough for robotics, and much less of it will be needed, so only the general amount of new construction will support it.	Requires more care than much other manufacturing-related work, but robots will be doing it before 2033.

Job Name	Paper Goods Machine Setters, Operators, and Tenders	Paperhangers	Paralegals and Legal Assistants	Parking Enforcement Workers
Occupation Group	Production	Construction and Extraction	Legal	Protective Service
Local-Boundness	Medium	High	Low	High
Resistance to Robotics	Low	Medium	High	Low
Resistance to Computing and Connectivity	High	High	Low	High
Pertinent Principles (Good)		3		3
Pertinent Principles (Maybe Good)		5, 12	5	5
Pertinent Principles (Bad)	17			
2010 Number of Workers	90,900	9,100	256,000	35,340
Chance for Good Living Wage	Low	Medium	High	Low
2010 Median Pay	Low	Low	Medium	Low
Median Quality of Work Conditions	Medium	Medium	High	Low
Family and Outside Activities Compatibility	High	High	High	High
Forecast for 2010-2020 Change	-6%	10%	18%	10%
Forecast for 2033	Poor	Fair	Fair	Poor
Comments	The outlook for paper products is better than for most manufactured goods, but the weaknesses of other machine operation jobs still dominate here.	Wallpaper and wall fabric seem to be out of fashion, and that may not change. Still an in-person, skilled job not overcrowded.	Will expand their scope. Many have great knowledge despite their lack of certification, and that will be used. Automation, though, will limit their numbers.	Robots and automated systems mean fewer will be needed, and there will not be much call to bring them back.

Job Name	Parking Lot Attendants	Patternmakers, Wood	Personal Assistants, Personal Organizers, and Task Completers	Personal Financial Advisors
Occupation Group	Transportation and Material Moving	Production	Personal Care and Service	Business and Financial
Local-Boundness	High	Medium	High	Medium
Resistance to Robotics	High	Low	High	High
Resistance to Computing and Connectivity	High	Low	High	Medium
Pertinent Principles (Good)	1, 3, 7, 8		1, 3, 7, 8	8
Pertinent Principles (Maybe Good)	5		5, 14, 19	
Pertinent Principles (Bad)		2, 17		
2010 Number of Workers	125,100	1,200	NA	206,800
Chance for Good Living Wage	Low	Low	Low	High
2010 Median Pay	Low	Low	Low	Medium
Median Quality of Work Conditions	High	Medium	High	High
Family and Outside Activities Compatibility	High	High	High	High
Forecast for 2010-2020 Change	-2%	4%	NA	32%
Forecast for 2033	Fair	Poor	Excellent	Fair
Comments	Valet parking, which may become more common, will still provide jobs, but other parking lots are completely automatable.	As with model makers, will be replaced with CAD and 3D printing technology.	An emerging job, involving a variety of personal tasks, from shopping and running errands to scheduling and booking things.[302] Can be virtual as well as in person.[303] Will grow tremendously in the next two decades.	How well this occupation performs will depend on how much it needs to be done in person. If clients will respond to automated or telephone-only customer service, it will shrink dramatically.

Job Name	Pest Control Workers	Petroleum Engineers	Petroleum Pump System Operators, Refinery Operators, and Gaugers	Pharmacists
Occupation Group	Building and Grounds Cleaning	Architecture and Engineering	Production	Healthcare
Local-Boundness	High	Low	Medium	Low
Resistance to Robotics	Medium	High	Low	High
Resistance to Computing and Connectivity	High	Medium	Medium	Low
Pertinent Principles (Good)	3			
Pertinent Principles (Maybe Good)	5			11, 19, 20
Pertinent Principles (Bad)			17	
2010 Number of Workers	68,400	30,200	44,200	274,900
Chance for Good Living Wage	Low	High	High	High
2010 Median Pay	Low	High	Medium	High
Median Quality of Work Conditions	Medium	High	Medium	High
Family and Outside Activities Compatibility	High	High	High	High
Forecast for 2010-2020 Change	26%	17%	-14%	25%
Forecast for 2033	Good	Fair	Poor	Poor
Comments	Steady, local work that may be reduced by technology, but only slightly.	Petroleum still overwhelms all other transportation energy sources, and that may not change even by 2033. While many are against new drilling, a lot of American oil wells have reached the stage where they need new extraction methods, which will provide opportunities.	Remote workers, or robots using the same systems humans follow, will take over these jobs.	Is maintained as a profession through antiquated prescription-filling requirements and the absence of all-inclusive electronic medical records. Some will be needed to oversee the algorithms, but by 2033 that will be about all.

Job Name	Pharmacy Aides	Pharmacy Technicians	Photographers	Photographic Process Workers and Processing Machine Operators
Occupation Group	Healthcare	Healthcare	Media and Communications	Production
Local-Boundness	High	Low	High	Medium
Resistance to Robotics	Medium	High	Medium	Low
Resistance to Computing and Connectivity	Low	Medium	Medium	High
Pertinent Principles (Good)	3, 4		3	
Pertinent Principles (Maybe Good)	14, 19, 20	5, 14, 19, 20		
Pertinent Principles (Bad)	2			2
2010 Number of Workers	50,800	334,400	139,500	58,700
Chance for Good Living Wage	Low	Low	Low	Low
2010 Median Pay	Low	Low	Low	Low
Median Quality of Work Conditions	High	High	High	Medium
Family and Outside Activities Compatibility	High	High	High	High
Forecast for 2010-2020 Change	29%	32%	13%	-8%
Forecast for 2033	Poor	Fair	Fair	Poor
Comments	Pharmacy jobs will be consolidated, but they will go to those more skilled than aides, who mainly record information awaiting automated interfaces to take over.	Job listings increased 43% from August 2011 to August 2012.[304] Better prospects than those for pharmacists, as they will increasingly be allowed to fill in for them, but with precounted pills and dose-sized liquids they will have less to do.	Common, but can be very skilled. Their special occasion and industrial niches should stay much the same, though they will lose some work to ever-improving technology.	One effect of the replacement of film cameras with digital ones is that the vast majority of photos are never printed, and many more are done at the professional or amateur photographers' homes and businesses.

Job Name	Physical Therapist Assistants and Aides	Physical Therapists	Physician Assistants	Physicians and Surgeons
Occupation Group	Healthcare	Healthcare	Healthcare	Healthcare
Local-Boundness	High	High	High	High
Resistance to Robotics	High	High	High	High
Resistance to Computing and Connectivity	High	High	High	High
Pertinent Principles (Good)	1, 3	1, 3	1, 3	1, 3
Pertinent Principles (Maybe Good)	5, 14, 19, 20	5, 11, 14, 19, 20	5, 14, 19, 20	5, 10, 11, 19, 20
Pertinent Principles (Bad)				
2010 Number of Workers	114,400	198,600	83,600	691,000
Chance for Good Living Wage	Medium	High	High	High
2010 Median Pay	Low	Medium	High	High
Median Quality of Work Conditions	High	High	High	High
Family and Outside Activities Compatibility	High	High	High	Medium
Forecast for 2010-2020 Change	45%	39%	30%	24%
Forecast for 2033	Excellent	Very Good	Excellent	Very Good
Comments	Demand for their work, a lower-cost and often more effective alternative to drugs or surgery, will continue to rise, and, as with others in supporting medical occupations, they will take over tasks from those they help.	Excellent, with ever more patients, except for the prospect of assistants doing more.	One of several that will increasingly take over work now done by physicians, its prospects are superb. The only possible problem is being priced out of itself. The number-one job overall.	More older people mean a rising need, and their supply will probably continue to be kept artificially low. But with their pay as high as it is, the search for lower-priced alternatives will continue apace.

Job Name	Physicists and Astronomers	Pipelayers	Plasterers and Stucco Masons	Plumbers, Pipefitters, and Steamfitters
Occupation Group	Life, Physical, and Social Science	Construction and Extraction	Construction and Extraction	Construction and Extraction
Local-Boundness	Low	High	High	High
Resistance to Robotics	High	Medium	Medium	High
Resistance to Computing and Connectivity	High	High	High	High
Pertinent Principles (Good)	1	3	3	1, 3
Pertinent Principles (Maybe Good)	11	5	5, 12	5, 12
Pertinent Principles (Bad)				
2010 Number of Workers	20,600	53,100	27,900	419,900
Chance for Good Living Wage	High	Medium	Medium	High
2010 Median Pay	High	Low	Low	Medium
Median Quality of Work Conditions	High	Medium	Medium	Medium
Family and Outside Activities Compatibility	High	High	High	Medium
Forecast for 2010-2020 Change	14%	25%	17%	26%
Forecast for 2033	Very Good	Good	Good	Very Good
Comments	Quantum mechanics, formerly an exclusively academic province, will move into more practical realms, opening spots in private industry. A real growth field.	Will connect with upcoming extensive infrastructure work, which will include sewer systems. Low but appreciable chance of competition from robots.	Harder for machines to do than some construction tasks, and real demand in the future.	Except for some prefabrication, there has been no substitute for a human plumber when many things go wrong, and there probably won't be by 2033 either.

Job Name	Podiatrists	Police and Detectives	Police, Fire, and Ambulance Dispatchers	Political Scientists
Occupation Group	Healthcare	Protective Service	Office and Administrative Support	Life, Physical, and Social Science
Local-Boundness	High	High	Low	Low
Resistance to Robotics	High	High	High	High
Resistance to Computing and Connectivity	High	High	High	High
Pertinent Principles (Good)	1, 3	1, 3	1	1
Pertinent Principles (Maybe Good)	5, 11, 19, 20	5, 15	5, 14, 15	
Pertinent Principles (Bad)				
2010 Number of Workers	12,900	794,300	100,100	5,600
Chance for Good Living Wage	High	High	Medium	High
2010 Median Pay	High	Medium	Low	High
Median Quality of Work Conditions				
Family and Outside Activities Compatibility	High	Low	Medium	High
Forecast for 2010-2020 Change	High	High	High	High
Forecast for 2033	20%	7%	12%	8%
Comments	Very Good	Good	Fair	Fair
	Paid less than doctors for similar tasks but with comparable skills, they will be increasingly in demand, though, as with other occupations just short of M.D. compensation, others will be sought to do their tasks.	Will gain, with little competition from automation or globalization. Could grow even more if they are stationed more often in schools and in other public places. Their job responsibilities may evolve to make it more of a helping profession.	Will be damaged less than other clerical positions, as operators must be human, must understand colloquial American English, and must be able to coordinate quickly and effectively.	Most of the small minority not in the academic world work for the federal government and its uncertain funding. Political campaigns, if they increase emphasis on issues, can use more.

Job Name	Postal Service Workers	Postmasters and Mail Superintendents	Postsecondary Education Administrators	Postsecondary Teachers
Occupation Group	Office and Administrative Support	Management	Management	Education, Training, and Library
Local-Boundness	High	Medium	Medium	Medium
Resistance to Robotics	Medium	High	High	High
Resistance to Computing and Connectivity	Medium	High	High	Medium
Pertinent Principles (Good)	3	1	1	
Pertinent Principles (Maybe Good)				11
Pertinent Principles (Bad)				
2010 Number of Workers	524,200	24,500	146,200	1,756,100
Chance for Good Living Wage	Medium	High	High	Medium
2010 Median Pay	Medium	Medium	High	Medium
Median Quality of Work Conditions	High	High	High	High
Family and Outside Activities Compatibility	High	High	High	High
Forecast for 2010-2020 Change	-26%	-28%	19%	17%
Forecast for 2033	Poor	Poor	Poor	Fair
Comments	The Postal Service of 2033 will have weekly delivery, small offices in non-dedicated buildings, much lower mail volumes, and greater automation than today. It may not employ even 100,000 people, and pay will have come down as well.	Once, each small town had a postmaster, but it may soon be closer to one in each county or even group of counties.	Colleges will be seeing real enrollment drops, and hiring fewer administrators will be a common way for them to save money.	BLS statistics do not include the ever-increasing mass of adjunct professors, who teach ever more college courses for a few thousand dollars apiece. College attendance will fall as well. Helped by the relative lack of people with Ph.D's, however, a requirement that will increasingly be imposed on adjuncts as well as on full-time staff.

Job Name	Power Plant Operators, Distributors, and Dispatchers	Preschool and Childcare Center Directors	Preschool Teachers	Pressers, Textile, Garment, and Related Materials
Occupation Group	Production	Management	Education, Training, and Library	Production
Local-Boundness	Low	High	High	High
Resistance to Robotics	Low	High	High	Low
Resistance to Computing and Connectivity	Medium	High	High	High
Pertinent Principles (Good)		1, 3	1, 3, 8	3, 7, 8
Pertinent Principles (Maybe Good)		14	6, 14	
Pertinent Principles (Bad)				
2010 Number of Workers	55,900	63,600	456,800	57,800
Chance for Good Living Wage	High	Medium	Low	Low
2010 Median Pay	High	Medium	Low	Low
Median Quality of Work Conditions	Medium	High	High	Low
Family and Outside Activities Compatibility	High	High	High	High
Forecast for 2010-2020 Change	-2%	25%	25%	-12%
Forecast for 2033	Poor	Fair	Good	Poor
Comments	Robotics should take over this field and eliminate the need for these people to be in harm's way, especially at nuclear plants.	There may or may not be more preschool childcare centers, but fewer people working will mean fewer people needing their services.	Are low-paid enough to hold off cheaper alternatives, but the drop in parents working will shrink demand for them. Will increasingly cater to the 1% and to those working long hours.	Most are employed in drycleaning, an industry in general decline. Others are susceptible to the same robot and foreign-worker competition as other machine operators.

Job Name	Printing Workers	Private Detectives and Investigators	Probation Officers and Correctional Treatment Specialists	Producers and Directors
Occupation Group	Production	Protective Service	Community and Social Service	Entertainment and Sports
Local-Boundness	Medium	Medium	High	Medium
Resistance to Robotics	Low	High	High	High
Resistance to Computing and Connectivity	Medium	High	Medium	High
Pertinent Principles (Good)		1	3	1
Pertinent Principles (Maybe Good)		5	5, 14, 15	
Pertinent Principles (Bad)	17			
2010 Number of Workers	304,600	34,700	93,200	122,500
Chance for Good Living Wage	Low	Medium	High	High
2010 Median Pay	Low	Medium	Medium	Medium
Median Quality of Work Conditions	Medium	Medium	Medium	High
Family and Outside Activities Compatibility	High	High	High	Medium
Forecast for 2010-2020 Change	-4%	21%	18%	11%
Forecast for 2033	Poor	Fair	Very Good	Fair
Comments	A lot of material is printed in the United States, and that will continue, though it will be made by end-to-end robotic systems instead of by people running machines.	Their work has become less of an in-person proposition, and that will continue, with electronic means for tracking people becoming more common and available. Still, the job calls for knowledge Americans are most likely to have.	Some of their tasks can be done remotely, but sentences rate to involve probation or lengthier parole more often.	Still needed to implement productions at many different levels. Often well-paid, even when their performers are not.

Job Name	Proofreaders and Copy Markers	Property, Real Estate, and Community Association Managers	Prostitutes (Legal)	Psychiatric Technicians and Aides
Occupation Group	Office and Administrative Support	Management	Personal Care and Service	Healthcare
Local-Boundness	Low	High	High	High
Resistance to Robotics	High	High	High	High
Resistance to Computing and Connectivity	Medium	High	High	High
Pertinent Principles (Good)		1, 3	1, 3, 6, 7, 8	1, 3
Pertinent Principles (Maybe Good)	5, 14		5, 14	5, 14, 20
Pertinent Principles (Bad)				
2010 Number of Workers	14,000	303,900	NA	142,500
Chance for Good Living Wage	Low	High	Medium	Low
2010 Median Pay	Low	Medium	Medium	Low
Median Quality of Work Conditions	High	High	Low	Medium
Family and Outside Activities Compatibility	High	High	Low	High
Forecast for 2010-2020 Change	5%	6%	NA	15%
Forecast for 2033	Poor	Fair	Very Good	Good
Comments	Are squeezed between spell- and grammar-check software, which will improve further, and full-scale editors.	This in-person function will need to be filled somehow but can also be consolidated, with property managers handling multiple subdivisions or apartment complexes.	May well be legal in many states, or even the whole country, by 2033. The nature of the work will of course be unacceptable to the vast majority, but conditions, once the job is lawful, will be greatly improved. Ultimately a middle-class personal service job impervious to Work's New Age disadvantages.	Fewer people with mental disorders will end up in hospitals, which hire the plurality of these technicians. Still, for what they do they are remarkably low paid, making them less vulnerable and more likely to take on sophisticated tasks.

Job Name	Psychologists	Public Relations Managers and Specialists	Pump Operators, Except Wellhead Pumpers	Purchasing Managers, Buyers, and Purchasing Agents
Occupation Group	Life, Physical, and Social Science	Management	Transportation and Material Moving	Business and Financial
Local-Boundness	Medium	Medium	High	Medium
Resistance to Robotics	High	High	Low	High
Resistance to Computing and Connectivity	High	High	High	Medium
Pertinent Principles (Good)	1	1	3	
Pertinent Principles (Maybe Good)	11, 14	14		
Pertinent Principles (Bad)				
2010 Number of Workers	174,000	320,000	10,800	487,200
Chance for Good Living Wage	High	High	Medium	High
2010 Median Pay	Medium	Medium	Medium	Medium
Median Quality of Work Conditions	High	High	Medium	High
Family and Outside Activities Compatibility	High	High	High	Medium
Forecast for 2010-2020 Change	22%	21%	4%	7%
Forecast for 2033	Good	Fair	Poor	Good
Comments	One of several mental-health-related fields, it has been both oversold and underrated. Should fall out at a good level with demand in many different settings.	Their duties could, in smaller organizations, be covered more by other managers, but in the large ones the jobs will remain and are relatively low-paid.	Robots should have taken over most of their work by 2033.	Still a face-to-face job, with that touch likely to stay highly valued. An unusual area where business travel may increase, to visit foreign suppliers.

Job Name	Quality Control Inspectors	Radiation Therapists	Radio Operators	Radio, Cellular, and Tower Equipment Installers and Repairers
Occupation Group	Production	Healthcare	Media and Communications	Installation, Maintenance, and Repair
Local-Boundness	Medium	High	Low	Medium
Resistance to Robotics	Medium	High	High	Medium
Resistance to Computing and Connectivity	High	High	Low	High
Pertinent Principles (Good)		1, 3		
Pertinent Principles (Maybe Good)		5, 14, 20		5
Pertinent Principles (Bad)	17			
2010 Number of Workers	416,100	16,900	1,200	9,900
Chance for Good Living Wage	Low	High	Low	Medium
2010 Median Pay	Low	Medium	Medium	Medium
Median Quality of Work Conditions	High	High	High	Low
Family and Outside Activities Compatibility	High	High	High	Low
Forecast for 2010-2020 Change	8%	20%	7%	29%
Forecast for 2033	Fair	Good	Poor	Good
Comments	One of the better manufacturing occupations, as it will need to be done periodically and often in person, even with more reliable equipment and processes. As product quality improves, customer expectations rise, maintaining the need for this work.	High paid for a position with so many algorithmic and routine tasks, but still subsituting for medical doctors at half of their average wage.	A small, niche field once common in the military. For now, those needed can be anywhere, and speech recognition software will soon be able to replace them.	There may be a large increase in the number of towers, which are suited for only a limited set of robotic applications. Even changing light bulbs on them usually calls for one of these workers.

Job Name	Radiologic Technologists	Railroad Conductors and Yardmasters	Rail-Track Laying and Maintenance Equipment Operators	Real Estate Brokers and Sales Agents
Occupation Group	Healthcare	Transportation and Material Moving	Construction and Extraction	Sales
Local-Boundness	High	Medium	High	Low
Resistance to Robotics	Medium	Medium	Medium	High
Resistance to Computing and Connectivity	High	High	High	Low
Pertinent Principles (Good)	3		3	
Pertinent Principles (Maybe Good)	5, 14, 20		5, 12	5, 14
Pertinent Principles (Bad)				
2010 Number of Workers	219,900	40,800	15,000	466,100
Chance for Good Living Wage	High	High	High	Medium
2010 Median Pay	Medium	Medium	Medium	Medium
Median Quality of Work Conditions	High	High	Medium	High
Family and Outside Activities Compatibility	High	Medium	High	Medium
Forecast for 2010-2020 Change	28%	5%	2%	11%
Forecast for 2033	Fair	Fair	Good	Poor
Comments	Can substitute for higher-paid employees, but headed for a drop in salary or possibly replaced themselves, if the danger from medical X-rays is considered small, or removed in favor of robots if it is not.	Rail travel is cheapest on land for heavy, low-unit-value freight, and it will stay that way. Although such things as ticket taking could easily be done by machines, this field is already quite labor-unintensive in general.	New rail lines, including subway systems, will be built over the next two decades and for the most part will require humans with machines rather than robots.	This area is heading for a fall, as fewer Americans will be able to afford to own real estate, commissions may change to reflect "easy" and "hard" money, and agents spend too much time not working with clients. Expect far fewer people here by 2033.

Job Name	Receptionists	Recreation Workers	Recreational Therapists	Recreational Vehicle Service Technicians
Occupation Group	Office and Administrative Support	Personal Care and Service	Healthcare	Installation, Maintenance, and Repair
Local-Boundness	High	High	High	High
Resistance to Robotics	Medium	High	High	Medium
Resistance to Computing and Connectivity	High	High	High	High
Pertinent Principles (Good)	3	1, 3, 4	1, 3	3
Pertinent Principles (Maybe Good)	5, 14	14	5, 14, 19, 20	5, 9, 19
Pertinent Principles (Bad)				
2010 Number of Workers	1,048,500	339,100	22,400	9,900
Chance for Good Living Wage	Low	Low	Medium	Low
2010 Median Pay	Low	Low	Medium	Low
Median Quality of Work Conditions	High	High	High	Medium
Family and Outside Activities Compatibility	High	High	High	High
Forecast for 2010-2020 Change	24%	19%	17%	22%
Forecast for 2033	Fair	Fair	Very Good	Very Good
Comments	Provide a front-desk presence, will still be valued, and can do other work during slack times. May become the only office clerks at many locations.	An ongoing proposition but susceptible to being hired for only one season or part time. A classic type of job once commonly held by high school and college students, and pay scales are still low.	Not many are in this field, which is usually an adjunct to other mental health services. Its prospects are promising but will depend on how highly this work is viewed.	One of the best repairing occupations, as it ties into increased travel, has many customers over 65, and is an ongoing, locally-provided need.

Job Name	Refractory Materials Repairers, Except Brickmasons	Registered Nurses	Rehabilitation Counselors	Reinforcing Iron and Rebar Workers
Occupation Group	Installation, Maintenance, and Repair	Healthcare	Community and Social Service	Construction and Extraction
Local-Boundness	High	High	Medium	High
Resistance to Robotics	Medium	High	High	Medium
Resistance to Computing and Connectivity	High	High	High	High
Pertinent Principles (Good)	3	1, 3	1	3
Pertinent Principles (Maybe Good)	5	5, 14, 19, 20	5, 11, 14, 19	5, 13
Pertinent Principles (Bad)				
2010 Number of Workers	2,100	2,737,400	129,800	19,100
Chance for Good Living Wage	Medium	High	Medium	Medium
2010 Median Pay	Medium	Medium	Low	Low
Median Quality of Work Conditions	Medium	High	High	Medium
Family and Outside Activities Compatibility	High	High	High	High
Forecast for 2010-2020 Change	9%	26%	28%	49%
Forecast for 2033	Fair	Very Good	Very Good	Good
Comments	Steady-seeming work, but any rise in jobs may be cut by more robust equipment needing less attention.	Have more expertise than either doctors or LPNs in many different areas and will be in demand indefinitely. The choice between them and LPNs will be a hard one for many health care providers, and both will have opportunities.	Some remote work possibilities, but relatively low pay means they will be less of a priority to eliminate. Will have high demand from the aging population.	Rebar and reinforcing iron are needed for highways, bridges, and other infrastructure. Against that, its implementation may become less labor intensive.

Job Name	Reporters, Correspondents, and Broadcast News Analysts	Residential Advisors	Respiratory Therapists	Respiratory Therapy Technicians
Occupation Group	Media and Communications	Personal Care and Service	Healthcare	Healthcare
Local-Boundness	Low	High	High	High
Resistance to Robotics	High	High	High	High
Resistance to Computing and Connectivity	High	High	High	High
Pertinent Principles (Good)	1	1, 3, 4	1, 3	1, 3
Pertinent Principles (Maybe Good)		5, 14, 19	5, 14, 19, 20	5, 14, 19, 20
Pertinent Principles (Bad)				
2010 Number of Workers	58,500	72,600	112,700	13,800
Chance for Good Living Wage	Low	Low	High	High
2010 Median Pay	Low	Low	Medium	Medium
Median Quality of Work Conditions	High	High	High	High
Family and Outside Activities Compatibility	Medium	High	High	High
Forecast for 2010-2020 Change	-6%	25%	28%	4%
Forecast for 2033	Fair	Excellent	Good	Very Good
Comments	Because fewer have been writing for more publications, their number has shrunk. That will not continue indefinitely, but bloggers, writing for little or no money, will fill most gaps. Reporters of local news will still be needed.	A real growth area, with nursing homes and a variety of community settings attracting older people. Protected by low pay and capability to take on other tasks, which make them easily justifiable.	A solid physician-replacing medical specialty. But, strangely enough, the decline of smoking will hurt demand.	With about nine respiratory therapists for every technician, this field has a long way to grow, especially as its workers have high levels of skill and knowledge.

Job Name	Retail Sales Workers	Riggers	Rock Splitters, Quarry	Roof Bolters, Mining
Occupation Group	Sales	Installation, Maintenance, and Repair	Construction and Extraction	Construction and Extraction
Local-Boundness	High	High	High	High
Resistance to Robotics	High	Medium	Low	Low
Resistance to Computing and Connectivity	High	High	High	High
Pertinent Principles (Good)	1, 3, 4	3	3	3
Pertinent Principles (Maybe Good)	5, 14	5	5	5
Pertinent Principles (Bad)			16	16
2010 Number of Workers	4,465,500	15,200	3,500	5,700
Chance for Good Living Wage	Low	Medium	Low	High
2010 Median Pay	Low	Medium	Low	Medium
Median Quality of Work Conditions	Medium	Medium	Medium	Low
Family and Outside Activities Compatibility	High	High	High	High
Forecast for 2010-2020 Change	17%	11%	12%	2%
Forecast for 2033	Good	Good	Poor	Poor
Comments	Will fare much better than cashiers, as human contact is needed, and the tendency of big-box stores to have as few as possible may have reached a limit.	A dangerous job if heights are involved, though not a good target for robots. Will continue to grow.	Another extraction task that will be covered robotically by 2033, though the number of human workers is small already.	Harder for robots to handle than operating mining equipment but dangerous enough that people will be pushed out of the work.

Job Name	Roofers	Sales Engineers	Sales Managers	School and Career Counselors
Occupation Group	Construction and Extraction	Sales	Management	Community and Social Service
Local-Boundness	High	Medium	Medium	Medium
Resistance to Robotics	Medium	High	High	High
Resistance to Computing and Connectivity	High	High	High	Medium
Pertinent Principles (Good)	3	1	1	
Pertinent Principles (Maybe Good)	5	5		5, 14
Pertinent Principles (Bad)				
2010 Number of Workers	136,700	66,400	342,100	281,400
Chance for Good Living Wage	Medium	High	High	High
2010 Median Pay	Low	High	High	Medium
Median Quality of Work Conditions	Low	High	High	High
Family and Outside Activities Compatibility	High	Medium	Medium	High
Forecast for 2010-2020 Change	18%	14%	12%	19%
Forecast for 2033	Good	Good	Fair	Good
Comments	As with plumbers, they seem like they will always be needed, and the automation possibilities appear quite limited. Better quality materials, however, may reduce the need for as many workers.	More complex, high-ticket products will require humans to explain them, to make reasonably judicious cases for them, and to work out custom contracts, even if future generations value face-to-face contact less.	Have different responsibilities at different companies. Some are subject to computer takeover, but much of sales is, and will probably remain, in-person work.	Best for school counselors, since the sensitivity of students, particularly about bullying and discrimination, is a rising topic, and face-to-face meetings won't be replaced. Career counseling is much less secure.

Job Name	Secretaries and Administrative Assistants	Securities, Commodities, and Financial Services Sales Agents	Security and Fire Alarm Systems Installers	Security Guards and Gaming Surveillance Officers
Occupation Group	Office and Administrative Support	Sales	Installation, Maintenance, and Repair	Protective Service
Local-Boundness	Medium	Low	High	Medium
Resistance to Robotics	High	High	Medium	Medium
Resistance to Computing and Connectivity	High	High	High	High
Pertinent Principles (Good)	1	1	3	7
Pertinent Principles (Maybe Good)	5, 14	5	5	5
Pertinent Principles (Bad)				
2010 Number of Workers	4,010,200	312,200	63,800	1,090,600
Chance for Good Living Wage	Medium	High	Medium	Low
2010 Median Pay	Low	Medium	Low	Low
Median Quality of Work Conditions	High	High	High	Medium
Family and Outside Activities Compatibility	High	Medium	High	Medium
Forecast for 2010-2020 Change	12%	15%	33%	18%
Forecast for 2033	Fair	Fair	Good	Fair
Comments	Will be valued for their helping tasks in general and less for anything resembling clerical production. If empowered, they can take over many aspects of a manager's job; if not, they may plummet in numbers.	Human brokers are no longer required for most stock trades, but people with knowledge are needed to help with more complicated financial transactions such as initial public offerings, and they still will be in 2033.	An installation job that, due to too much difference between sites, is less likely to be lost to robots than most.	More and more areas, especially gated subdivisions and apartment complexes, will be secured, which is good news for this still generally in-person occupation facing a moderate challenge from robotics. Casinos will need many as well.

Job Name	Segmental Pavers	Self-enrichment Teachers	Semiconductor Processors	Separating, Filtering, Clarifying, Precipitating, and Still Machine Setters, Operators, and Tenders
Occupation Group	Construction and Extraction	Education, Training, and Library	Production	Production
Local-Boundness	High	Medium	Low	Medium
Resistance to Robotics	Low	High	Low	Low
Resistance to Computing and Connectivity	High	Medium	Low	High
Pertinent Principles (Good)	3	18		
Pertinent Principles (Maybe Good)	5, 13	14		
Pertinent Principles (Bad)			17	17
2010 Number of Workers	1,300	252,800	21,100	38,400
Chance for Good Living Wage	Low	Low	Low	Low
2010 Median Pay	Low	Low	Low	Low
Median Quality of Work Conditions	Medium	High	Medium	Medium
Family and Outside Activities Compatibility	High	High	High	High
Forecast for 2010-2020 Change	33%	21%	-18%	5%
Forecast for 2033	Good	Fair	Poor	Poor
Comments	A growing construction specialty, connected with road repair, which will stay better suited to machines other than robots.	Except for upcoming demand for recreational teaching, which may be considerable, it is hard to see many of them kept on payrolls when others can be hired course by course at college adjunct instructor rates or less.	Automation and globalization have badly damaged this once-prosperous job source, and both will continue. This work is made for robotics, so even low-wage countries will have few opportunities in the field.	More manufacturing-related machine operation done better by robots or for less by foreign workers.

Job Name	Septic Tank Servicers and Sewer Pipe Cleaners	Set and Exhibit Designers	Sewers and Tailors	Sewing Machine Operators
Occupation Group	Construction and Extraction	Arts and Design	Production	Production
Local-Boundness	High	Low	Medium	Medium
Resistance to Robotics	Medium	High	Low	Low
Resistance to Computing and Connectivity	High	Medium	High	High
Pertinent Principles (Good)	3		7, 8	
Pertinent Principles (Maybe Good)	5	14	5, 14	14
Pertinent Principles (Bad)				17
2010 Number of Workers	25,300	11,700	57,500	163,200
Chance for Good Living Wage	Low	Medium	Low	Low
2010 Median Pay	Low	Medium	Low	Low
Median Quality of Work Conditions	Low	High	Medium	Medium
Family and Outside Activities Compatibility	High	High	High	High
Forecast for 2010-2020 Change	21%	10%	1%	-26%
Forecast for 2033	Good	Fair	Fair	Poor
Comments	Their unpleasant set of tasks is necessary to some extent or another for the tens of millions of Americans not on sewer lines.	The software used will evolve, but, as in other design propositions, it will open up new possibilities to offset the time it saves.	Except for repair work and a few custom and very high-end items, the entire garment manufacturing process will be fulfilled by robots and other machines by 2033.	Far cheaper overseas, and robotic competition will soon almost end this once common occupation.

Job Name	Sheet Metal Workers	Shoe and Leather Workers and Repairers	Shoe Machine Operators and Tenders	Signal and Track Switch Repairers
Occupation Group	Construction and Extraction	Production	Production	Installation, Maintenance, and Repair
Local-Boundness	High	Medium	Medium	Medium
Resistance to Robotics	Medium	Medium	Low	Medium
Resistance to Computing and Connectivity	High	High	High	High
Pertinent Principles (Good)	3			
Pertinent Principles (Maybe Good)	5, 12			5
Pertinent Principles (Bad)		17	17	
2010 Number of Workers	136,100	10,200	3,200	7,100
Chance for Good Living Wage	Medium	Low	Low	High
2010 Median Pay	Medium	Low	Low	Medium
Median Quality of Work Conditions	Medium	Medium	Medium	High
Family and Outside Activities Compatibility	High	High	High	Low
Forecast for 2010-2020 Change	18%	-14%	-53%	-2%
Forecast for 2033	Good	Poor	Poor	Poor
Comments	New buildings need sheet metal, and its workers do a variety of tasks, which are more difficult to automate than those in many construction fields.	Almost a hopeless area in America, but repair has a small amount of potential, as prices are sometimes high enough that buying new is prohibitive.	The job with the single worst 2020 BLS projection, it won't come back either. It will be a rare shoe that is made by machine in the United States.	A railroad specialty that may be combined with others as crossings require less work than before.

Job Name	Skincare Specialists	Slaughterers and Meat Packers	Small Engine Mechanics	Social and Community Service Managers
Occupation Group	Personal Care and Service	Production	Installation, Maintenance, and Repair	Management
Local-Boundness	High	Medium	High	Medium
Resistance to Robotics	High	Low	High	High
Resistance to Computing and Connectivity	High	High	High	High
Pertinent Principles (Good)	1, 3, 7		1, 3	1
Pertinent Principles (Maybe Good)	5, 14		5	14
Pertinent Principles (Bad)				
2010 Number of Workers	47,600	89,100	68,800	134,100
Chance for Good Living Wage	Low	Low	Medium	High
2010 Median Pay	Low	Low	Low	Medium
Median Quality of Work Conditions	High	Low	Medium	High
Family and Outside Activities Compatibility	High	High	High	High
Forecast for 2010-2020 Change	25%	8%	21%	27%
Forecast for 2033	Very Good	Poor	Good	Good
Comments	Almost any job that can't be automated or globalized, includes a high share of women, and caters to the 1% has fine prospects. The pay may stay higher than for many personal care positions.	Another set of tasks where robots will take over. It is already viable to automate the entire process, beginning to end.	Many small engines are of old enough technology that they will need significant repairs and are a bit too expensive for replacement to be the norm. Some of this work may not be done in person, but generally, especially in rural areas where many small engines are, it will continue to be.	As communities take over more social services, they will need to be organized and managed, opening up new opportunities.

Job Name	Social and Human Service Assistants	Social Media Managers	Social Science Research Assistants	Social Workers
Occupation Group	Community and Social Service	Management	Life, Physical, and Social Science	Community and Social Service
Local-Boundness	High	Low	Low	High
Resistance to Robotics	High	High	High	High
Resistance to Computing and Connectivity	Medium	High	High	High
Pertinent Principles (Good)	3, 18	1	1	1, 3, 18
Pertinent Principles (Maybe Good)	5, 14, 15	15	14	5, 14, 15
Pertinent Principles (Bad)				
2010 Number of Workers	384,200	NA	29,700	650,500
Chance for Good Living Wage	Low	High	Low	Medium
2010 Median Pay	Low	High	Medium	Medium
Median Quality of Work Conditions	High	High	High	High
Family and Outside Activities Compatibility	High	High	High	High
Forecast for 2010-2020 Change	28%	NA	15%	25%
Forecast for 2033	Good	Good	Poor	Good
Comments	In-person services with a growing set of clients. At the assistant level, much work may be taken over by unpaid community people, but professionals may be needed to train them.	Job listings increased 48% from August 2011 to August 2012.[305] A rising occupation not listed in the BLS data, it will become well established in some form, but who knows what role social media will have for businesses in 2033?	Any academic helping job with low requirements in a field with many undergraduate majors and graduate students is susceptible, as universities cut costs, to being done by others for very little money.	Clinical social workers who provide psychiatric help will do the best; many others may be replaced by skilled but less trained community volunteers.

Job Name	Sociologists	Software Developers	Special Education Teachers	Speech-Language Pathologists
Occupation Group	Life, Physical, and Social Science	Computer and Information Technology	Education, Training, and Library	Healthcare
Local-Boundness	Low	Low	High	High
Resistance to Robotics	High	High	High	High
Resistance to Computing and Connectivity	High	Medium	High	High
Pertinent Principles (Good)	1		1, 3	1, 3
Pertinent Principles (Maybe Good)	14		14	5, 14, 20
Pertinent Principles (Bad)				
2010 Number of Workers	4,000	913,100	459,600	123,200
Chance for Good Living Wage	High	High	High	High
2010 Median Pay	Medium	High	Medium	Medium
Median Quality of Work Conditions	High	High	High	High
Family and Outside Activities Compatibility	High	High	High	High
Forecast for 2010-2020 Change	18%	30%	17%	23%
Forecast for 2033	Fair	Poor	Fair	Good
Comments	As with anthropology, commercial sociology seems to have gone almost nowhere. That may well improve, but there are huge numbers of sociology majors who would like to work in the field and are nowhere near it.	Job listings increased 74% from August 2011 to August 2012,[306] but this position requires communication with programmers, which, though complex, may only reward developers who are from the same country. That does not rate to be the United States.	Mainstreaming and the Americans with Disabilities Act are both well established, meaning no further fundamental growth in the number of special education teachers. Employment should continue at rates similar to other K-12 instructors.	More personal than many other medical areas, so will need to be conducted face to face, even when it may seem that treatment could be done remotely.

Job Name	Stationary Engineers and Boiler Operators	Statistical Assistants	Statisticians	Structural Iron and Steel Workers
Occupation Group	Production	Office and Administrative Support	Math	Construction and Extraction
Local-Boundness	High	Low	Low	High
Resistance to Robotics	Low	High	High	Medium
Resistance to Computing and Connectivity	High	Low	High	High
Pertinent Principles (Good)	3		1	3
Pertinent Principles (Maybe Good)		5		5, 12, 13
Pertinent Principles (Bad)	17			
2010 Number of Workers	37,600	16,600	25,100	59,800
Chance for Good Living Wage	High	Medium	High	Medium
2010 Median Pay	High	Low	Medium	Medium
Median Quality of Work Conditions	Medium	High	High	Low
Family and Outside Activities Compatibility	Medium	High	High	High
Forecast for 2010-2020 Change	6%	6%	14%	22%
Forecast for 2033	Poor	Poor	Fair	Good
Comments	Better than many related propositions but will decline as the machines need less maintenance and their operation becomes trivial. This job will hardly become extinct, but there may be about one-third as many in 2033 as today.	As with other mathematical occupations, the algorithmic and non-local nature of the work means poor prospects for Americans.	The need to interpret data will greatly surpass the need to collect it, if it hasn't already. That may offset the complete nonrequirement for statisticians to be local or even to be employed by specific companies.	A rare, dangerous occupation that robots may not take over, as they may not prove viable in high-steel work settings. Construction demand will remain strong.

Job Name	Substance Abuse and Behavioral Disorder Counselors	Subway and Streetcar Operators	Surgical Technologists	Survey Researchers
Occupation Group	Community and Social Service	Transportation and Material Moving	Healthcare	Life, Physical, and Social Science
Local-Boundness	High	Medium	High	Low
Resistance to Robotics	High	Medium	High	High
Resistance to Computing and Connectivity	High	High	High	Medium
Pertinent Principles (Good)	1, 3		1, 3	
Pertinent Principles (Maybe Good)	5, 14, 15, 20		5, 14, 19, 20	
Pertinent Principles (Bad)				
2010 Number of Workers	85,500	6,500	93,600	19,600
Chance for Good Living Wage	Medium	High	High	Medium
2010 Median Pay	Low	Medium	Medium	Medium
Median Quality of Work Conditions	High	High	High	High
Family and Outside Activities Compatibility	High	High	High	High
Forecast for 2010-2020 Change	27%	10%	19%	24%
Forecast for 2033	Very Good	Fair	Very Good	Fair
Comments	Demand will continue, whether recreational drugs are legalized or not, and could grow as the set of "substances" may expand to include, for example, gambling and pornography. Must be done in person, and counseling is much cheaper than extensive medical care or prison.	Automation does not seem to be a job killer in this field, with too many irregularities and customer safety concerns to let the machines take over entirely, and there are few extra employees as it is.	The number of surgical operations will continue to increase, and skilled people are needed to support them. Pay for these workers is low enough that alternatives, at the level of diligence needed, will not be sought out for them. Some of their tasks, though, can also be done by nurses.	May be better in the short run, but principles could be defined algorithmically to the point where software would produce good surveys, which would need to be only slightly adjusted for use.

Job Name	Surveying and Mapping Technicians	Surveyors	Switchboard Operators, Including Answering Service	Tank Car, Truck, and Ship Loaders
Occupation Group	Architecture and Engineering	Architecture and Engineering	Office and Administrative Support	Transportation and Material Moving
Local-Boundness	Low	Low	Low	High
Resistance to Robotics	Medium	Medium	Low	Medium
Resistance to Computing and Connectivity	Medium	Medium	Low	High
Pertinent Principles (Good)				3
Pertinent Principles (Maybe Good)	5	5	5, 14	
Pertinent Principles (Bad)			2	
2010 Number of Workers	56,900	51,200	142,500	10,400
Chance for Good Living Wage	Low	Medium	Low	Medium
2010 Median Pay	Low	Medium	Low	Medium
Median Quality of Work Conditions	High	High	High	Medium
Family and Outside Activities Compatibility	Medium	Medium	High	High
Forecast for 2010-2020 Change	16%	25%	-23%	2%
Forecast for 2033	Poor	Poor	Poor	Poor
Comments	As with cartographers and surveyors, they are mostly working in maintenance mode, and computer systems should take over most of their efforts within a decade or so.	GPS-related technology should be able to define boundaries. Somebody needs to put down markers, but it need not be people as highly trained and well paid.	A job getting obsolete quickly, with physicians and a few others the only customers requiring domestic human contact for after-hours phone calls.	Robots will not take over this work right away, but they will by 2033, when they have progressed enough to handle these operations.

Job Name	Tax Examiners and Collectors, and Revenue Agents	Tax Preparers	Taxi Drivers and Chauffeurs	Teacher Assistants
Occupation Group	Business and Financial	Business and Financial	Transportation and Material Moving	Education, Training, and Library
Local-Boundness	Low	Medium	High	High
Resistance to Robotics	High	High	High	High
Resistance to Computing and Connectivity	Low	Medium	High	High
Pertinent Principles (Good)		8	1, 3, 7, 8	1, 3
Pertinent Principles (Maybe Good)	15	14	5, 9	14, 15
Pertinent Principles (Bad)				
2010 Number of Workers	74,500	81,500	239,900	1,288,300
Chance for Good Living Wage	Medium	Low	Low	Low
2010 Median Pay	Medium	Low	Low	Low
Median Quality of Work Conditions	Medium	High	Medium	High
Family and Outside Activities Compatibility	High	High	High	High
Forecast for 2010-2020 Change	7%	10%	20%	15%
Forecast for 2033	Good	Good	Very Good	Very Good
Comments	Will be needed over the phone and, in some cases, in person. More may well be hired.	Not to be confused with full accounting service providers, they help those who want to check their own preparing ability or who require assistance for one reason or another. Tax laws will remain mystifying to many, so there will be jobs here.	The connection with increased travel and lower future car ownership, along with a low automation threat, makes taxi, limousine, and private auto driving all resilient jobs.	May replace teachers more, and, with pay as low as it is, there is plenty of room to add educational qualifications, which many practicing and prospective ones have already, along with more money.

Job Name	Technical Writers	Telecommunications Equipment Installers and Repairers Except Line Installers	Telemarketers	Telephone Operators
Occupation Group	Media and Communications	Installation, Maintenance, and Repair	Sales	Office and Administrative Support
Local-Boundness	Low	High	Low	Low
Resistance to Robotics	High	High	Medium	Low
Resistance to Computing and Connectivity	High	High	Medium	Low
Pertinent Principles (Good)	1	1, 3	4	
Pertinent Principles (Maybe Good)	14, 15	5		5, 14
Pertinent Principles (Bad)				2
2010 Number of Workers	49,500	194,900	290,700	18,500
Chance for Good Living Wage	High	Medium	Low	Low
2010 Median Pay	Medium	Medium	Low	Low
Median Quality of Work Conditions	High	Medium	Low	High
Family and Outside Activities Compatibility	High	Medium	High	High
Forecast for 2010-2020 Change	17%	15%	7%	-17%
Forecast for 2033	Good	Good	Poor	Poor
Comments	Products need clear explanations in American English. Although this work can be done remotely, few foreigners from countries with low labor costs are good enough at it.	As with other forms of equipment repair, while less is needed per piece, there will be more in service, and promptness is more necessary than ever.	Foreigners will be recruited for this job, which may shrink in numbers anyway, given high consumer resistance.	Once perhaps the most common position for American women working outside their homes, now just about replaced by voice recognition software and other technology.

Job Name	Tellers	Textile Bleaching and Dyeing Machine Operators and Tenders	Textile Cutting Machine Setters, Operators, and Tenders	Textile Knitting and Weaving Machine Setters, Operators, and Tenders
Occupation Group	Office and Administrative Support	Production	Production	Production
Local-Boundness	High	Medium	Medium	Medium
Resistance to Robotics	Low	Low	Low	Low
Resistance to Computing and Connectivity	Medium	High	High	High
Pertinent Principles (Good)	3			
Pertinent Principles (Maybe Good)	5, 14			
Pertinent Principles (Bad)		17	17	17
2010 Number of Workers	560,000	13,900	14,900	22,500
Chance for Good Living Wage	Low	Low	Low	Low
2010 Median Pay	Low	Low	Low	Low
Median Quality of Work Conditions	High	Medium	Medium	Medium
Family and Outside Activities Compatibility	High	High	High	High
Forecast for 2010-2020 Change	1%	-15%	-22%	-18%
Forecast for 2033	Poor	Poor	Poor	Poor
Comments	There is no need for automation at banks to end with ATMs. Many functions could be handled by robot systems. Some employees will still be needed, but their numbers will come way down.	The textile industry, even as mechanized as it is, has almost left the United States and has no reason to return.	Similarly, there is little hope for these or many other textile jobs in this country anymore.	Another textile machine job belonging almost exclusively to America's past.

Job Name	Tile and Marble Setters	Tire Builders	Tire Repairers and Changers	Title Examiners, Abstracters, and Searchers
Occupation Group	Construction and Extraction	Production	Installation, Maintenance, and Repair	Legal
Local-Boundness	High	Medium	High	Low
Resistance to Robotics	Medium	Low	Medium	High
Resistance to Computing and Connectivity	High	High	High	Low
Pertinent Principles (Good)	3		3	
Pertinent Principles (Maybe Good)	5, 12, 13	9	5, 9	5, 14
Pertinent Principles (Bad)		17		
2010 Number of Workers	58,700	15,500	99,000	59,000
Chance for Good Living Wage	Medium	Medium	Low	Medium
2010 Median Pay	Low	Medium	Low	Medium
Median Quality of Work Conditions	Medium	Medium	Medium	High
Family and Outside Activities Compatibility	High	High	High	High
Forecast for 2010-2020 Change	25%	-6%	19%	-1%
Forecast for 2033	Good	Poor	Fair	Poor
Comments	Related to the other stone flooring trades, will both remain necessary and benefit from high demand, but will have real exposure to robotics and other mechanization.	A machine operating position calling for more skill than most, but still can be done better by robots and, as well, by cheaper overseas workers.	The number of older cars with older tires will increase, but tires are lasting longer, and are more likely than ever to be replaced instead of repaired.	Must be done separately for each transaction, but algorithmic, susceptible to improved computer connectivity, and can be performed from anywhere.

Job Name	Tool Grinders, Filers, and Sharpeners	Top Executives	Tour Guides and Escorts	Traffic Technicians
Occupation Group	Production	Management	Personal Care and Service	Transportation and Material Moving
Local-Boundness	Medium	Medium	Medium	Low
Resistance to Robotics	Low	High	High	High
Resistance to Computing and Connectivity	High	High	High	Low
Pertinent Principles (Good)		1	1, 4	
Pertinent Principles (Maybe Good)		11	9, 14, 19	
Pertinent Principles (Bad)	17			
2010 Number of Workers	13,100	2,136,900	34,900	6,900
Chance for Good Living Wage	Low	High	Low	Medium
2010 Median Pay	Low	High	Low	Medium
Median Quality of Work Conditions	Medium	High	High	High
Family and Outside Activities Compatibility	High	Medium	Low	High
Forecast for 2010-2020 Change	7%	5%	18%	11%
Forecast for 2033	Poor	Fair	Very Good	Poor
Comments	One more manufacturing spot headed for job losses, high skill or not.	Their numbers won't increase much, as companies and other organizations will have only so many of them, but they generally don't spend long times in the position, especially in private industry.	A fine opportunity that can't be automated and caters to travel, especially by tourists able enough to handle it but still needing some help.	A job very susceptible to replacement, or near-replacement, by computer-generated optimal traffic scenarios.

Job Name	Train Engineers and Operators	Training and Development Managers	Training and Development Specialists	Transportation Attendants, Except Flight Attendants
Occupation Group	Transportation and Material Moving	Management	Business and Financial	Transportation and Material Moving
Local-Boundness	Medium	Medium	Medium	Medium
Resistance to Robotics	Medium	High	High	Medium
Resistance to Computing and Connectivity	High	High	Medium	High
Pertinent Principles (Good)		1		
Pertinent Principles (Maybe Good)		14	14	5, 9, 14
Pertinent Principles (Bad)				
2010 Number of Workers	67,100	29,800	217,700	24,800
Chance for Good Living Wage	High	High	High	Low
2010 Median Pay	Medium	High	Medium	Low
Median Quality of Work Conditions	High	High	High	High
Family and Outside Activities Compatibility	Low	High	Medium	Medium
Forecast for 2010-2020 Change	1%	15%	28%	11%
Forecast for 2033	Fair	Fair	Fair	Fair
Comments	As with subway and streetcar drivers, not really automatable, so will remain.	Job listings increased 41% from August 2011 to August 2012.[307] Corporate training has been controversial lately, with less of it provided, despite increasingly specialized job requirements. Managers dedicated to it will mostly be confined to larger organizations and will be limited in number.	Corporate training, weak in general, will get worse in an employer's market. The scripts for online alternatives, however, must still be written or adapted.	More may be needed to assist travelers over 65, though increasingly streamlined processes will stop this form of help from becoming a real growth area.

Job Name	Transportation Inspectors	Transportation, Storage, and Distribution Managers	Travel Agents	Travel Guides
Occupation Group	Transportation and Material Moving	Management	Sales	Personal Care and Service
Local-Boundness	High	Medium	Low	Medium
Resistance to Robotics	Medium	High	High	High
Resistance to Computing and Connectivity	High	High	Medium	High
Pertinent Principles (Good)	3	1	7	1, 7
Pertinent Principles (Maybe Good)			5, 9, 14	9, 14, 19
Pertinent Principles (Bad)				
2010 Number of Workers	27,400	98,600	82,800	4,200
Chance for Good Living Wage	High	High	Low	Low
2010 Median Pay	Medium	High	Low	Low
Median Quality of Work Conditions	Medium	High	High	High
Family and Outside Activities Compatibility	High	High	High	Low
Forecast for 2010-2020 Change	14%	10%	10%	24%
Forecast for 2033	Fair	Fair	Fair	Very Good
Comments	Should grow slightly, with more travel offsetting higher efficiency. If there are more major domestic terrorism incidents, demand could become enormous.	A management function resistant to automation but with little prospect for growth. Pay may decrease.	Routine travel booking or information collecting no longer requires people, but there is real potential on the high end for custom services, especially arranging difficult itineraries and providing high-quality information.	Over the next two decades, there will be more demand for specialized tourism engagements that cannot easily be booked online. Those in this field can help facilitate all aspects of that.

Job Name	Umpires. Referees, and Other Sports Officials	Upholsterers	Urban and Regional Planners	Ushers, Lobby Attendants, and Ticket Takers
Occupation Group	Entertainment and Sports	Production	Life, Physical, and Social Science	Personal Care and Service
Local-Boundness	Medium	High	Medium	High
Resistance to Robotics	High	Medium	High	Low
Resistance to Computing and Connectivity	Medium	High	Medium	High
Pertinent Principles (Good)		3		3, 4
Pertinent Principles (Maybe Good)				14
Pertinent Principles (Bad)				
2010 Number of Workers	19,500	46,900	40,300	109,100
Chance for Good Living Wage	Low	Low	High	Low
2010 Median Pay	Low	Low	Medium	Low
Median Quality of Work Conditions	High	Medium	High	High
Family and Outside Activities Compatibility	Medium	High	High	High
Forecast for 2010-2020 Change	20%	4%	16%	10%
Forecast for 2033	Fair	Fair	Fair	Poor
Comments	Automation may make inroads on their number; otherwise, they will be needed in proportion to the number of professional and collegiate sporting events, which will stay substantial.	More of a craft than manufacturing, this field may hold on, saved by the high shipping cost of furniture, which prevents both cheap replacement and most overseas work.	Compared with other related jobs, such as geographers, there are a lot of them at work. That number may not get much higher, and, with mostly remote job duties, they can be shared effectively.	People in these fields are neither fully necessary nor greatly wanted by customers, so their numbers will shrink.

Job Name	Veterinarians	Veterinary Assistants and Laboratory Animal Caretakers	Veterinary Technologists and Technicians	Waiters and Waitresses
Occupation Group	Healthcare	Healthcare	Healthcare	Food Preparation and Serving
Local-Boundness	High	High	High	High
Resistance to Robotics	High	High	High	Medium
Resistance to Computing and Connectivity	High	High	High	High
Pertinent Principles (Good)	1, 3	1, 3, 4	1, 3	3, 4, 7
Pertinent Principles (Maybe Good)	5, 11, 14	5, 14	5, 14	5, 14
Pertinent Principles (Bad)				
2010 Number of Workers	61,400	73,200	80,200	2,260,300
Chance for Good Living Wage	High	Low	Low	Low
2010 Median Pay	High	Low	Low	Low
Median Quality of Work Conditions	Medium	Medium	Medium	Medium
Family and Outside Activities Compatibility	High	High	High	High
Forecast for 2010-2020 Change	36%	14%	52%	9%
Forecast for 2033	Very Good	Very Good	Good	Fair
Comments	Most of their work is with pets, which, with smaller households especially benefitting from companionship, have become even more common. That trend may reverse or at least level off, but they remain a relative bargain, and are invaluable to many.	A popular field despite low pay, but these employees are at the bottom of the hierarchy, so stand to pick up tasks.	Will continue to supplement veterinarians but not replace them. Will not do as well relatively as other medical assistant positions, as most vets' offices are small.	A low-paying, in-person job, but one ripe for robotics or automated systems, if customers will accept them. May be combined with related positions or be mainly at high-end places.

Job Name	Watch Repairers	Water and Wastewater Treatment Plant and System Operators	Water Transportation Occupations	Welders, Cutters, Solderers, and Brazers
Occupation Group	Installation, Maintenance, and Repair	Production	Transportation and Material Moving	Production
Local-Boundness	Medium	High	Medium	Low
Resistance to Robotics	High	Medium	Medium	Low
Resistance to Computing and Connectivity	High	High	High	High
Pertinent Principles (Good)	1	3	7	
Pertinent Principles (Maybe Good)	5		9	13
Pertinent Principles (Bad)				17
2010 Number of Workers	2,500	110,700	82,600	337,300
Chance for Good Living Wage	Medium	Medium	High	Low
2010 Median Pay	Low	Medium	Medium	Low
Median Quality of Work Conditions	High	High	Medium	Low
Family and Outside Activities Compatibility	High	High	Low	High
Forecast for 2010-2020 Change	6%	12%	20%	15%
Forecast for 2033	Poor	Fair	Good	Poor
Comments	Newer watches seldom require repairs, so the best opportunities in this field are for understanding antique and valuable timepieces, which can support a few of these workers.	Maintaining the water supply will prove surprisingly hard to automate, with intake variations and very large volumes involved.	Container ships carry ever more amounts of freight at tiny per-unit costs, and cruise ships require a lot of marine crew members, two strengths for these occupations unlikely to be lost by 2033.	As robotics improves, more of these functions will be taken over at an increasing number of work sites.

Job Name	Wellhead Pumpers	Wholesale and Manufacturing Sales Representatives	Woodworkers	Word Processors and Typists
Occupation Group	Transportation and Material Moving	Sales	Production	Office and Administrative Support
Local-Boundness	Low	Medium	Medium	Low
Resistance to Robotics	Low	High	Low	High
Resistance to Computing and Connectivity	High	Medium	Medium	Low
Pertinent Principles (Good)				
Pertinent Principles (Maybe Good)		5		5, 14
Pertinent Principles (Bad)	16		17	
2010 Number of Workers	15,100	1,830,000	217,200	115,300
Chance for Good Living Wage	Medium	High	Low	Low
2010 Median Pay	Medium	Medium	Low	Low
Median Quality of Work Conditions	Medium	Medium	Medium	High
Family and Outside Activities Compatibility	Medium	Medium	High	High
Forecast for 2010-2020 Change	5%	16%	18%	-11%
Forecast for 2033	Poor	Fair	Poor	Poor
Comments	Replaceable, either by automated systems, robots, or people from elsewhere.	Job listings increased 35% from August 2011 to August 2012.[308] An in-person but high-travel occupation, with employees who often offer little more information than on company websites, so one that will be hurt if the human touch is not valued in 2033.	Yet another manufacturing position that will be almost eliminated in America, first by foreign competition and soon thereafter by robotics and other automation.	The typing pool belongs to American working history, and human word processors didn't last either, with most managers doing that themselves.

Job Name	Writers and Authors	Zoologists and Wildlife Biologists
Occupation Group	Media and Communications	Life, Physical, and Social Science
Local-Boundness	Low	Medium
Resistance to Robotics	High	High
Resistance to Computing and Connectivity	High	High
Pertinent Principles (Good)	1	1
Pertinent Principles (Maybe Good)		14
Pertinent Principles (Bad)		
2010 Number of Workers	145,900	19,800
Chance for Good Living Wage	Medium	High
2010 Median Pay	Medium	Medium
Median Quality of Work Conditions	High	High
Family and Outside Activities Compatibility	High	Medium
Forecast for 2010-2020 Change	6%	7%
Forecast for 2033	Fair	Fair
Comments	Millions of books are published each year in America alone, and that will increase greatly with further acceptance of electronic versions. The problem is funding, profitability, or lack of either.	In this field where massive amounts are yet to be learned, the problem is getting sources other than universities to pay for it. Most work for governments, which means susceptibility to budget cuts.

Part III: Careers in the Longer Term

Chapter 8: Preparing for 2033 and Beyond

The cultural revolution in which we are immersed is no more a tale of bits and bytes than the story of Galileo is about paired lenses. —Joel Garreau[309]

If you are 20 in 2013, then in 2033 you will be only 40. As of 2007, men aged 20 had an average life expectancy of 56-plus more years, and women had more than 61,[310] meaning that, if those numbers stay the same, most will still be alive in 2070.

There will be careers then. Or will there be?

According to some writers, we are within decades of changes immeasurably beyond anything we have personally experienced, or for that matter, what the *world* has experienced. These shifts have potential to dwarf even the monumental transformation of the Industrial Revolution.

What am I talking about?

What? The Future Won't Need Us?

Bill Joy co-founded Sun Microsystems in 1982.[311] In April 2000, he wrote a long article in *Wired* magazine, titled "Why the future doesn't need us." In it, Joy discussed developments in the areas of robotics, genetic engineering, and nanotechnology, and he explained why they presented dangers well beyond those of the classic "weapons of mass destruction"—nuclear, biological, and chemical armaments—from the century then just ending, thereby presenting an article-length exposition of Joel Garreau's Hell scenario. He noted that, because of their military emphasis and use of controlled materials, the older technologies would be implemented only by governments that could limit their proliferation, something not true of the newer ones, with their history of much smaller-scale research. Joy wrote about the potential of worldwide disaster each could cause, especially through replication; as he put it, "a bomb is blown up only once - but one bot can become many, and quickly get out of control." Each of the three has perils along this line: genetic modification could be used to create a plague-like disease that would kill huge numbers of people quickly; self-reproducing robots might dominate the world; and nanotechnology could cause what Joy and other observers have called the "gray goo problem," in which self-replicating man-made bacteria could "reduce the biosphere to dust in a matter of days."[312]

So why did Bill Joy think the future wouldn't need us? If we all die from a worldwide disaster, nobody will have one. If no such thing happens, what might? What would that, in turn, mean for careers after 2033?

Merging with Computers—Would We Still Be Conscious?

Ray Kurzweil, a staunch believer in Joel Garreau's Heaven scenario, wrote in 2005 not only that "within several decades information-based technologies will encompass all human knowledge and proficiency, ultimately including the pattern-recognition powers [and] problem-solving skills" but that they would "display the full range of emotionally rich behavior exhibited by biological humans" and would also contain "the emotional and moral intelligence of the human brain itself."[313] For Kurzweil, human nature is "a pattern of information,"[314] meaning it can be transferred to other platforms, and even with massive enhancements nobody would lose their humanity.[315] Through merging with or being uploaded onto computers, people would be allowed to live the length of time they choose.[316] In the 2040s, we may be able to create new parts of ourselves, either of organic material or not.[317] In 2005 Kurzweil projected the Singularity, allowing us to go beyond the human brain's restrictions, for 2045, with the amount of machine intelligence thus far created being one billion times the human variety.[318] After that, we, or our human-cyborg descendants, would reconfigure matter and energy to acquire its own intelligence, limited only by, as far as we know now, the speed of light.[319] Kurzweil pointed out that, due to the nature of exponential growth, his projections would be delayed remarkably short times if the computational requirements proved much greater than expected; if he underestimated the total amount of speed and memory needed by a factor of one thousand, one million, or even one billion, the additional time needed would be only, respectively, 8, 15, and 21 years.[320]

There is a problem here, though. Could uploaded minds really think? In other words, what is awareness, and from where does it arise?

Roger Penrose, Oxford mathematics professor and author on consciousness, saw four general reasonable opinions on its nature. In the first, it is algorithmic and arises from carrying out computational procedures. Second, it originates in the brain and would not come from calculating in itself but can be simulated by machines. Third, it also emanates from the brain but cannot be replicated elsewhere. Fourth, it has no physical source, so cannot even be approximated through any kind of technology.[321]

Ray Kurzweil, a strong disciple of the first position, saw a steady transition from the unimproved humans of centuries ago, through technology already achieved in the form of computerized neural implants, to exponential advancement of these enhancements, and on to electronic brain components becoming their major parts.[322] Most important, he wrote, will be a "gradual transfer of our intelligence, personality, and skills to the nonbiological portion of our intelligence."[323]

The Turing test, named after computing pioneer Alan Turing, is given when someone remotely poses questions to a computer and one or more people and tries to identify which respondent is not human.[324] Ray Kurzweil claimed computers would pass it by 2029.[325] One who advocated Roger Penrose's first possibility would consider any computer passing the Turing test to be conscious itself. Yet it has a conceptual shortcoming. Although Kurzweil defined the human respondents as being "average educated,"[326] the outcome could vary depending on the knowledge of the assessor. I once proudly told a friend that I had served an ace—a starting shot that was inbounds and not returned—at tennis. He asked, "Against whom?" Indeed, all tennis opponents are not equal in ability, and there is no such thing as an ace in the abstract. As well, what would deceive someone unfamiliar with a range of machines, or for that matter with an assortment of humans, might not fool one knowing more.

In the second case above, even if a mechanical device could always act indistinguishably from a person, it would not have consciousness at all; therefore, no robot could actually understand its own actions.[327] Computers could potentially pass any Turing test, no matter how challenging or how sophisticated the judge, but here they would have no more knowledge of what they were doing than this laptop does when running Microsoft Word.

Roger Penrose himself advocated the third position, having concluded that technologies cannot even fully simulate intelligence, since, as he saw it, the mind itself is more than algorithmic.[328] Therefore, we would need to do more than replicate the structure of the brain to generate actual intellect, as opposed to making something only seeming to be intelligent, since for him the source of consciousness involves quantum physics[329] and so cannot be precisely reproduced. The fourth viewpoint was endorsed by philosophy professor John Searle, who said that awareness was too subjective for us to ever know what it was, and that nobody could ever be sure that it was really there.[330] That could be described as a religious view or one of a unified universe-level consciousness.

The potential downside of uploading a mind is the greatest possible. If awareness ends when a brain is destroyed and does not continue even if the exact molecular arrangement is recreated elsewhere, then, as ethics professor Nicholas Agar put it, uploading is the same as death and would "turn out the light of conscious experience just as surely as does a gunshot to the head."[331] It is possible that the *Star Trek* characters, after being repeatedly teleported from one place to another, had all long since lost their awareness.[332] Another problem with uploaded humans is that of the morality such entities could have, as they could determine that others should get the same treatment and force that on them.[333]

In any event, we cannot be sure whether a computer, no matter how faithfully designed, would be conscious. Even Ray Kurzweil agreed that advanced machines would "claim to have emotional and spiritual experiences, just as we do today," and he admitted there was no unbiased test to determine the presence of awareness, something we only assume exists in other people.[334] He thought that, eventually, since "'they' will be us," it would be accepted that such human-like machines would be conscious, but conceded that a world without awareness was as good as nonexistent.[335]

That is what we need to avoid. A planet of unconscious robots might seem to some to contain life, as an air conditioner turning on might to one who had never seen a house. The problem of other minds, in which we cannot conclusively know other people are aware, is ancient to philosophy but is essentially meaningless to us now, as all of our ways of thinking point to others being conscious.[336] That will be different with nonbiological entities seeming to be intelligent. Roger Penrose's four viewpoints, while well defined, are at the level of understanding human anatomy was before discovery of the circulation of blood, which points up how undeveloped our comprehension of awareness actually is.

Outside of trusting our minds to machines, what other profound, but less drastic, improvements might be here soon or are already?

Beyond Glasses and Hearing Aids: Super Powers and Other Improvements Through Technology

A less extreme use for technology than uploading mental capacity is, and has been, augmenting the body. Devices to do that have been around at least since eyeglasses were invented in 1200s Italy[337] and now include installed items such as cochlear implants for hearing and lenses after cataract surgery. Enhancements need not be physical; author and political scientist Francis Fukuyama proposed that selective serotonin reuptake inhibitors such as Prozac might also constitute a step toward what might be called "posthumanism."[338]

Many superhuman abilities depicted in comic books of the past already exist, though have not propagated. Telekinetics—the ability to make something move simply by thinking certain thoughts—has been practiced by an owl monkey that moved robot arms in Massachusetts from North Carolina.[339] Brain-to-brain communication was achieved in late 2012.[340] As of 2005, an extremely strong nanotech exoskeleton suit was under development, and Superman-style telescopic and X-ray vision are current military realities. Gene doping, or changing DNA to improve physical capabilities, has worked with laboratory animals.[341]

Many technical solutions to health and anatomical problems have recently arrived, or are expected to appear this decade. Implants are being developed to allow blind people to see in some fashion,[342] blinded rats have had their vision restored in fewer than 24 hours,[343] two men with retinitis pigmentosa had some vision restored by electronic implants,[344] and Stanford scientists made a working prototype of a light-powered bionic eye.[345] The exoskeletons mentioned above are being modified to allow non-ambulatory people to walk,[346] and a paralyzed person succeeded in traversing all 26.2 miles of a May 2012 marathon, using one.[347] Previously nonambulatory rats have done even better, managing to run very quickly after electrochemical therapy.[348] Northwestern University scientists pioneered a human brain-to-computer interface to allow muscle movement in incapacitated limbs from thoughts alone,[349] and a system allowing people to communicate by only thinking of specific letters of the alphabet has reached the proof-of-concept stage.[350] Genes causing cystic fibrosis, sickle-cell anemia, and hemophilia in humans have been swapped out.[351] And, as many people saw, in the 2012 Olympics sprinter Oscar Pistorius competed, at world-class speeds, using only artificial appliances below his knees.[352]

Technology will not only replace defective structures in the body but has the potential to maintain health in ones already there. Per Ray Kurzweil, we should expect to improve everything in the brain and body through reengineering.[353] Nanobots, or microscopic robots, may be introduced internally and serve such purposes as reversing aging,[354] serving as extra red-blood cells,[355] removing toxins and pathogens, working in the brain to increase intelligence, and even creating virtual reality through contact with nerve cells.[356] Tiny particles designed to imitate parts of a rat's immune system were found by Duke University researchers in 2012 to strengthen responses to vaccines.[357] In 2005 Kurzweil expected nanobots in the 2020s to improve human "sensory processing and memory, moving on to skill formation, pattern recognition, and logical analysis."[358] Since then, researchers have successfully used magnetic resonance imaging devices to steer bacteria through the body.[359]

How many would actually consent to using these things? Although people often think they would resist such enhancements for themselves or their families, they are not consistent. Journalist David Ewing Duncan asked groups for a show of hands on three questions: first, if they would give their children a pill to improve their memory by up to 25%; second, if they would give them that pill if it were safe and could improve them from B to A students; third, if they would if all of the others were taking them as well. The results were typically more than 80% saying no to the first but almost half responding yes to the second and nearly all agreeing with the third.[360] Technological augmentations may also be required for people in some careers; bioethicist Thomas H. Murray claimed it could someday be considered immoral for a surgeon to decline to take a drug to make his hand steadier.[361]

What could be the downside of massive genetic or physical improvement? As with uploaded humans, observers are concerned with the possibility of technically upgraded people dominating others, as well as with the chance of war between the two varieties, if the unenhanced take preemptive measures against those technologically superior.[362] Artificially created intelligent, or pseudo-intelligent, beings could cause similar and severe problems, as they could replace any directive they had to be benign with hostile strategies consistent with their other purposes.[363]

In all, there are many things in use, in development, or projected for the next few decades that could greatly enhance people without any need to resort to uploading. How much further could that go, without moving humans to a whole new physical platform? Maybe as far as in a BBC science fiction series, *Doctor Who*, which had characters called "cybermen" who had replaced all of their flesh except their brains with metal and other nonorganic materials.[364] So how might technology be used to improve the most important thing we have—our life spans?

The 150-Year (or Longer) Life

Aging in general prevents people from going beyond the current longevity range. As its causes, author and gerontologist Aubrey DeGrey identified seven components. They are the loss of important cells, the taking on of unwanted cells such as with cancer, two varieties of DNA mutations, waste accumulation within and outside of cells, and crosslinking of proteins, which causes problems such as hardening of the arteries.[365] Some of these, such as intracell garbage, are never factors with current lifespans but would be after multiple centuries.[366] How can we stop them? Future methods could include deactivating destructive genes, treatment to change an individual's genetic code, cell cloning for regeneration, and advanced metabolic medications, which if combined could maintain a person's overall health equivalent to that of someone in his or her 30s,[367] along with preventing cancer, a disease which could preclude indefinite life, by removing the telomerase gene, which normally controls cell division.[368] A drug to help with the problem of waste within cells was already identified by University of Michigan researchers in 2012.[369] Per author K. Eric Drexler, nanobots may "soon work like Pac-Man, gobbling up diseased cells and keeping the human body perpetually in tune."[370]

The greatest advantages of these technologies would not be restricted to those born after their availability. In order for people to live endlessly, he or she would need only to achieve what Aubrey DeGrey has termed "longevity escape velocity," when methods to stop aging add to remaining life expectancy quicker than it decreases naturally.[371] So how might that happen? In 2003, President George W. Bush signed legislation to provide $3.7 billion in possible medical nanobot research funding.[372] Beyond that, the cost of an all-out program to reverse aging would cost in the tens of billions of dollars, and, as with the Apollo space program, such an effort would call for advancements in science.[373] That could still have massive appeal; per DeGrey, it is likely that money spent on radical lifespan increases could provide more healthy person-years than any other project, including peacekeeping, feeding hungry people, or curing any disease.[374]

Another way people have hoped to continue after their lives would otherwise end is through cryonics. Participants in that procedure make arrangements for their bodies, or only their heads, to be preserved at far subzero temperatures in the hopes of being revived and their causes of death reversed someday.[375] That is nothing new, and, aside from technical maintenance matters, its possible problems include how future generations might deal with such "corpsicles."[376]

One thought-provoking issue sure to arise if lifespans shoot up is on attitudes toward risk. Many people might become extremely opposed to it, even declining to drive or ride in cars, if they knew an accident could cost not decades but centuries of life.[377] Nicholas Agar predicted that those not aging biologically would "retreat from the world," engaging only or mostly in the virtual equivalents of sex and travel while indulging heavily in food, alcohol, and tobacco, knowing those things could not kill them.[378] On the other hand, indefinite lifespans could produce such things as inventing new art forms, listening to extremely sophisticated and as yet uncomposed music, extensively playing games more rich and complex than any known now, and doing prodigious amounts of volunteer work.[379] My own informal survey of intelligent people without special knowledge in the field precipitated seven responses: three said indefinite natural lives would have little or no effect on risk tolerance, two said they would make people more risk-averse, one said they would result in higher acceptance analogous to physical risk-taking peaking at around age 20 when remaining time alive is perceived to be very long, and one maintained there would be too much individual variation for any pattern to be identified. Therefore, what is clearest to me is that we don't know what effect on risk attitudes potentially vastly longer lives would bring.

In all, what Aubrey DeGrey called "engineered negligible senescence"[380] has real potential and could bring different attitudes. It would not carry the same concerns as uploading but would, however, have other philosophical, societal, and logistical problems, which I will leave to the reader.

What Else by 2045?

One trend seems sure to continue: The United States will keep aging. The ratio of people aged 65 and over to those 20 to 64 is projected by some to increase further, to 36.8% in 2040, 39.2% in 2060, and 43.2% in 2080.[381] In 2050, there may be more than 600,000 Americans 100 or older.[382] The significances of advanced ages will continue to evolve, with many more 70, 80, and beyond still working. Baby boomers turning 81 to 99 in 2045 may well have the general health and vitality of those in their 60s in 2013 and, if the pattern established by their generation endures,[383] will often want full-time jobs.

Other long-range predictions have already been made. Urban futures expert Joel Kotkin saw two important trends for work in 2050: the continuing tendency for jobs to become virtual, which we have discussed; and the growing ability of Americans to choose the areas in which they live without regard to their work, resulting in movement between cities reversing its long-term increase.[384] The 2011 *New York Times* reader survey mentioned previously also named more distant developments, specifically enhanced electronic brainpower "available to most people" by 2058, a computer program with all features of human intelligence by 2063, entire full-brain memory backups by 2114, and ability to download knowledge mentally from a gigantic database by 2259.[385] These forecasts may be component parts of the Singularity, should the Heaven scenario come to pass.

Where Are We Going?

Technical predictions often fail. Joel Garreau named five general reasons why they do.[386] First, what was projected may turn out to be much more complicated than expected, such as understanding how cancer starts or how we can get electricity from nuclear fusion. Second, costs can be prohibitive, which explains, for example, the lack of magnetic levitation trains in America. Third, new and perhaps unexpected technologies may replace those involved, revealing why each home does not contain a mainframe computer. Fourth, negative experiences about the possibility can dampen or eliminate its use, which have prevented establishment of a nationwide identification database. Fifth, human behavior may conflict with the technology in unforeseen ways or to an unexpected extent, which is why we are still using so much private transportation. We should always view forecasts through these filters, as any one of them could cause the most informed, well thought out, and well analyzed prognostications to go the way of flying cars.

These are not the only problems with forecasting great technical change. Innovations, even when developed, produced, and accepted, are not always readily available, or even obtainable at all.[387] As profound as they could be, even the gains of the Singularity could face insufficient marketability, as many would require extremely high investments in the face of a small and shrinking set of those with the work income or other resources to afford them.[388] As one instance, moon-landing technology, now almost 50 years old, now goes unused and un-updated for lack of any funding source.

As for the brain, regardless of which of Roger Penrose's consciousness possibilities is correct, it is not clear that comprehending it will progress exponentially. Although Moore's Law, the doubling of speed and capacity of computing resources every 18 months, and as of 2005 down to about 12, also relates to the total of human knowledge,[389] it does not always apply to understanding specific things, many of which have been elusive. Strengths of human intelligence over what machines can do include identifying patterns, especially those with subtle common threads, and ability to learn not only from personal experience but through language.[390] We also do not know enough to determine if memories and feelings are entirely products of cell or even molecule arrangement.[391] In all, we could easily miss something, even if our technology allows scanning and uploading of entire brains, or, for that matter, billions of them. If these issues become critical, or if, as author Peter D. Kramer has contended, the brain is unknowable,[392] even computers becoming much faster due to their integrated circuits being replaced by nanotubes, their emerging ability to design themselves,[393] and the promise of quantum technology[394] will not be enough for us to comprehend the brain well enough to fully upload it.

There is another real objection to projecting a civilization improving at or nearly at the rate of computer speed. Not everything will progress along with it. Applying even the most conservative rate of Moore's Law to the time from 2004 to 2013 gives a 64-fold increase, during which, in addition to swifter electronics, we have had a variety of technical improvements and even breakthroughs, particularly in the area of genetics. The first genomic map of the entire human brain was created in the summer of 2012,[395] and a fundamentally more detailed view of human genetic structure, with 80% of all DNA being determined to serve a specific function, was completed later that year.[396] But how different are our lifestyles?[397] Ray Kurzweil and others have often seemed to downplay the difference between the current cutting edge and what people are actually using; embedded bases are not automatically updated by technology that is improved, even radically. Many American automobiles in use today do not approach the sophistication of concept cars designed this year, and even the features of the latest production models do not make their way to people without them. As author William Gibson wrote, "The future is already here — it's just not evenly distributed."[398]

On irregular allocation, what if advantages from the Singularity occur but do not spread through the entire population? American people could split into two groups, a division much more profound than the 1% and 99%. The more advanced could have extremely high machine-implemented intelligence and superhuman life expectancies and might be described, as British journalist Andrew Orlowski put it, as "rich people building a lifeboat and getting off the ship."[399] Joel Garreau saw three possible clusters in such a world: "The Enhanced," who are and greatly so; "The Naturals," who decline opportunities to become technologically improved; and "The Rest," never offered the choice.[400] In the view of geneticist Lee Silver, genetic enrichment could even create a new species, with upgraded body structures actually preventing normal reproduction[401] and the differences between the two groups, even if breeding between them were made possible, widened by lower romantic interest for people in the other set.[402]

What about jobs, and careers, if the Heaven scenario of the Singularity materializes? They could both just about go away. Yet, though Ray Kurzweil wrote about abundant prosperity, it is not clear how people, especially those of average intelligence and ordinary skills, could then earn significant money. As I pointed out in *Work's New Age*, markets can work only if there is demand as well as supply,[403] and if the realities of automation, globalization, scalability, and efficiency mean that many have little salable to offer, businesses will need different methods to get the new customers they require, which, per Jim Clifton and former Treasury secretary Robert Reich, is the largest predictor of new jobs.[404] As Martin Ford put it, "The technologists who speculate about the Singularity don't seem too concerned about this problem," and he pointed out that without consumer demand spurring production, we would no longer have a market economy, free or otherwise.[405] Indeed, in *The Singularity Is Near*, Kurzweil devotes four pages to the effect of the Singularity on work, mentioning that there will be more and more automation, but does not discuss the problem of people still being paid,[406] and in a 2012 *Washington Post* article, titled "Ray Kurzweil on the Future Workforce," he talked about both open-source information providing basic needs and the requirement that businesses have markets for their products, but not at all on how ordinary citizens could be either buyers or sellers.[407]

In all, with 32 years until Ray Kurzweil's projected Singularity date of 2045, the Prevail scenario seems most likely. If that holds, then while technological improvement will affect almost all areas of our society, it will not dominate. Most likely, we will still have jobs and careers, though the number of people in them will drop precipitously. Will the future need us? Yes. How? We will see.

Appendix:

Detailed Meanings of Job Field Items

Job Field Item	Value	Meaning
Job		The Detailed Occupation from the Bureau of Labor Statistics, when available.
Occupation Group		The name of the occupation from the Bureau of Labor Statistics.
Local-Boundness (HML)	High	The job must always or almost always be performed locally by someone living within commuting distance from the work location.
	Medium	One of two situations: 1) The job will usually be performed locally, as above, or 2) The job will always or almost always be performed locally with high likelihood of someone living elsewhere and traveling to different work locations.
	Low	The job will have little or no need to be performed locally in 2033.
Resistance to Robotics (HML)	High	The job has little or no chance to be replaced by robot technology by 2033.
	Medium	The job has a significant chance to be replaced by robot technology by 2033.
	Low	The job has a high chance to be replaced by robot technology by 2033.
Resistance to Computing Algorithms and Connectivity (HML)	High	The job has little or no chance to be made unnecessary to be worked by humans, due to direct applications of computing algorithms or improved computing connectivity, by 2033.
	Medium	The job has a significant chance to be made unnecessary to be worked by humans, due to direct applications of computing algorithms or improved computing connectivity, by 2033.
	Low	The job has a high chance to be made unnecessary to be worked by humans, due to direct applications of computing algorithms or improved computing connectivity, by 2033.
Pertinent Principles (Good)	1	Rating of High in both Resistance to Robotics, and Resistance to Computing Algorithms and Connectivity fields.

	3	Rating of High in Local-Boundness field.
	4	Less than 40% of those working the job have, according to BLS 2012 statistics, or according to author's judgment when statistics are not available, access to an employer-sponsored health insurance plan.
	6	The job has little or no potential to allow more production or results during less time, either through different procedures or better technology.
	7	At least 40% of the goods and services produced by the job will, by 2033, be consumed by people in the top 1% of income or net worth.
	8	The job produces goods and services with special appeal to those working over 45 hours per week.
	18	The job has potential for work teaching people how to do unpaid activities for their own sake.
Pertinent Principles (Maybe Good)	5	A majority of the job activity involves working for one customer at a time.
	9	The job produces goods and services with a strong connection to non-business travel, except local errands, of any kind.
	10	The job can be performed successfully at professional standards by less than 5% of the population, even if training or education is made generally available.
	11	The job requires construction-related skills at a specific task or tasks requiring extensive training or experience.
	12	The job produces goods and services required for highway, road, bridge, or airport repair, design, or construction.
	13	The job requires a doctoral or professional degree, or requires credentials not obtainable through merit or effort by the general population.
	14	At least 60% of people in the job are, or are often perceived to be, women.
	15	Either 1) people in the job are strongly preferred by employers or customers to be Americans, or 2) the job has cultural or linguistic requirements strongly likely to be only possessed by Americans.
	19	The job produces goods and services designed to enhance physical or mental health.
	20	Over 50% of the goods and services produced by the job will be, as of 2033, consumed by people aged 65 and over.

Pertinent Principles (Bad)	2	The job exists only or almost only because of technology, or lack of technology, expected to be replaced by 2033.
	16	Work in the job is primarily simple extraction of resources, such as farming, mining, or fishing.
	17	Work in the job is primarily manufacturing, or producing goods from resources, with the exception of food production.
Number of People In It, as of 2010 (OOH)		The number of people working full-time at that job, for an outside employer, as of 2010 (OOH, pp. 26-991).
Chance for Good Living Wage for Those Working In It (HML)	High	The job, when held, is very likely to pay the equivalent of at least $40,000 per year, with typical benefits at that level adjusted if not.
	Medium	The job, when held, is moderately likely to pay the equivalent of at least $40,000 per year, with typical benefits at that level adjusted if not.
	Low	The job has little or no potential to pay the equivalent of at least $40,000 per year, with typical benefits at that level adjusted if not.
2010 Median Pay and Benefits (HML)	High	As of 2010, median pay for the job was over $80,000 per year, with typical benefits at that level adjusted if not. (OOH, pp. 26-991)
	Medium	As of 2010, median pay for the job was between $40,000 and $80,000 per year, with typical benefits at that level adjusted if not. (OOH, pp. 26-991)
	Low	As of 2010, median pay for the job was under $40,000 per year, with typical benefits at that level adjusted if not. (OOH, pp. 26-991)
Median Quality of Work Conditions (HML)	High	Work circumstances and settings, both physical and emotional, are generally good or better.
	Medium	Work circumstances and settings, both physical and emotional, have significant shortcomings, but are not clearly a detraction.
	Low	One or more aspect of work circumstances and settings would be considered by the majority of people to be seriously detrimental.
Family Life and Outside Activities Compatibility (HML)	High	The job is limited in hours, regular in scheduling, and limited in travel enough to allow for a commonly regular family life and extensive work on unrelated projects and efforts.
	Medium	The job has one or more requirement with a high chance of impeding, but not preventing, regular family life and extensive work on outside projects, such as very long or irregular hours or a large amount of overnight travel.

	Low	The job has a requirement or requirements severe enough to effectively prevent regular family life or extensive work on outside projects.
Forecast for 2010-2020 Change (OOH)		The number of people projected by the BLS to be working in the job in 2020, as expressed as a percentage change from 2010 (OOH, pp. 26-991)
Forecast for 2033	Excellent	The job is projected to have one of the largest increases in workers in the United States of any occupation between 2013 and 2033.
	Very Good	The job is projected to have a large increase in workers in the United States between 2013 and 2033.
	Good	The job is projected to have a moderate increase in workers in the United States between 2013 and 2033.
	Fair	The job is projected to have about the same number of workers in the United States in 2033 as it has in 2013.
	Poor	The job is projected to have significantly fewer, maybe far fewer, workers in the United States in 2033 as compared with 2013.

Endnotes

Introduction: Which Careers Will Last?

1 Dizzy Dean Official Website, http://www.dizzydean.com/.

Chapter 1: Work's New Age

2 Joyce, Frank, "The Jobless Model," *Salon*, May 1, 2012.

3 Wikipedia entry on "Industrial Revolution," http://en.wikipedia.org/wiki/Industrial_Revolution.

4 See Beck, Ulrich (2000), translated by Patrick Camiller, *The Brave New World of Work*, pp. 12-13. Cambridge, United Kingdom: Polity Press.

5 W. Bridges, cited in Dooley, David and Joann Prause (2004), *The Social Costs of Underemployment: Inadequate Employment as Disguised Unemployment,* p. 7. Cambridge, United Kingdom: Cambridge University Press.

6 Eichengreen, Barry, "Introduction." In Aerts, Erik and Barry Eichengreen (eds.) (1990), *Unemployment and Underemployment in Historical Perspective: Session B-9, Proceedings of Tenth International Economic History Congress, Leuven, August 1990,* p. 9. Leuven, Belgium: Leuven University Press.

7 Rifkin, Jeremy (2004). *The End of Work: The Decline of the Global Labor Force and the Dawn of the Post-Market Era*, pp. 64-65. New York: Jeremy P. Tarcher/Penguin.

8 U.S. Department of Labor, cited in Kaufman, Harold G. (1982), *Professionals in Search of Work: Coping with the Stress of Job Loss and Underemployment*, p. 13. New York: John Wiley & Sons.

9 V. C. Perrella, cited in Kaufman, *Professionals in Search of Work,* p. 13.

10 Wikipedia entry on "1973 Oil Crisis," http://en.wikipedia.org/wiki/1973_oil_crisis.

11 Lakshman Achuthan, cited in Goodman, Peter S., "The New Poor: Millions of Unemployed Face Years Without Jobs," *The New York Times*, February 21, 2010.

12 Zuckerman, Mortimer B., "Unemployment Rate Is Worse Than It Looks," *U.S. News & World Report*, August 20, 2010.

13 Ryan, Mary Meghan (ed.), (2009). *Handbook of U.S. Labor Statistics: Employment, Earnings, Prices, Productivity, and Other Labor Data* (12th ed.), p. 9. Lanham, MD: Bernan Press; Bureau of Labor Statistics.

14 See Huntington, James B. (2012), *Work's New Age: The End of Full Employment and What It Means to You*, pp. 21-23. Eldred, NY: Royal Flush Press.

15 Peck, Don, "How a New Jobless Era Will Transform America," *The Atlantic*, March 2010.

16 Meyerson, Harold, "Corporate America, Paving a Downward Economic Slide," *The Washington Post*, January 5, 2011.

17 Bureau of Labor Statistics.

18 Goodman, "The New Poor"; Silverblatt, Rob, "Why the Unemployment Rate Refuses to Budge," *U.S. News & World Report*, April 2, 2010; Hauser, Christine, "Private Sector Improves Jobs Picture Only Moderately," *The New York Times*, January 7, 2011; Peck, "How a New Jobless Era Will Transform America"; Wolgemuth, Liz, "Why the December Jobs Report Is Such a Bust," *U.S. News & World Report*, January 8, 2010; Rich, Motoko, "Few New Jobs as Jobless Rate Rises to 9.8%," *The New York Times*, December 3, 2010; Center for Economic and Policy Research, "We Need 90,000 Jobs Per Month to Keep Pace With the Growth of the Population," July 9, 2011, http://www.cepr.net/index.php/blogs/beat-the-press/we-need-90000-jobs-per-month-to-keep-pace-with-the-growth-of-the-population; Cook, Robert, "Ryan: "We Want a Safety Net," Hampton–North Hampton Patch, September 18, 2012.

19 Ryan, *Handbook of U.S. Labor Statistics,* pp. 9, 92; Bureau of Labor Statistics.

20 Calculated from Ryan, *Handbook of U.S. Labor Statistics,* pp. 83, 103; Bureau of Labor Statistics.

21 Calculated from Ryan, *Handbook of U.S. Labor Statistics,* pp. 30, 39; Bureau of Labor Statistics. The 2012 data is the average of the first six months.

22 Davidson, Adam, "The Dwindling Power of a College Degree," *The New York Times*, November 23, 2011.

23 Ryan, *Handbook of U.S. Labor Statistics,* p. 140; Bureau of Labor Statistics. The trend line is not shown, as it is very close to the actual data.

24 Bureau of Labor Statistics.

25 Brownstein, Ronald, "Our Upside-Down Workforce," *The Atlantic*, June 2011.

26 Plumer, Brad, "The Incredible Shrinking Labor Force," *The Washington Post*, May 4, 2012.

27 Huntington, *Work's New Age,* pp. 23-37.

28 Ibid., pp. 27-28.

29 Ibid., p. 31; Huntington, James B., "Introducing the American Job Shortage Number," Work's New Age blog, September 4, 2012, http://worksnewage.blogspot.com/2012/09/introducing-works-new-age-american-job.html.

30 See Huntington, *Work's New Age,* pp. 34-36.

31 Huntington, "Introducing the American Job Shortage Number."

32 Bureau of Labor Statistics. All unadjusted data; calculated from U.S. Census Bureau.

33 Clifton, Jim (2011). *The Coming Jobs War,* p. 2. New York: Gallup Press.

34 "Fed Boss: It Will Take Years for Jobs to Come Back," *U.S. News & World Report*, January 7, 2011.

35 Zuckerman, Mortimer P., "The American Jobs Machine is Clanging to a Halt," *U.S. News & World Report,* October 1, 2010.

36 Zuckerman, Mortimer P., "The Great Jobs Recession Goes On," *U.S. News & World Report*, February 11, 2011.

37 Johnson, Simon, "Employment vs. Corporate Profit," Room for Debate blog, *The New York Times*, January 17, 2011, http://www.nytimes.com/roomfordebate.

38 Samuelson, Robert J., "The Big Hiring Freeze," *Newsweek*, July 23, 2010.

39 Toles, Tom, "Works for him," *The Washington Post*, November 28, 2010.

40 Toles, Tom, "Shape of things to come," *The Washington Post*, February 22, 2011.

41 Ford, Martin (2009), *The Lights in the Tunnel: Automation, Accelerating Technology, and the Economy of the Future*, p. 112. Acculant Publishing.

42 See Huntington, *Work's New Age,* pp. 43-45.

43 Skandalaris, Bob (2006). *Rebuilding the American Dream: Restoring American Jobs and Competitiveness Through Innovation and Entrepreneurship*, p. 18. Bloomfield Hills, MI: Pembrook Publishing.

44 Pelton, Joseph N. and Peter Marshall (2010). *MegaCrunch!: Ten Survival Strategies for 21st Century Challenges*, p. 44. Bethesda, MD: PMAssociates.

45 Pelton and Marshall, *MegaCrunch!,* p. 45.

46 Skandalaris, *Rebuilding the American Dream,* p. 18.

47 Pelton and Marshall, *MegaCrunch!,* p. 45.

48 Bureau of Labor Statistics, cited in Ford, *The Lights in the Tunnel,* p. 60.

49 Markoff, John, "Armies of Expensive Lawyers, Replaced by Cheaper Software," *The New York Times*, March 4, 2011.

50 Zuckerman, "The American Jobs Machine Is Clanging to a Halt."

51 Rifkin, *The End of Work*, p. 5.

52 Zuckerman, "The Great Jobs Recession Goes On."

53 Ford, *The Lights in the Tunnel,* p. 3.

54 Pelton and Marshall, *MegaCrunch!,* p. 7.

55 Ford, *The Lights in the Tunnel,* p. 64.

56 Ibid., pp. 72-73.

57 Rifkin, *The End of Work*, p. xxii; Ford, Martin, "What If There's No Fix for High Unemployment?," CNNMoney.com, June 10, 2010, http://money.cnn.com/.

58 Rifkin, *The End of Work*, p. 289.

59 Brooks, David, "The Experience Economy." *The New York Times*, February 14, 2011.

60 Ford, *The Lights in the Tunnel,* pp. 9, 67.

61 Vonnegut Jr., Kurt (1952). *Player Piano,* p. 199. New York: Avon Books.

62 Huntington, *Work's New Age,* p. 52.

63 Tom G. Palmer, cited in Wikipedia entry on "Globalization," http://en.wikipedia.org/wiki/Globalization.

64 Cited in Steingart, Gabor (2008), *The War for Wealth: The True Story of Globalization, or Why the Flat World is Broken*, p. 135. New York: McGraw-Hill.

65 McKinsey Global Institute, cited in Foroohar, Rana, "Joblessness is Here to Stay," *Newsweek*, December 12, 2009.

66 Cited in Steingart, *The War for Wealth,* p. 201.

67 Foroohar, "Joblessness is Here to Stay."

68 Ford, *The Lights in the Tunnel,* p. 86.

69 Shin, Hyon-hee, "Robotic Helpers Coming to Homes, Offices," *The Korea Herald*, January 19, 2011.

70 Ford, *The Lights in the Tunnel,* p. 87.

71 Ibid., p. 113.

72 See Huntington, *Work's New Age,* pp. 52-58.

73 Ibid., pp. 52-57.

74 Ford, *The Lights in the Tunnel,* p. 133.

75 See Huntington, *Work's New Age,* pp. 58-63.

76 Clifton, *The Coming Jobs War,* p. 146.

77 Ibid., p. 150.

78 See Huntington, *Work's New Age,* p. 129.

79 David M. Cutler and Brigitte C. Madrian, cited in Eibner, Christine (2008), *The Economic Burden of Providing Health Insurance: How Much Worse Off Are Small Firms?*, p. 2. Santa Monica, CA: The RAND Corporation.

80 Cowen, Tyler, "Some Jobs Aren't Needed," Room for Debate blog, *The New York Times*, January 17, 2011, http://www.nytimes.com/roomfordebate.

81 Beck, *The Brave New World of Work,* p. 114.

82 Zuckerman, Mortimer B., "The Jobless Recovery Remains Issue Number One," *U.S. News & World Report*, May 28, 2010.

83 Calculated from Ryan, *Handbook of U.S. Labor Statistics,* p. 258; Bureau of Labor Statistics. The 2012 data is the average of the first three quarters.

84 Ryan, *Handbook of U.S. Labor Statistics,* p. 256.

85 Reich, Robert B., "The Limping Middle Class," *The New York Times*, September 4, 2011.

86 Wellner, Alison Stein, "Tapping a Silver Mine," *HR Magazine*, March 2002.

87 AARP (2004). *Baby Boomers Envision Retirement II: Survey of Baby Boomers' Expectations for Retirement.* Washington, DC, http://www.aarp.org/research/work/employment/.

88 Newman, Rick, "Why Baby Boomers Are Bummed Out," *U.S. News & World Report*, December 29, 2010.

89 Ted Fishman, cited in Brandon, Emily, "The Baby Boomers Turn 65," *U.S. News & World Report*, December 20, 2010.

90 Bureau of Labor Statistics.

91 Newman, "Why Baby Boomers Are Bummed Out."

92 Newman, Rick, "New Rules for a Darwinian Economy," *U.S. News & World Report*, January 19, 2010.

93 Bureau of Labor Statistics.

94 Thompson, Derek, "The Four Horsemen of the Job-Pocalypse," *The Atlantic*, August 2010.

95 See Huntington, *Work's New Age,* pp. 71-73.

96 Samuelson, Robert J., "The Mystery of Stubborn Unemployment," *Newsweek*, October 8, 2010.

97 Cappelli, Peter, "If There's a Gap, Blame It on the Employer," *The New York Times*, July 9, 2012.

98 Green, Alison, "10 Mistakes Employers Make in Hiring," *U.S. News & World Report*, July 21, 2008.

99 Shapiro, Cynthia (2008). *What Does Somebody Have to Do to Get a Job Around Here?*, p. 192. New York: St. Martin's Press.

100 See Samuelson, "The Mystery of Stubborn Unemployment."

101 Pearlstein, Steven, "The Bleak Truth About Unemployment," *The Washington Post*, September 7, 2010.

102 See Huntington, *Work's New Age,* pp. 69-71.

103 Cappelli, "If There's a Gap, Blame It on the Employer."

104 Cappelli, Peter (2012*). Why Good People Can't Get Jobs: The Skills Gap and What Companies Can Do About It*, pp. 43-44. Philadelphia: Wharton Digital Press.

105 Cited in O'Brien, Matthew, "I Can't Stop Looking at These Terrifying Long-Term Unemployment Charts," *The Atlantic*, December 2012.

106 Bureau of Labor Statistics.

107 Cited in Gutting, Gary, "What Work Is Really For," Opinionator blog, *The New York Times*, September 8, 2012, http://opinionator.blogs.nytimes.com/2012/09/08/work-good-or-bad/.

108 Kahn, Herman, William Brown, and Leon Martel (1976). *The Next 200 Years: A Scenario for America and the World*, p. 22. New York: William Morrow and Company, Inc.

109 Cited in Gutting, "What Work Is Really For."

110 Joyce, "The Jobless Model."

111 Ford, "What If There's No Fix for High Unemployment?"

112 Heather Boushey, cited in "Can Obama Create More Jobs Soon?", Room For Debate blog, *The New York Times*, June 24, 2010, http://www.nytimes.com/roomfordebate.

113 Rosen, Nick (2010). *Off the Grid: Inside the Movement for More Space, Less Government, and True Independence in Modern America*, p. 13. New York: Penguin Books.

114 See Huntington, *Work's New Age*, pp. 132-133.

115 Fisker, Jacob Lund (2010). *Early Retirement Extreme: A Philosophical and Practical Guide to Financial Independence*, pp. 85, 135, 176, 177. USA: softcover book published by www.earlyretirementextreme.com.

116 Clyatt, Bob (2007). *Work Less, Live More: The Way to Semi-Retirement* (2nd ed.), p. 78. Berkeley, CA: Nolo.

117 See Huntington, *Work's New Age*, p. 135.

118 Posner, Richard A., "Working 9 to 12," *The New York Times*, August 19, 2012.

119 Gallup Monthly, cited in Gorz, Andre (1999), translated by Chris Turner. *Reclaiming Work: Beyond the Wage-Based Society*, p. 63. Cambridge, United Kingdom: Polity Press.

120 Baird, Julia, "Redefining Failure," *Newsweek*, September 12, 2010.

121 See Huntington, *Work's New Age*, pp. 155-157.

Chapter 2: What's Ahead for Workers, and the Rest of Us

122 Davidson, Adam, "Vote Obamney!," *The New York Times*, October 9, 2012.

123 Douthat, Ross, "The Magic Is Gone," *The New York Times*, September 8, 2012.

124 Davidson, "Vote Obamney!."

125 Reich, Robert, "The Factory Jobs Aren't Coming Back," *Salon.com*, February 17, 2012.

126 Romney for President website, http://www.mittromney.com/jobsplan.

127 Full Text of Obama's State of the Union Address," *The News-Herald* website, http://www.thenewsherald.com.

128 Ibid.

129 "We Don't Turn Back. We Leave No One Behind. We Pull Each Other Up: President Barack Obama's Prepared Remarks at the DNC," *Slate Magazine*, September 7, 2012.

130 "Full Text of Obama's State of the Union Address."

131 Ibid.

132 Ibid.

133 Ibid.

134 "Full Text of Obama's State of the Union Address"; Romney for President website.

135 Davidson, "Vote Obamney!."

136 Sharma, Ruchir, "Obama Won Because Voters Understand Economics," *The Atlantic*, November 2012.

137 Weisman, Jonathan, "Senate Passes Legislation to Allow Taxes on Affluent to Rise." *The New York Times*, January 1, 2013.

138 Yglesias, Matthew, "How Obama Can Beat Gridlock: The Bush Tax Cut Expiration Will Force Compromise," *Slate Magazine*, September 6, 2012.

139 Yglesias, "How Obama Can Beat Gridlock."

140 Douthat, "The Magic Is Gone."

141 Yglesias, "How Obama Can Beat Gridlock."

142 Per Friedman, Thomas L., "Hope and Change: Part 2," *The New York Times*, November 7, 2012, in October 2010, Senate Minority Leader Mitch McConnell was quoted as saying, "The single most important thing we want to achieve is for President Obama to be a one-term president."

143 Douthat, "The Magic Is Gone."

144 Brooks, David, "Character, Not Audacity," *The New York Times*, September 6, 2012.

145 Ezra Klein, cited in Douthat, "The Magic Is Gone."

146 See "Full Text of Obama's State of the Union Address" and "We Don't Turn Back."

147 McManus, Doyle, "Gridlock Likely in Washington No Matter Who Wins Presidential Race," *Los Angeles Times*, August 23, 2012.

148 DeLong, Brad, "Full Transcript Plus Video from Chairman Bernanke's Press Conference: December 12, 2012," http://delong.typepad.com/sdj/2012/12/transcript-of-chairman-bernankes-press-conference-december-12-2012.html.

149 Samuelson, Robert J., "The Fed Rolls the Dice," *The Washington Post*, December 16, 2012; Reich, Robert, "Why The Fed's Jobs Program Will Fail," Robert Reich blog, http://robertreich.org/.

150 Brooks, "Character, Not Audacity."

151 Calmes, Jackie, "Obama Criticizes Republicans Over Student Loan Rates," *The New York Times*, June 7, 2012.

152 Martin, Andrew and Andrew Lehren, "A Generation Hobbled by the Soaring Cost of College," *The New York Times*, May 12, 2012.

153 FinAid.org, cited in Carrns, Ann, "College Students Don't View Debt as Burden," Bucks blog, *The New York Times*, June 15, 2011, http://bucks.blogs.nytimes.com/2011/06/15/college-students-surprising-attitude-toward-debt/.

154 "Heavy Debt, but No Degree," *The New York Times*, May 29, 2012.

155 Martin and Lehren, "A Generation Hobbled by the Soaring Cost of College."

156 FinAid.org, cited in Carrns, "College Students Don't View Debt as Burden."

157 Lewin, Tamar, "Burden of College Loans on Graduates Grows," *The New York Times*, April 11, 2012; Lewin, Tamar, "College Graduates' Debt Burden Grew, Yet Again, in 2010," *The New York Times*, November 2, 2011.

158 Lewin, "College Graduates' Debt Burden Grew, Yet Again, in 2010."

159 Hamilton, Walter, "Average student-loan debt rises again – to more than $26,000," *Los Angeles Times*, October 18, 2012.

160 Ripley, Amanda, "College Is Dead. Long Live College!," *Time*, October 29, 2012.

161 Lewin, "College Graduates' Debt Burden Grew, Yet Again, in 2010."

162 Rampell, Catherine, "Report Details Woes of Student Loan Debt," *The New York Times*, July 20, 2012.

163 Lewin, "College Graduates' Debt Burden Grew, Yet Again, in 2010."

164 Lewin, Tamar, "Student Loan Default Rates Rise Sharply in Past Year," *The New York Times*, September 12, 2011.

165 Rampell, "Report Details Woes of Student Loan Debt."

166 Lewin, "Student Loan Default Rates Rise Sharply in Past Year."

167 Martin and Lehren, "A Generation Hobbled by the Soaring Cost of College."

168 "Heavy Debt, but No Degree."

169 Lewin, "Student Loan Default Rates Rise Sharply in Past Year."

170 Calmes, "Obama Criticizes Republicans Over Student Loan Rates"; Lewin, "Burden of College Loans on Graduates Grows."

171 Rampell, "Report Details Woes of Student Loan Debt."

172 Lewin, "Burden of College Loans on Graduates Grows."

173 Cited in Lewin, "College Graduates' Debt Burden Grew, Yet Again, in 2010."

174 Carrns, "College Students Don't View Debt as Burden."

175 Martin, Andrew, "Well-Off Will Benefit Most From Change to Student Debt Relief Plan, Study Says," *The New York Times*, October 16, 2012.

176 Associated Press, "Education Department Announces New 'Pay as You Earn' Student Loan Repayment will Start Dec. 21," *The Washington Post*, December 6, 2012.

177 Calmes, "Obama Criticizes Republicans Over Student Loan Rates."

178 Kantrowitz, Mark, and O'Shaughnessy, Lynn, "Much Ado About Double or Nothing," *The New York Times*, May 9, 2012.

179 Martin and Lehren, "A Generation Hobbled by the Soaring Cost of College."

180 Ripley, "College Is Dead. Long Live College!."

181 Martin and Lehren, "A Generation Hobbled by the Soaring Cost of College."

182 Cited in Lewin, "College Graduates' Debt Burden Grew, Yet Again, in 2010."

183 Ripley, "College Is Dead. Long Live College!."

184 See Huntington, *Work's New Age,* p. 18.

185 Brooks, David, "Après Rahm, Le Déluge," *The New York Times*, September 12, 2012.

186 See Huntington, James B., "Historical American Job Shortage Number Data, and How the AJSN Fits In," Work's New Age blog, September 16, 2012, http://worksnewage.blogspot.com/2012/09/historical-american-job-shortage-number.html, and posts since then on more recent values of the AJSN.

187 Cited in Clifton, *The Coming Jobs War*, p. 151.

188 See, for example, Farrell, Warren (2005). *Why Men Earn More: The Startling Truth Behind the Pay Gap and What Women Can Do About It.* New York: AMACOM.

189 Slaughter, Anne-Marie, "Why Women Still Can't Have It All," *The Atlantic*, July/August 2012.

190 Kurzweil, Ray (2005). *The Singularity Is Near: When Humans Transcend Biology*, p. 298. New York: Penguin Books.

191 Raymond Kurzweil, cited in Vance, Ashlee, "Merely Human? That's So Yesterday," *The New York Times*, June 11, 2010.

192 Kurzweil, *The Singularity Is Near,* pp. 338, 339.

193 Ibid., pp. 341-342.

194 Garreau, Joel (2005). *Radical Evolution: The Promise and Peril of Enhancing Our Minds, Our Bodies—and What It Means to Be Human*, pp. 130-131, 184-185, 224-225. New York: Broadway Books.

195 Ibid., p. 130.

196 Ibid., p. 184.

197 Ibid., pp. 224-225.

198 Actually, the first life form, a bacterium producing insulin, was manufactured in 1978, and the first patent for a living organism, a bacterium to consume oil spills, was issued in 1981. See, for example, http://www.thenakedscientists.com/HTML/content/interviews/interview/1110/.

199 Lin, Thomas, and Jonathan Huang, "Imagining 2076: Connect Your Brain to the Internet," *The New York Times*, December 12, 2011.

200 Kotlikoff, Laurence J. and Scott Burns (2004). *The Coming Generational Storm: What You Need to Know About America's Economic Future*, pp. xvii, 7. Cambridge, MA: The MIT Press.

Chapter 3: What All This Means for Our Career Choices

201 Thinkexist.com website, http://thinkexist.com/quotation/i_skate_to_where_the_puck_is_going_to_be-not/149961.html.

202 See, for example, Ripley, "College Is Dead. Long Live College!."

203 Indiviglio, Daniel, "The Importance of College: A Self-Fulfilling Prophecy," *The Atlantic*, June 2011.

204 Steingart, *The War for Wealth*, p. 138.

205 See Rampell, Catherine, "Degree Inflation? Jobs That Newly Require B.A.'s," Economix blog, *The New York Times*, December 4, 2012, http://economix.blogs.nytimes.com/2012/12/04/degree-inflation-jobs-that-newly-require-b-a-s/.

206 Friedman, Thomas L. and Michael Mandelbaum (2011). *That Used to Be Us: How America Fell Behind in the World*, p. 224. New York: Farrar, Straus and Giroux.

207 Rendell, Ed, "Strengthening Our Infrastructure," *Parade*, November 4, 2012.

208 Lewin, Tamar, "At Colleges, Women Are Leaving Men in the Dust," *The New York Times*, July 9, 2006; Brooks, David, "Why Men Fail," *The New York Times*, September 10, 2012.

209 The companies were Frontier Communications, PayPal, and Citibank.

210 Krikorian, Mark (2008). *The New Case Against Immigration: Both Legal and Illegal*, p. 134. New York: Sentinel.

211 Kahn, Brown, and Martel, *The Next 200 Years,* pp. 22, 23, 53.

212 See Huntington, *Work's New Age*, pp. 147-148.

213 Yglesias, Matthew, "Sectoral Shifts in the U.S. Labor Market," Moneybox blog, *Slate Magazine*, September 7, 2012, http://www.slate.com/blogs/moneybox/2012/09/07/sectoral_shifts_in_the_u_s_economy_more_waitresses_nurses_fewer_teachers_and_factory_workers_.html .

214 Ford, *The Lights in the Tunnel*, pp. 58-61.

215 Ibid., pp. 59-60.

216 Shatkin, Laurence (2012). *Best Jobs for the 21st Century* (6th ed.), p. 17. St. Paul, MN: JIST Publishing.

217 Brienza, Victoria, "Jobs Rated 2012: Ranking 200 Jobs from Best to Worst," CareerCast website, http://www.careercast.com/jobs-rated/2012-ranking-200-jobs-best-worst; "The 25 Best Jobs," *U.S, News & World Report* website, http://money.usnews.com/careers/best-jobs/rankings/the-25-best-jobs.

218 Shatkin, *Best Jobs for the 21st Century*, p. 17.

219 Graves, Jada A., "6 Careers to Watch in 2012," *U.S. News & World Report*, January 19, 2012.

220 See, for example, Light, Joe, "The Best and Worst Jobs," *The Wall Street Journal*, January 4, 2011; Auerbach, Debra, "7 Jobs That Pay $75,000 a Year," *The Chicago Tribune*, July 23, 2012; "Best Business Jobs," *U.S. News & World Report* website, http://money.usnews.com/careers/best-jobs/rankings/best-business-jobs; Auerbach, Debra, "9 Well-Paying Jobs That Don't Require a Degree," *The Chicago Tribune*, July 10, 2012.

221 Strieber, Andrew, "The 10 Worst Jobs of 2011," CareerCast website, http://www.careercast.com/jobs-rated/10-worst-jobs-2011.

222 See, for example, Rotherham, Andrew J., "The Next Great Resource Shortage: U.S. Scientists," *Time*, May 26, 2011.

223 NSF survey, cited in Vastag, Brian, "U.S. Pushes for More Scientists, But the Jobs Aren't There," *The Washington Post*, July 8, 2012.

224 *Nature* and *The Economist*, cited in Lemetti, Daniel, "Is a Science Ph.D. a Waste of Time?," *Slate Magazine*, August 31, 2012.

225 Challenger, Gray, and Christmas, cited in Vastag, "U.S. Pushes for More Scientists, But the Jobs Aren't There."

226 Vastag, "U.S. Pushes for More Scientists, But the Jobs Aren't There."

Chapter 4: The Careers: How They Compare

227 LexiYoga website, http://www.lexiyoga.com/career-quotes.

228 U.S. Department of Labor (2013). *Occupational Outlook Handbook*, pp. iii-vi. St. Paul, MN: JIST Publishing.

229 Bureau of Labor Statistics.

230 U.S. Department of Labor, *Occupational Outlook Handbook*, pp. iii-vi, 967-991.

231 Ibid., pp. 26-991.

232 Ibid.

233 Ibid.

234 Ibid.

235 Ibid.

Chapter 5: The Best Jobs, in Different Ways and in General

236 Famous Quotes and Authors website, http://www.famousquotesandauthors.com/topics/work_quotes.html.

237 U.S. Department of Labor, *Occupational Outlook Handbook*, pp. 26-991.

Chapter 6: Self-Employment: What's the Real Story?

238 Williams, Bruce, with Warren Sloat (1991). *In Business for Yourself*, p. 260. Lanham, MD: Scarborough House.

239 Thinkexist.com website, http://thinkexist.com/quotation/whenever_you_see_a_successful_business-someone/167688.html.

240 Williams, *In Business for Yourself*, p. 13.

241 Ibid., p. 14.

242 Young Entrepreneur Council, "10 Things to Consider Before Becoming a Full-Time Entrepreneur," *U.S. News & World Report*, December 14, 2011.

243 Tyson, Eric, and Jim Schell (2008). *Small Business for Dummies* (3rd ed.), p. 101. Indianapolis, IN: Wiley Publishing, Inc.

244 Ibid., p. 42.

245 Nemko, Marty, "Overrated Career: Small Business Owner," *U.S. News & World Report*, December 11, 2008.

246 Tyson and Schell, *Small Business for Dummies,* p. 48.

247 Nemko, "Overrated Career."

248 Tyson and Schell, *Small Business for Dummies,* pp. 18-21.

249 Williams, *In Business for Yourself,* pp. 21-22, 28.

250 Ibid., p. 30.

251 Warner, Ralph, and Laurence, Bethany (2009). *Save Your Small Business: 10 Crucial Strategies to Survive Hard Times or Close Down and Move On*, p. 6. Berkeley, CA: Nolo.

252 Tyson and Schell, *Small Business for Dummies,* pp. 22-23.

253 Ibid., pp. 24-25.

254 Ibid., pp. 31, 34.

255 Nemko, "Overrated Career."

256 Samuelson, Robert J., "The Real Jobs Machine: Entrepreneurs," *The Washington Post*, October 4, 2010.

257 Thompson, Derek, "Actually, America Isn't a Small Business Country At All," *The Atlantic*, August 2009.

258 Newman, Rick, "Why Startups Surged During the Recession," *U.S. News & World Report*, May 20, 2010.

259 Rob Fairlie, cited in Shane, Scott A., "How the Health Care Mess Affects Entrepreneurship," Economix blog, *The New York Times*, July 27, 2009, http://economix.blogs.nytimes.com/.

260 Shane, "How the Health Care Mess Affects Entrepreneurship."

261 Wolgemuth, Liz, "Why Start-Ups Could Make or Break the Job Recovery," *U.S. News & World Report*, July 19, 2010.

262 John C. Haltiwanger, Ron S. Jarmin, and Javier Miranda, cited in Indiviglio, Daniel, "Young, Not Small, Businesses Drive Job Growth," *The Atlantic*, September 2010.

263 Huntington, *Work's New Age,* pp. 121-122.

264 Ibid., pp. 123-124.

265 Williams, *In Business for Yourself,* p. 6.

266 Ibid., p. 16.

267 Huntington, *Work's New Age,* pp. 123-124.

268 Tyson and Schell, *Small Business for Dummies,* p. 47.

269 See Huntington, *Work's New Age,* p. 74.

270 Tyson and Schell, *Small Business for Dummies,* p. 47.

271 Ibid.

272 McDonald's website, http://aboutmcdonalds.com/mcd/franchising/us_franchising/aquiring_a_franchise.html.

273 See Huntington, *Work's New Age,* pp. 105-107.

274 Gehring, Abigail R. (2012). *Odd Jobs: How to Have Fun and Make Money in a Bad Economy* (2nd ed.), pp. 6-7. New York: Skyhorse Publishing.

275 Ibid., pp. 105-106.

276 Ibid., pp. 9-11.

277 Ibid., pp. 22-23.

278 Ibid., pp. 25-27.

279 Ibid., pp. 29-31, 167-168.

280 Ibid., pp. 96-98.

281 Gehring, *Odd Jobs,* pp. 15-17; Freed, Dolly (1978, reprinted 2010). *Possum Living: How to Live Well Without a Job and With (Almost) No Money*, p. 27. Portland, OR: Tin House Books.

282 Gehring, *Odd Jobs,* pp. 13-15.

283 Ibid., pp. 67-68, 77-79, 84-86.

284 Ibid., pp. 110-112, 115-117.

285 Ibid., pp. 191-192.

286 Freed, *Possum Living,* p. 27.

287 Gehring, *Odd Jobs,* pp. 132-134.

288 Ibid., pp. 162-163.

289 Freed, *Possum Living,* pp. 28, 29.

290 Pendrith, Mike, "12 Reasons Why New Businesses Fail," Evan Carmichael website, http://www.evancarmichael.com/Starting-A-Business/866/12-REASONS-WHY-NEW-BUSINESSES-FAIL.html.

Chapter 7: The Outlook, Job by Job

291 Famous Quotes and Authors website, http://www.famousquotesandauthors.com/topics/work_quotes.html.

292 Gehring, *Odd Jobs,* pp. 68-71, 75-76, 80-81, 83-84, 200-202.

293 Ricker, Susan, "10 Jobs That Have Grown Over 30 Percent in the Last Year," *The Chicago Tribune*, September 11, 2012.

294 Ibid.

295 Gehring, *Odd Jobs,* pp. 74-76, 82-83.

296 Ricker, "10 Jobs That Have Grown Over 30 Percent in the Last Year."

297 Ibid.

298 Ibid.

299 Khanna, Parag and Smith, Aaron, "5 Future Jobs, and What They'll Replace," *The Chicago Tribune*, August 28, 2012.

300 Ibid.

301 Gehring, *Odd Jobs,* pp. 13-15.

302 Wortham, Jenna, "Gofer Does Your Bidding, for a Price," *The New York Times*, August 28, 2011; Gehring, *Odd Jobs,* pp. 6-7, 18-21, 42-44.

303 Gehring, *Odd Jobs,* pp. 51-53.

304 Ricker, "10 Jobs That Have Grown Over 30 Percent in the Last Year."

305 Ibid.

306 Ibid.

307 Ibid.

308 Ibid.

Chapter 8: Preparing for 2033 and Beyond

309 Garreau, *Radical Evolution,* p. 11.

310 Actuarial Life Table, U.S. Social Security Administration.

311 Wikipedia entry on "Bill Joy," http://en.wikipedia.org/wiki/Bill_Joy.

312 Joy, Bill, "Why the Future Doesn't Need Us," *Wired*, April 2000.

313 Kurzweil, *The Singularity is Near,* pp. 8, 377.

314 Ibid., p. 258.

315 Kurzweil, Ray (1999). *The Age of Spiritual Machines: When Computers Exceed Human Intelligence*, pp. 52-53. New York: Penguin Books.

316 Kurzweil, *The Singularity is Near,* p. 9.

317 Ibid., p. 258.

318 Ibid., pp. 20, 136.

319 Ibid., pp. 21, 29.

320 Ibid., p. 123.

321 Penrose, Roger (1994). *Shadows of the Mind: A Search for the Missing Science of Consciousness*, p. 12. New York: Oxford University Press.

322 Kurzweil, *The Singularity is Near,* p. 28.

323 Ibid., p. 201.

324 "Computing Machines and Intelligence," *Mind* 59 (1950), cited in Kurzweil, *The Age of Spiritual Machines,* p. 61.

325 Kurzweil, *The Singularity Is Near,* p. 25.

326 Ibid., p. 263.

327 Penrose, *Shadows of the Mind,* pp. 14, 393.

328 Ibid., p. vi.

329 Ibid., pp. 393, 406.

330 Cited in Garreau, *Radical Evolution,* p. 177.

331 Agar, Nicholas (2010). *Humanity's End: Why We Should Reject Radical Enhancement*, p. 59. Cambridge, MA: The MIT Press.

332 Kurzweil, *The Age of Spiritual Machines,* pp. 54-55.

333 Agar, *Humanity's End,* p. 77.

334 Kurzweil, *The Singularity Is Near,* pp. 377, 378.

335 Ibid., pp. 378, 380.

336 That is because it is unreasonable to think other humans are not alive. We can see, though, a sense of the problem we would face if we try to determine if other animals are conscious. See, for example, Harmon, Katherine, "Octopuses Gain Consciousness (According to Scientists' Declaration)," *Scientific American*, August 21, 2012.

337 Wikipedia entry on "Glasses," http://en.wikipedia.org/wiki/Glasses.

338 Cited in Agar, *Humanity's End,* p. 59.

339 Garreau, *Radical Evolution,* pp. 19-20.

340 Templeton, Graham, "Father-Daughter Duo Have the World's First Brain-to-Brain 'Telepathic' Conversation," ExtremeTech website, http://www.extremetech.com/extreme/143148-father-daughter-duo-have-the-worlds-first-brain-to-brain-telepathic-conversation.

341 Garreau, *Radical Evolution,* p. 21.

342 Duncan, David Ewing, "How Science Can Build a Better You," *The New York Times*, November 4, 2012.

343 Garreau, *Radical Evolution,* p. 27.

344 Collins, Nick, "Eye Implant Restores Vision to Blind Patients," *The Telegraph*, May 3, 2012.

345 Gallagher, James, "Light-Powered Bionic Eye Invented to Help Restore Sight," BBC website, May 14, 2012, http://www.bbc.co.uk/news/health-18061174.

346 Duncan, "How Science Can Build a Better You"; Kooser, Amanda, "NASA Exoskeleton Suit is Half Way to Iron Man," CNET website, September 15, 2012, http://news.cnet.com/8301-17938_105-57532729-1/nasa-exoskeleton-suit-is-half-way-to-iron-man/.

347 "Paralysed Claire Lomas finishes London Marathon 16 days after it began," *The Guardian*, May 8, 2012.

348 "Walking and Running Again After Spinal Cord Injury," Science Daily website, May 31, 2012, http://www.sciencedaily.com/releases/2012/05/120531145714.htm.

349 Anthony, Sebastian, "Researchers create brain-computer interface that bypasses spinal cord Injury paralysis," ExtremeTech website, April 20, 2012, http://www.extremetech.com/extreme/126773-researchers-create-brain-computer-interface-that-bypasses-spinal-cord-injury-paralysis.

350 "Mental Scanner Lets Paralyzed People Spell Their Thoughts," LiveScience website, June 29, 2012, http://www.livescience.com/21303-mental-scanner-lets-paralyzed-people-spell-their-thoughts.html.

351 Garreau, *Radical Evolution,* p. 116.

352 Duncan, "How Science Can Build a Better You."

353 Kurzweil, *The Singularity Is Near,* p. 27.

354 Ibid., p. 28.

355 Freitas, Robert A., cited in Kurzweil, *The Singularity Is Near,* p. 28.

356 Kurzweil, *The Singularity Is Near,* pp. 28, 256.

357 "Nanoparticle trick 'boosts Body's Vaccine Response,'" BBC website, January 22, 2012, http://www.bbc.co.uk/news/health-16654182.

358 Kurzweil, *The Singularity Is Near,* pp. 201-202.

359 Grifantini, Kristina, "Voyage of the Bacteria Bots," *MIT Technology Review*, October 31, 2008.

360 Duncan, "How Science Can Build a Better You."

361 Cited in Duncan, "How Science Can Build a Better You."

362 George Annas, Lori Andrews, and Rosario Isasi, cited in Agar, *Humanity's End,* p. 153.

363 Agar, *Humanity's End,* p. 75.

364 Ibid., p. 14.

365 Cited in Agar, *Humanity's End,* pp. 88-89.

366 Agar, *Humanity's End,* p. 99.

367 Kurzweil, *The Singularity Is Near,* pp. 256-257.

368 Agar, *Humanity's End,* p. 94.

369 University of Michigan, "Biologists Find Potential Drug That Speeds Cellular Recycling," Medical Xpress website, March 13, 2012, http://medicalxpress.com/news/2012-03-biologists-potential-drug-cellular-recycling.html.

370 Cited in Garreau, *Radical Evolution,* p. 177.

371 Cited in Agar, *Humanity's End,* p. 84.

372 Garreau, *Radical Evolution,* pp. 11-12.

373 Agar, *Humanity's End,* pp. 84, 102-103.

374 Cited in Agar, *Humanity's End,* p. 164.

375 Agar, *Humanity's End,* p. 65.

376 See, for example, Niven, Larry (1976), *A World Out of Time*, pp. 1-33. New York: Ballantine Books.

377 Agar, *Humanity's End,* pp. 116-117.

378 Ibid., pp. 123, 127.

379 Bostrom, Nick, cited in Agar, *Humanity's End,* p. 148.

380 Cited in Agar, *Humanity's End,* p. 83.

381 Kotlikoff and Burns, *The Coming Generational Storm,* p. 7.

382 John W. Rowe and Robert L. Kahn, cited in Kotlikoff and Burns, *The Coming Generational Storm,* p. 1. Cambridge, MA: The MIT Press. Kotlikoff and Burns noted that "other sources have smaller projections"; for example, 473,000 American 2050 centenarians by the United Nations.

383 See Huntington, James B. (2007), *Prospects for Increased Post-65 Career Employment for the Baby Boom Generation*, p. 30. Ann Arbor, MI: ProQuest Information and Learning Company.

384 Cited in Bandyk, Matthew, "The Future of the U.S. Economy: 2050," *U.S. News & World Report*, February 2, 2010.

385 Lin and Huang, "Imagining 2076."

386 Garreau, *Radical Evolution,* pp. 211-212.

387 See Clifton, *The Coming Jobs War*, pp. 88-89.

388 Ford, *The Lights in the Tunnel,* p. 240.

389 Kurzweil, *The Singularity Is Near,* p. 25.

390 Ibid., pp. 25-26.

391 See Agar, *Humanity's End,* pp. 46-47.

392 Cited in Agar, *Humanity's End,* p. 45.

393 Kurzweil, *The Singularity Is Near,* p. 27.

394 See, for example, "Researchers Claim Quantum Breakthrough," ABC Science website, April 26, 2012, http://www.abc.net.au/science/articles/2012/04/26/3489504.htm.

395 Bardin, Jon, "First Human Whole-Brain Genetic Map Created," *Los Angeles Times*, September 28, 2012.

396 Walsh, Fergus, "Detailed Map of Genome Function," BBC website, September 5, 2012, http://www.bbc.co.uk/news/health-19202141.

397 As another example, from 2007: Despite accelerating technology, airplane travel, along with "cars and oil rigs and credit cards and the operations of the New York Stock Exchange" seem much the same as they did 30 years before, and "[A]side from the telephones, almost all the objects and daily habits in Steven Spielberg's twenty-five-year-old film *E.T.* are about the same as they are today." (Bodanis, David, "Is the West Already on a Downhill Course?" In Brockman, John (Ed.) (2007), *What Is Your Dangerous Idea?*, pp. 279-280. New York: HarperCollins Publishers.

398 Cited in Garreau, *Radical Evolution,* p. 15.

399 Cited in Vance, "Merely Human? That's So Yesterday."

400 Garreau, *Radical Evolution,* pp. 156-157.

401 Cited in Agar, *Humanity's End,* p. 29.

402 Agar, *Humanity's End,* p. 31.

403 Huntington, *Work's New Age,* p. 147.

404 Clifton, *The Coming Jobs War*, p. 87; Reich, Robert, "Why is Washington Obsessing About the Deficit and Not Jobs and Wages?," Robert Reich blog, http://www.robertreich.org.

405 Ford, *The Lights in the Tunnel*, pp. 102-103.

406 Kurzweil, *The Singularity Is Near*, pp. 337-341.

407 Wadhwa, Vivek, and Kurzweil, Ray, "Ray Kurzweil on the Future Workforce," *The Washington Post*, November 15, 2012.

Appendix: Detailed Meanings of Job Field Items

408 U.S. Department of Labor, *Occupational Outlook Handbook*, pp. 26-991.

409 Ibid.

410 Ibid.

411 Ibid.

412 Ibid.

Index

Page numbers followed by *f* indicate figures

About the Author

James B. Huntington is also the author of Independent Publisher Book Award (IPPY)-winning *Work's New Age: The End of Full Employment and What It Means to You*, from 2012. His 2007 doctoral dissertation, *Prospects for Increased Post-65 Career Employment for the Baby Boom Generation*, is the only book ever published on that subject. He is also the creator and keeper of the AJSN (American Job Shortage Number), the key economic indicator showing latent demand for jobs in the United States. He has a B.A. in sociology from the University of Wisconsin-Milwaukee, an M.B.A. from the University of Phoenix, and a Ph.D. in Applied Management and Decision Sciences from Walden University. Since November 2011, he has spoken on Work's New Age on more than 130 American radio stations coast to coast. He has also been a business professor, teacher, and professional speaker, and has written scholarly works on leadership, organizational change, and human development. He is married and lives in Eldred, New York.

Keep up with *Choosing a Lasting Career*, the AJSN, and *Work's New Age* on James's blog at http://worksnewage.blogspot.com.

Also by James B. Huntington

WORK'S NEW AGE:
The End of Full Employment and What It Means to You

ISBN 978-0-9835006-3-6 (paperback)

For most of their lives, Americans have thought all good people could find work and support themselves. That is gone forever, and no economic recovery will bring it back. The recession is officially long over, yet almost 14 million people remain unemployed. As well, 9 million work part-time but want more, and another 9 million would take jobs if they thought they could get them. Yet negotiations in Washington to solve or even improve it, when they have happened at all, have stalled.

Neither political side is getting anywhere. Conservatives are wrong: cutting corporate taxes is not the answer. Liberals are wrong: blaming businesses, increasing the minimum wage, or encouraging unionization won't help either. Romney and Obama have shown that they do not understand the problem. Meanwhile, all signs point to even fewer jobs in the future. Today's innovations, such as eBay, Facebook, and Twitter, provide employment not for millions but only thousands or hundreds. Almost a quarter of 20 to 24-year-olds never work each year, along with ¾ of those 16 and 17. At the same time, many careers end around 50, leaving those that age with no clear course of action. Employment and workplace productivity have parted statistical company. These facts have huge implications for everyone, working or not.

A 2012 Independent Publisher Book Award winner, giving a fresh view on what is happening with American jobs, is also available. *Work's New Age: The End of Full Employment and What It Means to You* is a resource for all of us. It explains what we are experiencing in terms of numbers, trends, and social patterns, and what we can—and cannot—do about it. *Work's New Age* is the first full-length book in years to address this massive national concern. It shows why the gap between workers and jobs will get ever larger, and which possible solutions will only harm. It is well-documented and thoughtful but easy to understand. The book even provides hope, by demonstrating how we have the potential to transform this crisis into a new American golden age.

Work's New Age is available at www.amazon.com, www.barnesandnoble.com, at bookstores (on the shelves or special-ordered through Ingram Book Company), and directly from the publisher at www.royalflushpress.com or 845-456-0115. Kindle and Nook electronic versions are also on the market.

Royal Flush Press, P.O. Box 190, Eldred, NY 12732-0190 USA

Tel: 845.456.0115, Fax: 845.557.0353

jhuntington@royalflushpress.com http://www.royalflushpress.com

FAST ORDER FORM

Fax orders:
845-557-0353. Use this form.

Telephone orders, by credit card or PayPal:
845-456-0115.

Email orders:
Send to orders@royalflushpress.com.

Mail orders:
Royal Flush Press, P.O. Box 190, Eldred, NY 12732

Please send _____copy (or copies) of *Choosing a Lasting Career*, for US $14.95 apiece,

Please send _____copy (or copies) of *Work's New Age*, for US $17.95 apiece, to:

Name ____

Address ____

____

City __________________________________

State ______________________ ZIP Code ______________

Telephone ___________________________

Email address: ________________________

___ Cash or check (enclosed)

___ MasterCard, Visa, or Discover:
Card number and expiration date: ______________________________

___ PayPal: Use email address above, or ________________________________

Sales tax: Please add 6% for delivery to New York State.

Shipping for ***entire order*** (no extra charge for more than one book):

U.S. Media Mail $2.00,
U.S. Priority Mail $5.00,
Foreign Priority Mail $12.00

FAST ORDER FORM

Fax orders:
845-557-0353. Use this form.

Telephone orders, by credit card or PayPal:
845-456-0115.

Email orders:
Send to orders@royalflushpress.com.

Mail orders:
Royal Flush Press, P.O. Box 190, Eldred, NY 12732

Please send _____copy (or copies) of *Choosing a Lasting Career*, for US $14.95 apiece,

Please send _____copy (or copies) of *Work's New Age*, for US $17.95 apiece, to:

Name ____

Address ____

____

City ________________________________

State _____________________ ZIP Code _____________

Telephone __________________________

Email address: _______________________

___ Cash or check (enclosed)

___ MasterCard, Visa, or Discover:
Card number and expiration date: ____________________________

___ PayPal: Use email address above, or ______________________________

Sales tax: Please add 6% for delivery to New York State.

Shipping for ***entire order*** (no extra charge for more than one book):

U.S. Media Mail $2.00,
U.S. Priority Mail $5.00,
Foreign Priority Mail $12.00

FAST ORDER FORM

Fax orders:
845-557-0353. Use this form.

Telephone orders, by credit card or PayPal:
845-456-0115.

Email orders:
Send to orders@royalflushpress.com.

Mail orders:
Royal Flush Press, P.O. Box 190, Eldred, NY 12732

Please send _____copy (or copies) of *Choosing a Lasting Career*, for US $14.95 apiece,

Please send _____copy (or copies) of *Work's New Age*, for US $17.95 apiece, to:

Name ____

Address ____

____

City ________________________________

State _____________________ ZIP Code _____________

Telephone __________________________

Email address: _______________________

___ Cash or check (enclosed)

___ MasterCard, Visa, or Discover:
Card number and expiration date: ____________________________

___ PayPal: Use email address above, or ______________________________

Sales tax: Please add 6% for delivery to New York State.

Shipping for ***entire order*** (no extra charge for more than one book):

U.S. Media Mail $2.00,
U.S. Priority Mail $5.00,
Foreign Priority Mail $12.00

FAST ORDER FORM

Fax orders:
845-557-0353. Use this form.

Telephone orders, by credit card or PayPal:
845-456-0115.

Email orders:
Send to orders@royalflushpress.com.

Mail orders:
Royal Flush Press, P.O. Box 190, Eldred, NY 12732

Please send _____copy (or copies) of *Choosing a Lasting Career*, for US $14.95 apiece,

Please send _____copy (or copies) of *Work's New Age*, for US $17.95 apiece, to:

Name ____

Address ____

____

City ________________________________

State _____________________ ZIP Code _____________

Telephone __________________________

Email address: ________________________

___ Cash or check (enclosed)

___ MasterCard, Visa, or Discover:
Card number and expiration date: ____________________________

___ PayPal: Use email address above, or ______________________________

Sales tax: Please add 6% for delivery to New York State.

Shipping for ***entire order*** (no extra charge for more than one book):

U.S. Media Mail $2.00,
U.S. Priority Mail $5.00,
Foreign Priority Mail $12.00

Notes

Notes

Notes

Notes

Notes

Notes

Notes

Notes